GLAMOUR BLONDES

To Clarry,

hEE hEE

Love Debs.

x x.

GLAMOUR BLONDES

From Mae to Madonna
by David Evans

BRITANNIA PRESS PUBLISHING

British Library Cataloguing in Publication Data.
A Catalogue record for this book is available from the British Library.

Evans
Glamour Blondes
From Mae to Madonna

ISBN 1-899784-05-5 (Paperback)

Printed and bound in Great Britain by WBC, Bridgend.

Picture Credits: *Britannia Press Publishing would like to thank the following companies and individuals for supplying photographs and memorabilia for this book.* The Kobal Collection: Front cover (top left); p. 9; p. 31; p. 53; p. 71; p. 95; p. 139; p. 157; p. 195; p. 233; Rex Features: Front cover (bottom right); p. 181; p. 215; p.249; and Nigel Quiney for the use of his private collection of lobby cards and other memorabilia.

Britannia Press Publishing is a division of Britannia Crest International Ltd
72 Chalk Farm Road, London NW1 8AN

An affectionate look
at a lineage of legends...

This book is for

Ven Hart

and is also dedicated to the memory of
Kenny Everett and Cupid Stunt

and

Richard Perfitt

CONTENTS

Introduction

There's nothing more head-turning or eye-catching than a glamorous blonde. Even the words themselves, glamorous and blonde seem made to run together. Glamour blonde. A plain blonde, even sometimes a natural blonde, lacks the artifice, the inbuilt allure, the ensnaring purpose with which the glamour blonde is inherently endowed.

The dictionary tells us that glamour is an eighteenth century corruption of *gramarye*, an archaic term for magic, even for necromancy, the time-honoured black art of prediction through communication with the spirits. Spooky?

Not really. Making a glamorised image - for that is what the creation of any graven likeness is - is itself a form of communication; the application of make-up, the heightening or changing of hair colour and body, skin tones, bone structure, eye shape ... glamorising is designed to bewitch.

The glamorised radiate enchantment. They hold out the promise of excitement beyond our wildest dreams. They have indeed consulted the spirits of the selves they have killed off in order to be thus reborn. They have taken the best of what was and re-invented it for a greater purpose.

This greater purpose is to enhance the lives of others and by doing so, gain greater profit for themselves. As Marlene Dietrich is supposed to have said whilst passing through the motley at a passenger terminal: *"My God! Look at how ugly all those people are. No wonder people like me are paid so much money."*

The glamour, the image, the dedication, the perfectionism,

the expertise ... It's all for our benefit. The humdrum and the ordinary have always been made bearable by the allure of the delusive charms of magical, unreal and probably libidinous icons of humankind's own creation. The message is, 'It could happen to you, too!'

Dangerous?

'T was ever thus. Poor Moses ... Try as he and his college of prophets have done and still do, it's not enough for mankind to labour on merely looking at where the face of their invisible gods are supposed to be when there's a screen to look at. Humanity has always had to have its icons and of these, the twentieth century's blondes have been amongst the most potent.

Their potency and power have been so often vaunted that it must now be hailed as a universal truth that, whether natural or bottled, we all suppose that blondes have more fun.

Do they? Have they had?

Quantitatively, the answers to both those questions are indubitably yes and emphatically no, in equal measure.

How much *more* fun blondes are *supposed* to be heir to than we lesser mortals can perhaps be assessed by taking a look at the lives and times of some of the more celebrated blondes, those legends of the silver screen, those sirens of the vinyl disc, the goddesses of love and lust who not only inflamed the passions of men down the decades but also captured the imaginations and hearts of women for without the support of their female audience, these begotten, never-to-be-forgotten blondes would never have been allowed to exist in the first place.

Faced with a sackful of thumbs-down mail, there wasn't a blonde on their books who would have escaped being scrapped by the Louis B's, the Adolf Z's, the Laskys, the Schencks, the Warners, the Goldwyns, the Foxes, the Thalbergs, the Selznicks, the Skouras, the Levathes and all the moguls, managers and master-minders who have controlled the media this century for unlike the development of any other century's culture, our century's was man-made. It certainly wasn't naturally evolved. Who has time to wait for evolution? Who needs natural when you can get exactly what the recipe calls for from a bottle? Why bother with real when you can have instant? Why search when you can have whatever-it-is delivered?

Though sex appeal has changed over the years, sex certainly hasn't and whether suggested or supplied, sex was and is probably the most vital ingredient in the consumer cocktail which the entertainment industry purveys.

But for all the apparent winners, there have been the time-honoured losers. So often, the blondes in the picture have turned out to be the flies in the ointment and, more often than not, the ointment has been their own. More iconoclasm has been heaped upon and reaped by the glamour blondes than has either been right, proper or fair.

But then, that's life. For all of us, living life has brought its share of not right, not proper and not fair and that is why the pain of Harlow, the anguish of Monroe, the deception of Doris Day, the apotheosis of Grace Kelly has meant and means so much to so many people so many years on.

Conversely of course, it is the success of Mae West, the achievement of Dolly Parton and the triumph of Madonna which fuels all our own secret blonde ambitions, for these, being only wannabee dreams of course, can survive the under-lying reality.

Like dreams, peroxide is available in plenty. Anyone can dream and anyone can be a blonde, even if you're one already.

CHAPTER 1

New World Blondes

New World Blondes

My review of our significant blondes lies snugly between the parameters of our century which, although not yet over, has surely been one of the most confusing and, in a sense, retrograde, especially for women. It seems ironic that at the beginning of the century, there was the towering presence of Miss Mae West as a role model for the progressive, emancipated woman and at the end, in our time, there stands Ms. Madonna Ciccone, who ranks as equivalent talking head.

I had an idea to write this book in the form of a memo, a fictitious missive sent by Mae, the former of these two Empresses of the Modern Woman, writing to the latter, Madonna who in turn, would reply. It seemed to me, from reading exhaustively about both of them, that they are extraordinarily alike. However, being avowedly not a woman's woman, I rather thought that such a memo would be doing a disservice to Miss West although I have a feeling that, always generous to those of her fellow performers who merited her praise, the off-duty Miss Mae would have rather taken to the un-alloyed Miss Madonna.

In beginning the romp through the blonde century, I don't think it will serve to theorise about the way things stand for women today for every woman will have her own idea, perspective and opinion of her contemporary space in place and time. But for those women and men whose curiosity has been tickled thus far, they might find it interesting to explore comparable life and time as generally existed when Mae West first breasted the century's tape on the Vaudeville stages of the Eastern United States of America.

Edna Ferber, the author of the novel SHOWBOAT which has steamed such a long way through our entertainment highways, wrote in her autobiography A PECULIAR TREASURE published in 1939, just before the Second World war, "*I feel sorry for anyone born after 1918. To have been an adult before the (First World) war and to have lived twenty years after it is to have known two worlds in one lifetime.*"

Our gorgeous blondes appear on the catwalk of our century's culture because of the successive emergence of three branches of the media, one of which wasn't even invented when the eight year old 'Baby' Mae first stamped her foot and demanded the spotlight on-stage at the Royal Theatre, Fulton Street, Brooklyn in 1900. Some of our blondes knew three lifetimes.

Remarkably, in 1900 there was no teevee.

No one then had a telly, not even Mr. Logie Baird who invented it. There were, however, moving pictures and there was recorded sound though both were nascent, unrecognisable in the forms and guises they were to adopt as the century ticked by. Edna Ferber remembers the novelty of going with her family to a showing of moving pictures by a machine called the Animatograph in 1897. The family opinion was that it was a fairground attraction, in no way rivalled the theatre and the consensus was that it wouldn't last. They were, of course, wrong. In the fullness of time, moving pictures became the movies and eclipsed theatre, vaudeville and burlesque although the new medium came to inhabit many of the dead theatre buildings.

Together with the flowering of the spread of movie theatres arose the phenomenon of the radio station. Radio played a big part in the growth of the movie industry and bridged the deadfall when movies in their turn were eclipsed by the arrival and indecently hasty spread of television. And, of course, it was radio which allowed the third of this century's mega-media phenomenon to emerge into what we nowadays know as the music business. The record companies which were spawned by Doris Day and Peggy Lee (amongst the legion other recording artists) didn't get fat off teevee; Decca, Warners, RCA, Atlantic, Columbia, Motown and all the myriad offshoots and indies were nurtured by radio and, ultimately, zombified radio by inhabiting its host corpse like a parasite. The zenith of radio as a cultural medium providing a richly imaginative diet of drama, the spoken word, classical music and appreciation as well as news, current affairs and popular music came and went in its turn and allotted time. It died first in America and then succumbed throughout the world for, of course, radio is for free. You don't have to pay to listen in the same way that, until the introduction of satellite and cable teevee, you didn't have to pay to watch. But watch and watch out. Things change. In Britain where radio culture yet clings to life in the teeth of commercialism and at the whim of politicians, it is indeed a still, small voice and its bequest to teevee will be a prediction of more of the same. The powers that be don't want us to see teevee for free ... They want our money and it looks as though they're going to get it.

So, thank you and bye-bye radio - it is now television which bolsters the stranglehold of the music business on world-wide popular culture, it being entirely co-incidental, surely, that the television screen evolved into the VDU for soon the vinyl disc, the cassette and the new ceedees ... These too shall pass when our music and our visuals can be ordered and paid for via a modem connecting our personal VDU to a master computer source which *could* take the place of Virgin mega-stores the world over. So, bye-bye to the executive pie? Make the most of it all you vice-presidents and marketing men and sales reps and pluggers and especially you A and R souls.

Of course, there is a very important fourth medium of communication and entertainment which has survived relatively unscathed. Although it may have wavered in style, content and quality during the ups and downs of the twentieth century, the book has come through pretty much unchanged. After all, you're reading one.

And, to tie up loose digressions, this particular book maintains that now, as we approach not only the end of a century but also the millennium, Madonna is the Queen of Blonde for Mae, sadly, is no longer with us.

A Queen is dead - Long live the Queen!

It must be of more than passing interest to note that Mae West's ascendancy occurred at a time when the industry in which she figured was in a state of flux and that the same conditions threaten now that Madonna has assumed her throne. The intervening period when the men had the whole kit and caboodle sussed and hog-tied, it seemed there was little the women could do except kick out, often forcibly although never as united as 'the men', against the pricks.

Madonna's blonde ambition can be seen as well as heard and, above all, purchased and taken home in all its forms. Mae's could only be had by marvelling from afar in a movie house or theatre with a lot of other people. Mae remained a dream, Madonna will soon be virtual reality. Madonna, thanks to technology, is really mistress of all who fall prey to her and she holds sway o'er all she surveys for she surveys us as individuals from the privacy of our own screens in the intimacy of our own homes.

Mae West commanded what media there were available to her at the beginning and in the middle of the century in the same way that Madonna operates now. Both are women able to understand *how* to achieve their goals and then devote themselves shamelessly to successfully doing so, un-distracted by conventional commitments, immune to masculine slings and arrows, their own outrageous fortune being vulnerable only to indifference. And, let's face it, the male-dominated world of show-business will never be as un-gallant to display indifference when a woman continues to command such wealth. Indifference doesn't pay.

So what happened to that relay of blondes who came in between Mae and Madonna who accepted and then, by example, passed on the baton of beauty and bewitchment to their successors in the race? If only they could all be garnered from their bubbles of time and assembled ... It would be like the start of a blonde marathon, an all-but endless series of races in which there have had to be both winners and losers.

If winning is achieving fame and wealth and losing is succumbing to oblivion and poverty, there were victims and martyrs in both categories. It can get pretty lonely sitting in a many-roomed mansion in Bel Air with no one to love and it is, of course, love which is the confusion, the stake to which many of our blondes were lead as victims and against which they were made martyrs.

To be loved and adored by so many nameless, faceless individuals for what you aren't and yet to be unable to find that one person who will love you for what you are; to have had your dreams made reality only because of a love generated for you and not by you; to have allowed yourself to be re-born with a different personality and psyche to cope with your celebrity and good fortune and yet still having to maintain the original self which underpins the whole edifice; to look at yourself in a mirror and be unable to find the person you once were ... The person you think you still are.

Some coped. Some couldn't. Some embraced the life that fame brought, trusting it, and triumphed. Some embraced the life that fame brought, trusted it and tottered. Some seemed to have no need of whom they'd once been; some were haunted and tortured by a past which simply could not equip them to deal with both the present and future perspective. Some fell. Some were pushed. Some picked themselves up. Some perished. For the industry to prosper, many a blonde sacrifice was required. In a way, as well as being the ultimate worshippers, the public rather than either the stars or the star-makers became the ultimate god and occasionally, the public had to be appeased.

But it was only by getting their feet wet, by jumping in the water that the blondes found out who were swimmers, who were sinkers and who would make the biggest splash. They had to strike out to find out and for every sinker, there was another on the pool-side under starter's orders.

And there were no life preservers. In those days there was only one Mae West.

CHAPTER 2

Mae West

Mae West

It is well known that Mae took her time about everything. Her lines, the delivery of them, the once down, once up look which took in every nook and cranny of the man she was sizing up ... She also took her time coming out to Hollywood and when she did so, she was out there with Ginger Rogers and Jean Harlow, women something of a decade younger than her.

Mae was born in Brooklyn in 1893 so if she had survived other than in legend, her flesh would have been a hundred and two this year, 1995. But then Barbara Cartland's ninety four so, with the marvels of modern science and cosmetic taxidermy, I would bet that Mae would have still fitted snugly into those hour glass frocks with which she shocked the world, couture which cantilevered and contorted her bosoms into a shape the Royal Airforce would use in 1941 to describe their life preservers in world war two. Believe it, folks, Mae West saved lives too!

"Yes," she tells us in her autobiography, GOODNESS HAD NOTHING TO DO WITH IT, *"first I had to create myself."* And indeed she did. Mae was on the vaudeville boards by her mid-teens and she was a star at twenty. Okay ... She was no Sarah Bernhardt or Alla Nazimova but she knew the Mae West her audiences liked and she wrought, then honed and finally fine-tuned the creation which her audiences came not only to like but to adore. They liked her to sing a little, dance a little, look gorgeous and wealthy and drip with diamonds - a stone she made her own - and if she had to act, then all they really wanted her to do was to be Mae West.

Mae's not-so-secret weapon was shock. She had an instinct

for the shocking. She capitalised upon it throughout her career and the vehicle she chose from the beginning to carry the message of shock was sex which she later cocktailed with a more-than-generous dash of religion ... No, Madonna, dear. You weren't the first!

Whether Mae's own sexual appetites were as gargantuan as she implied, we can but boggle about. She made a mistake in marrying very young but after she realised her mistake, husband Frank Wallace left and Mae never made the same mistake again. Although she and Wallace remained married until 1942, the piece of paper didn't seem to slow her down any. She seems to have taken great pleasure in seeing men physically fighting each other for her affection. Others' jealousies she revelled in and whilst always, it seems, appearing to be 'engaged' to whom-so-ever, she delighted in assignations and snatched moments of passion between her private and public lives. Mae knew what excited her and she also knew that most women's passions were excited by the same things. Men.

Mae learned a lot from the early days in vaudeville on the East Coast and she met a lot of people too, men of the theatre who would later be in a position to help her on the West Coast. Joe and the other Schencks, Jesse Lasky, William le Baron who produced all her pictures and whom she met on a Broadway show called A LA BROADWAY. She made money for these people in vaudeville and they never argued with the profit she turned.

There must also have been many contemporary performers from whom she learned but I fancy that there was a genre of artiste from whom she borrowed mercilessly - the female impersonator. This was a breed of performer much in vogue in vaudeville, the most famous of those whom Mae mentions being Julian Ettlinge. Let's face it, Mae West became every drag queen's dream with the drag queen's ability for irony and self-mockery. Mae's performances all but sent themselves up but she was queen of her craft and always forestalled the ludicrous. The fact she had a 'gay' following was not lost on Miss West who actually didn't have too many kind things to say about the homosexuals who must have made up a large part of her audience and around and about whom she wrote her second play, THE DRAG.

From the beginning of her career, Mae habitually tinkered with the songs and the lines which had been written for her and the early Nineteen Twenties saw her write and star in her own full length play. What was it called? What else but SEX.

It looked as though it would flop on its opening but, second night, word got out and the house was full of sailors on liberty. They loved it and so what else could the two lone critics in their allocated free seats that night say but that Mae's show was going to be a hit.

However, newspapers, fearful of moral backlash, refused to take ads for SEX and so Mae ordered her producers to fly-post the town, just like would be done for a circus. Result? Sure. SEX was a smash, the fly-posting being a shrewd move on Mae's part, forecasting the later trend for fly-posting which now accompanies all major rock and pop music record releases and concert tours.

It was a ploy worthy of Madonna.

SEX was so successful that Mae found that she could charge $10 for the best seats whereas the top Broadway seat price generally was a mere $2.80. Mae West certainly didn't die a pauper.

Her second play, THE DRAG, all about the turbulence, traps and turpitude of the homosexual life, was performed whilst she herself was still appearing in SEX. However, for appearing in SEX, she was accused of allowing her " ... *personality, looks, walk, mannerisms and gestures to make the lines and situations suggestive*" and brought to trial.

Mae, her manager and producer were found guilty of "*corrupting the morals of youth*" and Mae was in fact imprisoned for a few days in the jail on Welfare Island close to Manhattan in the Hudson River. Her celebrity status ensured good treatment and she was soon released but not before reflecting on the misfortunes which beset the other women with whom she was imprisoned. According to her autobiography, it was a sobering experience.

Mae was blooded but not bowed and she was to run into tougher censorship later in the movies.

Though in 1925 Variety announced in banner headlines - 'Vaudeville Will Go' - the prophesy didn't much affect Mae's career. Though she herself notes that the motion picture industry had come out of its rented stores and was building film palaces, Mae kept touring the vaudeville circuits and writing, observing that many of the theatres she had known for years were now given over mainly to showing movies which, in the true spirit of transition, were supported by live vaudeville acts. Her third play was THE WICKED AGE all about the bathing beauty scene in the nineteen twenties.

Her fourth play which she managed to mount despite her producers' misgivings about the relevance of a turn-of-the-century context for a contemporary show, was DIAMOND LIL all about a prostitute in New York's Bowery district in the 1890's. It was the show in which she sang her song FRANKIE AND JOHNNY which rendered her not only legendary but immortal.

DIAMOND LIL was good to Mae and Mae was good to LIL. She not only later turned LIL into a movie, she also wrote her as a novel in which form, she is pleased to inform us, LIL sold ninety five thousand copies for Mae and Macaulays, its publishers. Mae's younger sister Beverly, another blonde, was also in the show and later went on to make a career of impersonating her elder sister. Their joint appearance must have made their mother very proud and Mae was devoted to her German-born mother although of her prize-fighting Irish father, she always seems at arm's length.

1929 was a somewhat momentous year for Mae. Yes, she wrote THE PLEASURE MAN, her fifth play. Yes she toured in DIAMOND LIL in which she continued to appear to great box office acclaim despite the Wall Street Crash. The resulting slump in theatre box office created a vortex of unemployment in thespian circles to the tune of twenty five thousand talented souls. Later six million in less extolled trades would be unemployed across America.

Throughout all this Mae triumphed but also in 1929, her dearest Mama died. It does seem to have been a turning point for Mae who always based herself in New York where she was close to the woman who had facilitated and encouraged her career from the outset.

However, her grief did not curtail her creative juices which flowed into her novel BABE GORDON, a story of an amoral lady of pleasure and set in Harlem. It was re-titled THE CONSTANT SINNER and published with great success by Macaulay. In Spring 1931, whilst touring in SEX and meeting all the world's underworld in prohibition-bound Chicago, Mae adapted THE CONSTANT SINNER as a play for the Schubert Brothers and their chain of theatres.

The aftermath of 'the Crash' had brought intense financial hardship. Movie audiences dropped fifty percent in the recession years to the extent that the Warners' studio was $30,000,000 in debt in 1932. The coming of sound had meant that 'the talkies' had wiped out many former screen idols who had not managed the transition and had left many Hollywood chairs vacant.

Coupled with this scenario of gloom, the 1932 Broadway season saw four fifths of Broadway openings or tryouts fold without a run. Was it any wonder that 1932 also saw Mae finally accept Hollywood's dollar?

Her business representative William Morris Jr. negotiated a ten week deal for her services with Paramount at $5000 a week. It was considerably less than the income she was generating in the theatre but Mae could read road signs; she knew her pulling power was undiminished but in the long run there had to be enough live theatres to pull the people into and in 1932 that possibility looked decidedly wobbly.

She left New York City with her business partner/manager/companion/minder and one time/some times/between times lover Jim Timony on June 16th 1932 and after the four day rail crossing of the States, arrived at Pasadena where she disembarked to be driven by Murray Feil of the West Coast William Morris office the last few miles to Hollywood. No one, but *no one* , ever took the train right in to Los Angeles.

Mae put up at an apartment in The Ravenswood building not a mile from Paramount Studios. She kept the apartment throughout her life.

The first offering which she was given by Emmanuel Cohen and Al Kaufman, Adolf Zukor's duly delegated producers, was NIGHT AFTER NIGHT, adapted from a short story by Louis Bromfield which had appeared in Cosmopolitan magazine. She didn't like it. She didn't like it so much that she wanted to go straight back to New York. Timony persisted and persevered and Mae was allowed the unheard of luxury of rewriting the script which was directed by Archie Mayo and co-starred George Raft. For a woman to achieve that in the early thirties in Hollywood was nothing short of miraculous.

She genuinely seems to have had a 'take-it-or-leave-it' attitude with her demands on the studio, probably banking not only upon her own not inconsiderable wealth but also on the fact that Zukor needed her more than she needed him. I don't think Mae *really* ever *truly* gambled, except on certs.

In 1933, she adapted her own play DIAMOND LIL and turned it into SHE DONE HIM WRONG in which Cary Grant played the lead and in which she uttered her immortally mutilated line, *"Come up ... See me sometime!"* Contrary to her assertion, she didn't 'discover' Cary Grant. He had been in pictures for some time. She merely saw him one day on the back-lot. Whether or not she launched Anthony Quinn's career as Mr. Quinn avows, is surely not for us to question but only, perhaps, to remark that the young and the old Mr. Quinn are equally discoverable.

And whilst flirting with the apocryphal, why bother to cap or top Mae's claim that DIAMOND LIL became more famous than any woman alive at that time ... ?

What is incontrovertible is that Mae West contributed to the sexing of this century. Her persona and the vehicles in which she let it and her diamonds ride, gave sexual confidence to more women than ever. Vanity Fair asked her to pose for them as The Statue of Liberty, emancipating the sexually repressed and terrified from the 'thou shalt nots' which bound and inhibited them. As the poet and critic George Jean Nathan said when he saw the resulting picture, *"... she looks more like the Statue of Libido."*

It was supposed to have been Mae - or was it the wicked work of a competitive drag queen - who uttered the invincible come-on line, *"Is that a gun in your pocket or are you just pleased to see me!"*

Mae's New York friend, the writer and publisher Lowell Brentano had given her a full outline of a movie idea he'd called THE LADY AND THE LIONS all about a female lion tamer. Mae wrote it as a full script and it was re-titled I'M NO ANGEL which, let's face it, had more of a Westian ring to it. Paramount had seventeen hundred of its own theatres to fill and THE LADY AND THE LIONS wasn't exactly a sexy title. Now, BORN FREE, there *was* a sexy title for Mae West.

Mae West, human being, was very aware of the construction of Mae West, star and as she became more and more successful, she was conscious of the other studios attempting to create their own Mae Wests and these rivals, she notes, had been put together with one part breastworks and the remainder, a torrent of crazy publicity. This cocktail was meant to be shaken up and then topped with *"a small dash of talent"* instead of a cherry. She notes that the results usually turned out like something from the laboratory of a mad scientist.

Her sympathy for what she calls *"the raw material for these experiments"* is evident. All very well, she remarks of the business of glamorising a wannabee, until someone, maybe even the public, notices that the object which has been created to bedazzle, is stuffed not with bright talent but with yellowing press clippings. So many 'starlets' with no background or theatrical achievement to talk about were thrown by their studios into the jaws of the news-hounds whose inky instinct was to try to rip them to shreds and who usually succeeded. There were few major stars who survived with little or no background and theatrical experience although one of those who did succeed and succeeded spectacularly is one of our later blondes, Miss Lana Turner.

By 1934, Mae must have been becoming respectable even, for her next picture, directed by Leo McCarey, originally entitled A SAINT LOUIS WOMAN was not finally titled IT AIN'T NO SIN but BELLE OF THE '90s. The evolution betrays not Mae's instinct to capitalise and project her own persona to 'pull 'em in' but that of the Front Office, who obviously wanted to capitalise on the success of DIAMOND LIL but more importantly to appease the censorship of the Hays Office, that Cerebus of moral guardianship whose heads were turned this way and that, usually barking to the terrific but entirely localised and factional pressure exerted by vociferous religious and women's groups. In the 1980's, the front office would have called the movie DIAMOND LIL II or DIAMOND LIL, "The Sequel."

But Mae had been censored all her life and Hays Office or no, Mae swaggered and strutted on, proclaiming, *"It is better to be looked over than overlooked."*

Mae knew the importance of censorship in advertising her product. When the Hays Office made a fuss, the public hurried to the box office. Mae despised imposed censorship, believing that everyone carried their own censor in their heads and hearts. She believed that outside censorship leaves a public feeling robbed of its precious right to exercise its own judgement. How right, how very right she was when she observed how feeble would have been the tirades and protests of the moral lobby against the very real obscenity of something as cruel and life-threatening as war.

By the time she made GOIN' TO TOWN, Mae was on a dollar roll. Her salary was $300,000 per picture and she received an additional $100,000 for a screenplay. Believe me, that was *a lotta money* in those days. Her star was at its zenith. She was courted and feted by international society, dining with Noel Coward and entertaining the Vanderbilts and she hadn't finished by a long chalk. She had Hollywood exactly where she wanted it.

To quote her own words, " ... *I always held it at arms' length like a would-be lover one didn't fully trust.*"

In 1935, she added religion to her platform of shock tactics and appeared in KLONDIKE ANNIE which she rewrote from an original script outline called 'FRISCO KATE. She was appalled that her studio bosses fully intended not to credit the original writing team who, at her insistence, were given screen credits.

Playing ANNIE, a missionary in Alaska, the last American frontier, Mae shocked the world as much as Madonna did sixty years later with her LIKE A VIRGIN material. When challenged on why she apparently deliberately set out to be controversial, Mae said, "*All I ever wanted to do is entertain people, make 'em laugh so hard they forget they'd like to cry ...*" The line could have been Madonna's.

Fuelled by indignation caused by Mae's annual salary at $480,000 being only $20,000 less than his, but more likely because he had a deal with the movie studio, W. R. Hearst, that *great* American, preceding only Rupert Murdoch on Onan's Field, complained about the immoral, nose-thumbing Mae to no less august an institution than the United States Congress itself.

Mae survived.

In 1936, Emmanuel Cohen left Paramount to start up an independent subdivision called Major Pictures and Ernst Lubitsch became production chief. For all that waxes, something wanes as sure as the moon has its phases and occasionally eclipses the sun.

Mae wanted to make a picture about Catherine the Great of Russia. Maybe because the essentially European Lubitsch really didn't see the all-American Mae West as the man-eating Catherine and also because the 1934 Marlene Dietrich SCARLET EMPRESS on the same subject had laid such a big box-office egg, Mae's project was turned down and she embarked instead in

1938 on EVERY DAY'S A HOLIDAY playing Peaches O'Day. Lubitsch later made the Catherine picture with Tallulah Bankhead. Another egg was duly laid. As Mae observed acidly, *"It played several of the smaller drive-ins."*

Lubitsch's arrival seemed to mark the beginning of Mae's exit from Paramount. Radio was all the rage, there being five hundred and sixty plus stations nationwide by the mid-1930s. Mae gave her first radio performance doing an Adam and Eve sketch with Don Ameche, written by Arch Oboler, nationwide out of KF1-LA. She conquered yet another medium.

With Louis Lurie, her lawyer and Jim Timony, Mae left Paramount and started the Mae West/Empire Pictures Corporation which would organise not only her personal appearance tours throughout America but also her cinematic services in future productions, the first of these being a venture with Universal with W. C. Fields. THE JAYHAWKERS became THE LADY AND THE BANDIT which became, finally, MY LITTLE CHICKADEE which was hugely successful.

It was to be the last of her screen-crackling movies although not to be out done, she did just what Marlene was to do twenty years later. She picked her favourite image of herself, froze it in time and took herself back to the boards.

The Royal Airforce's immortalising her figure in the Mae West life preservers in 1941 and Salvador Dali's sensational representation of her lips in the creation of his famous red sofa in 1942, only served to make of Mae an international institution. During the war and after her final divorce from her one and only husband Frank Wallace, Mae delved deeply into religion, taking a sabbatical from all her entertainment activities to explore matters spiritual and various areas of the occult. In the year 1943, she decided her lucky number was 8, the numerological prime number derived from tinkering with 1+9+4+3.

In that year, she made THE HEAT'S ON, directed by actor/producer Greg Ratoff and adapted from the Broadway play TROPICANA. In 1945 Mike Todd finally produced the stage version of her Catherine project entitled CATHERINE WAS GREAT on Broadway at The Schubert theatre, a production which, like all her others, she toured to eager out-of-state audiences.

The remainder of the 1940's saw her play DIAMOND LIL in London where she played eight months at The Prince of Wales Theatre and touring LIL, her best-remembered vehicle, throughout her own United States.

She was left alone in business when Jim Timony died in 1954 after having been first hospitalised with a bad heart condition in 1951. But she was far from through. She and Las Vegas began a mutual love affair in 1955 when she created her Muscle Boy Show which she produced at The Sahara for its owner Milton Prell and then toured in the new Theatre/Restaurant circuit spawned by the late-fifties and sixties.

Mae said that with her Muscle Boys, she wanted to give the women of America something to look at. She did that and beat The Chippendales into a cocked (sorry) hat by three decades. She encouraged the libidinous rumours by taking up with at least one of her hand-picked chorus whilst fighting an off/on/ off bout with the attentions of the jealous Victor Lopez, an All-American wrestler. Mae and Catherine the Great would appear to have had a *lot* in common.

Mae didn't really take to television although she stole the 1959 televised Academy Award Oscar presentations by singing BABY IT'S COLD OUTSIDE with Rock Hudson. She was sixty seven years young.

Always teetotal, she continued to take care of herself, telling us she washed each breast each day in very cold water. She re-invented herself after Rex Reed re-discovered her in MYRA BRECKINRIDGE and although she made it known she was available both for work and play, Mae lived out a more than comfortable retirement before her death.

It was a great life. She was a pioneer and despite being an easy target, was never even splashed by the mudslingers. I empathise with her. She was an original and she always enjoyed the luxury of being in control. Her legacy is summed up in her one-liner, *"Between two evils, I always pick the one I never tried before."*

CHAPTER 3

The Movie Masters

The Movie Masters

In his admirable book, AN EMPIRE OF THEIR OWN, Neal Gabler charts the rise and rise of the Hollywood moghuls from their small beginnings to their various pinnacles of success. For some lions roared and cocks crew; others found expression for their achievements in snow-capped mountains, imperially dominant broadcasting towers pulsing energy over the globe. Whatever. The studio founders and heads, the Mayers, the Zukors, the Laemmles, the Foxes, the Warners were all Jewish, either immigrants to the United States or first generation and they were hands-on bosses.

Unlike the majority of corporate executives, industry presidents and vice-presidents today, these founding movie men knew their trade. Most of them had been alive when Louis and Auguste Lumière projected the first publicly exhibited film on March 22nd 1895 in Paris. It was the first box office and the showmen who turned entertainment shamen knew all about bums on seats. They knew about turnover, grosses and costs because they'd all counted and banked the daily box office. Moreover, they had developed both from the balance sheets of their early businesses and endless hours spent watching those movies which brought the bums through the doors, an instinct for what their audiences wanted to watch.

Dynastic these men certainly were but dynasties can only be founded on families and it was the very family context from which these men operated which allowed the industry to grow and prosper. The family at home and at leisure in Jewish environments may have been headed by the husbands but it was effectively martialled by the wives. It was a family outing, arranged by the mothers, who went to the early moving pictures. The French initiative didn't take long to cross the Atlantic. By 1897 it had penetrated deep into the American hinterland as Edna Ferber remembers although overnight success was not the destiny of the early moving pictures. Going to see the silent strobing of these primitive movies gave many people headaches.

Family, both in concept and in reality, was all-important. Without family there could be no networking. After centuries of persecution, of being hounded from town to town, country to country and now, finally, - for there was nowhere else for Israel to move - in America, without the network the Jewish community felt more than usually vulnerable.

Whilst the East Coast invented the mechanics and then both spawned and continued to propagate the art content of the new movie medium, when the Jewish producers moved West, to the California coast where the industry had already settled its roots, the film business both in production and exhibition was ripe for industrialisation. The producers and the exhibitors combined - the Mayers and the Foxes got in bed with the Loews, the Keiths, the Orpheums and rationalised the business.

Along with this rationalisation went, strangely, a democratisation for most of these latter day Moses who distributed the tablets of entertainment, wanted to be assimilated into the wider American society. But what was American society? Who knew? Did *they*? No one else did or ever has.

So, lacking any coherent answers, the moguls concocted an answer and what they made up was an America which everyone - at least of non-colour - could feel part of too. What they made up was the America of human emotions, the America of sentiment and sentimentality, the America of small towns, main streets, apple pies and mom and pop, of heroes and villains and its own proud history. They created the America which is easily manipulable by the harangue, diverted by the dream, the short term moment, the America whose heart opens the same way as its purse strings.

America was sold to itself seat-by-seat. It was given a dream which, like the misconceived pre-Galileo notion of a flat earth borne on the back of a turtle, was floated on the carapace of romantic love, on the raft of good boy meets pure girl, repels wicked rival, marries and lives happily forever, together, two hearts united at the beck and call of nothing and no one other than God (sic) and the Flag.

America, all disparate elements of it, discovered itself when it looked upon its own face. God never believed that there was no other work to be done after the six days of creation. He wasn't resting. He was figuring out how to complete the work. It was all very well to have given the people discipline, but God knew that as well as needing to behave, humanity also needed to dream. However, because discipline and dreams do not flow comfortably or, ultimately, credibly from the same chalice, God bided his time.

When that time came he merely subcontracted the work to the Hollywood Dream Machine.

Because it was their own taste, the movie masters developed their product as a broad back on which the common denominators of public taste could comfortably sit. The movie masters were ably aided and abetted by the W. R. Hearst school of journalism. Yellow Journalism, as the ilk became branded, had already powerfully proved itself to be at once creator and arbiter of public opinion, genesis of morality and even dynamo of political will and direction.

The majority of the American press of the teens and twenties had become riddled through and through with what we know today as the shock-horror-sex-jingo genre of our own vulgarised press. In short, they ran stories which were calculated to sell copies. Hearst had even managed to send his country to war; though it had been ever so briefly, the United States went to war against Spain in 1898 supposedly over the question of Cuba. Supposedly. Whatever that episode didn't achieve, its major accomplishment was to irrevocably put the American politician firmly in the hands of the media barons. Popular support for any politician was in the gift of the newspaper magnates. Politicians had to sell themselves via the papers and thus became more important than the politics they pretended.

The movie men needed the shock/horror/sensation/!!! press to sell its movies. No wonder Mr. Hearst was so besotted with the movie industry. He above all realised that where a mutual need arises, industrial fortunes are made.

By the mid-1920's, the as yet silent movies were playing on 18,000 screens across America. Across the world, there were 47,000. (* Figures from GOODNESS HAD NOTHING TO DO WITH IT - Mae West) Throughout this decade and the thirties and forties, the publicity material for most American-made movies was printed in and therefore controlled by America. Lobby cards from out-of-the-way movie theatres in British Colonial India have merely a blank space for being locally overprinted with the Indian cinema names and programme times.

From whatever prime arena, the century's culture-vators had moved more by accident than design into the business of the store-front movie houses, those shops and vacant premises which were hastily furbished with seating for an eager public to flock to at prices way below those charged by the vaudeville houses, the only other alternative of mass entertainment, to watch the early one, two and three reel silent pictures. Some of these pictures in the very early days lasted only three or four minutes. Even when more reels were added, it would be some years before the full length movie we recognise today emerged.

The First World War was a watershed. Whilst the fighting itself, of course had not spread to have been experienced in every country of the world, the effects of the fighting were certainly globally felt for the balance of world power was changed.

The very sacrifice endured and supplied by the masses, by the workers and labourers and peasants of the world seemed to have had an empowering effect. Seemed ... The empowerment was probably illusory. Probably ... No! What *happened* was that sops were thrown and the various elites realised that they had to be *seen* to be more sensitised, more democratic, more a part of the whole ... But what whole? A whole is, after all, two halves. Or three thirds or four quarters. The whole is *all* the people, every individual. Men *and* women. Rich *and* poor. Black *and* white.

Women had at last re-joined men in the theatre, if not the field, of battle. The Women's Auxiliary Army Corps, the Women's Royal Naval Service and the Women's Royal Air Force were all created in the last year of the Great War and, in Britain, women were partially enfranchised in 1918 though it was not to be until 1928 that all women won the right to equal electoral participation in the choosing of their leaders.

In post-First World War America, where female enfranchisement had not long been established after the tireless respectable 'campaigning' by the Womens' Clubs, the inchoate voice of 'the people' rumbled first grudgingly and then angrily throughout the land. Revolution had swept through the old Russia, half of which it seemed to the American establishment, had immigrated into its own back-yard. For a time, those same 'dangerous' ideas took shape and form via the Communist Party of America for there was no other chord which could make heard the people's voice. This forgotten period, this swept-beneath-the-carpet era of American history has had the angry pride shamefully expunged from it. At the time, unrest and discontent were not only suppressed by the civil authorities' violence and brutal murder of militant protesting workers and intellectuals. Whilst literature did its best to give the people a voice, the press, the movies and the incipient radio medium ignored what those in power deemed a threat to their self-styled 'American way'. The perceived unrest threatened the economics of the very capitalism which had allowed the powerful to prosper.

Although later, very much later, Warren Beatty with REDS went a little way to putting over another side of the story of those times in his portrait of the idealistic journalist Jack Reed, Hollywood abetted by Hearstism gave the people of the nineteen teens, twenties and thirties a diet which was considered more politically digestible.

The movies, for the most part, ignored the big issues, going as far as vilifying 'troublemakers'. Sacco and Vanzetti were allowed to be fried in the electric chair and untold numbers of unsung martyrs were created on the killing fields of social protest and trade union activity.

The main constituent of the diet was very simple. Instead of heroes, the people, proletariat and patricians alike, were given stars.

In the same way that the press had made personalities out of politicians, Hollywood provided even bigger stars, huge, marquee-wide, hoarding-high, larger-than-life dream-pegs; hooks for hope, hangers for fantasy ...

In the front and back offices of the several Emerald Cities, the dream merchants traded overtime; the Marco Polos of fantasy and escapism raided whatever arsenal necessary, bought up material from whatever source to fashion graven images and house these in a whole galaxy of make-believe. Broadway was pillaged for talent, vaudeville was systematically drained of acts and ideas, publishing houses were ransacked to provide vehicles for the newly forged stellar giants who, however they appeared to be presented to the public, were designed to be perceived against an invisible backdrop of excitement, they mugged and hammed their way through an unspoken subtext of sex.

Sex sold stars. Sex made stars. As strong as the urge to eat, the urges of sex unite the human race. Sex can make everyone a star. For a few blinding moments, sex can nourish the soul.

The dream merchants' warehouses were stuffed with stars,

who, being only manufactures on a mortal frame, were therefore only human and, ergo, prey to all the vices and temptations and foibles and fears that sex and the sexes cause.

The closets-ful of stars were overflowing with sex.

Newsprint was therefore concomitantly stiff with the revelations of the stars' secrets and the sleaze and slang which came along for the ride. The worst aspects of basic human nature were employed by the publicity machinery updated from pre-war days by the demands of the film industry. Natural, over-the-fence gossip and rumour were legitimised as the cavorting of the famous and the beautiful were 'dutifully' reported in the press. Both the movies and the press assumed a moral stance - pro bono publico - which they have never shucked.

Lives and careers, marriages and sanities were therefore sacrificed daily on the altar of prurience-gone-mad. The studios produced stars which glittered as brightly in those tough times as the alternatives paled dull and unappealing. Who wanted to go without? Who wanted to risk what little they had when... Look! Look at Mae! Look at Harlow! They do alright for themselves in those movies ... If they can, so can we!

And so the American Dream was born, reinforcing the American Way, laying down the Yellow Brick Road along which no one was supposed to actually walk for no one was ever intended to meet The Wizard.

CHAPTER 4

Jean Harlow

Jean Harlow

By the standards of any age, Jean Harlow was a tragic figure. The tradition of being passed from pillar to post by man after man started at a very tender age way back when, way back home in Kansas City where she was born on March 3rd 1911. There were men who didn't want her and men who did. The men who did weren't so much of a problem for they were the great punting public. It was the men who didn't want her, who were cruel to her who caused the grief. Everyone from her grandfather Sam Harlow to Howard Hughes to Louis B. Mayer. Her life, as it developed, turned into an object lesson in what can happen to a perfectly sweet, adorable blonde baby who never gets the loving she deserved. In the end, she was merely used. By everyone.

She was referred to as 'The Baby' throughout her infancy and most of her childhood before she knew her name was Harlean. She had been christened Harlean Carpentier. Her father Montclair was a prominent dentist and her mother Jean Harlow was the daughter of a well-respected solidly middle class Kansas City family.

Harlean's parents' marriage floundered and they separated when Harlean was nine, just a year after her grandfather Sam had enrolled her in the private and costly Barstow School for girls. It is not too early to observe that Doctor Carpentier had thought his wife excessively vapid. Mama Jean as she was always known in Hollywood Harlow circles was rather a silly woman, with little intellectual curiosity, much given to lazing abed. She'd been brought up to be a little too grand for her roots and she always thought the world owed her rather than feeling herself honour-bound to do anything for that living. She had little willpower and her tears only served to galvanise her father Sam's intentions of properly bringing up his grand-daughter where he had palpably failed with his daughter.

Because of Sam's fear of diseases, the little Harlean was allowed few playmates. Harlean's mother, isolated from the only proper role available to her as Harlean's mother, took instead to the reading of Mary Baker Eddy's texts and blind adoption of the tenets of Christian Science and was encouraged in this by her own mother, Ella Harlow.

Thus the circumstances of Harlean's relationship with her mother were characterised very early on. The helpless led the helpless and the follow-my-leader bluff was to have tragic consequences.

I imagine Sam Harlow basically drove Mama Jean out. Untrained and unwilling to work and with a failed marriage behind her, she had no ability for employment and, let's face it, little chance of remarriage with little Harlean in tow in the close community in which the Harlows lived. Mama Jean left Kansas City for a weekend visit to some distant Chicago relatives and stayed. The weekend became an absence of some years.

The reason for her absence was Marino Bello and although he was patently the classic Latin moustachioed lover, he was bad news. He was an arrogant braggart of a man, slaked with pomposity and perfidy and with a repertoire of bragadoccio which boasted Sicilian and even murkier European aristocratic ancestry. Mama Jean, not Kansas' most classic beauty, was bowled over by the peacock display of her lover's charm, his dash, his energy and his lack of sexual inhibition and her orgasm appeared to assume command of her judgement. Marino was machismo. He obviously liked his women to moan.

It's a good enough reason to marry, I suppose, and marry they did although Sam Harlow threatened to have it annulled as soon as he heard about it. Marino, similarly, was not a little taken aback when Mama Jean finally told him about Harlean.

He refused to have anything to do with 'The Baby' and, concomitantly, Sam Harlow refused to have anything to do with Marino. Harlean decided she was going to have little to do with Sam.

Perfect.

Mama Jean and her new husband remained away for four years. The only ripple her divorce from Montclair caused was that news of it sent her eleven year old daughter screaming to hide in the depths of a closet. As Montclair and Sam Harlow didn't speak and after Sam had forbidden his Christian Scientist wife to consult her practitioner on the best way of 'curing' the hysterical child, it was left to the auspices of a kindly public nurse to coax the frightened Harlean out of her misery. For years, Harlean only saw her father at a once weekly meeting at his dental surgery. His only child became a time slot.

Harlean was physically womanly and prey to jealous cat-calls from her female school friends as well as wolf whistles from the local beaux. When her mother and Marino came to visit one Christmas, Mama Jean fell sick and, against her own and Mrs. Harlow's protestations, a doctor was called, diagnosed pernicious bronchitis and the result was that the Bellos stayed in Kansas City.

Sam Harlow never took to the strutting Marino whom he distrusted and whom he thought to be beating up on Mama Jean when he mistook her nightly moans of orgasmic ecstasy for cries of pain.

Frankly, my dears, sex was not a topic Sam Harlow even recognised and when Dr. Carpentier raised the subject with Harlean of those wolf whistles which had been getting loud enough for Marino to notice too, Carpentier enrolled his daughter in a boarding school. In 1926 Harlean entered Ferry Hall finishing school for girls near Chicago.

The assets that were to make Harlean famous as Jean Harlow were firmly in place; she knew about her breasts and knew that others wanted to know about them too, going to the lengths of refusing to wear the brassieres which Mama Jean forced her into. The brassieres made everything more obvious, lifting, pointing and aiming ... However, like her father and despite being in the thrall of sex herself, Mama Jean was unable to utter the words which might have put the phenomenon which her daughter was discovering into perspective. It seemed that the only Harlow upon whom was doomed to fall the mantle of sex was Harlean.

Harlean already knew how much boys liked her firm perfect breasts which had been further endowed by a naturally bequeathed matching pair of larger-than-designer-size nipples. Being otherwise ignorant, Harlean intuited from direct mammary experience that the boy who'd got there loved her. Away from the hawklike surveillance of her sex-vigilante grandpa, Harlean had already sneaked out of school and was seeing seventeen year old Chuck McGrew, the son an Illinois stockbroking family.

Two months later, in March 1927, the couple eloped to Waukegan and were married. It was all legal and aboveboard. They'd spent the night in an hotel and had obviously 'done it'. But being Mr. and Mrs. Chuck McGrew in name or no, the couple were immediately separated; Chuck was sent off East, Harlean was grounded and Sam Harlow, seething once again under the canopy of shame which his inexplicably wayward family had thrust him, paid for the Bellos and Harlean to move to California in summer 1927. To Los Angeles.

To Hollywood.

It was thought that there was a frontier there which would welcome the dash and verve of the buccaneering Bello. There was also a lot to involve a well-stacked, nubile, seventeen year old blonde in Hollywood 1927. It was the year that technology found its voice and passed it on to THE JAZZ SINGER. Only the year before, 1926, the greatest of the silent legends, Valentino, had died. It was the end of an era.

Even seen through the rosiest of rose tints, although they were hugely popular, silent black and white movies were mostly pretty banal. Saving Nazimova and the superb pictures of D. W. Griffith and his ilk, the content of only a mere twenty percent of films was artistically significant and the stories of the majority merely pegs on which were hung that all-time crowd-pulling cert, SEX. But it was just what the public wanted and thank God someone was finally pulling the old dinosaur out of the unhealthy closet.

Sex was dressed up this way and that way and, as far as could be gotten away with, the other. Movie audiences mushroomed. Movie palaces were built to accommodate the phenomenon and by 1929, most every picture talked and a lot of careers had crashed when the sound of their stars' recorded voices failed to match the stereotype of their images. A lotta dreams were up for grabs in 1929 and every girl fancied she was gonna be swept off her feet by Richard Dix or John Boles...

Or Howard Hughes.

Howard Hughes would have been much happier dating and marrying an aeroplane. Let's face it, he owned them, designed them, built them, flew them and he owned the hangars, offices, factories and airfields to do all these. If only he'd been able to exchange bodily fluids with one ... Anyway, when not doing any of the above, Hughes even made movies about aeroplanes in a studio he owned for the purpose, Metropolitan Studio on Romaine and Cahuenga in Hollywood.

Greta Nissen fondly thought she was to star in Hughes' HELLS ANGELS, a paen to the wartime heroics of the nascent Air Force Squadrons. Instead, Greta found herself on her ass and off the lot. Being Norwegian and vocally thus identifiable, Nissen had hardly been perfect casting for the role of the English rose in the movie. Her agent, Arthur Landau, blamed for the mis-casting by both Hughes and James Whale, the movie's new director, was despatched forthwith to seek a replacement. Preferably look-alike. Greta, by the way continued to make movies. We have an RKO lobby card advertising MELODY CRUISE in which she stars with Marjorie Gateson and Helen Mack. Greta looks incredibly like the as yet, in our tale at least, un-invented Jean Harlow.

Dorothy MacKaill, another blonde on Landau's client list whom Hughes and Whale had specifically requested, was unavailable.

What to do? There were hundreds of girls in Hollywood. Thousands. Why Harlow? It seems to me that the look-alike thing figured in the start of the Jean Harlow story.

Landau's tale is that he called in to the Hal Roach Studio and was chatting on their set to Stan Laurel and Oliver Hardy when he noticed Harlean who we shall now call Jean. The guys shared some smutty asides and then told Landau Jean'd extra-ed on a couple of their pictures, even doing a little business in DOUBLE WHOOPEE where her dress had been slammed in a car door and she'd stepped away in her smalls. Tee hee! Black and white movies? Art?

Landau talked to her. She was hungry, she was tired, she hadn't worked that week. She wasn't wearing a bra and she looked cheap, tarty and rough. But she was blonde and she *did* look a little like Greta Nissen. Jean, of course, thought Landau was coming on to her especially when he suggested a steak dinner to at least ease the hunger. According to Landau, he wasn't coming on to her and so, mollified and reassured, Jean of course told Arthur she had indeed heard of him and was duly impressed. She was blown away when he asked her if she'd screen test at Metropolitan. In fact she couldn't believe her luck and to validate it, her luck that is, wanted Arthur to give her a contract. So she'd *know*.

She also needed a loan.

The following morning, Arthur collected her from the little house in one of the streets between Sunset and Santa Monica. Mama Jean and Bello waved her goodbye, their greed and laziness wreathed in the smile of family values. They both saw their stars rising and Bello had already gambled away that initial loan. It was the first of a series of loans that could have cumulatively crippled the diminutive Landau. I sure hope he used better judgement when representing his other clients.

Jean's test was iffy, the guys on the sound stage were the first to be wowed by the chest and Hughes, immune to such mortal fancies remained unconvinced. *"I think she's nix,"* was how his appraisal of her abilities has been reported.

But Landau talked Jean into the part and a terrible deal. It was a bad start and it led to a shabby finish. Life as she came to know it would be un-sustainable. Hughes would only agree to $1500 for the six weeks of the movie, an exclusive contract with his Caddo Corporation for three years with a weekly salary of $200 off, $250 on. Of course, to Jean it was telephone numbers but as things were to work out, a star's 'phone calls didn't come cheap. And there were those good ol' family values. 'Til her dying day, Jean had to contend firstly with Marino Bello's ambitions to be her manager and always with her mother's expenses. When Bello failed to control Jean as a manager, he merely controlled her by spending her money.

HELLS ANGELS opened in 1930 and laid a big egg. But the people noticed Jean and when she went out on personal appearances to bolster the ailing, sputtering aeroplane movie, the public went wild for her body, her boobs and her famous bon mots. Recognising her propensity, Arthur arranged that she be coached in the art of the double entendre and that her apparently impromptu innuendo was thoroughly scripted.

Jean Harlow's success was literally overnight. She became, quite simply, the third of cinema's sex goddesses after Theda Bara and Clara Bow. The Harlow succession seemed almost vindicated by her having appeared, 'though too-too briefly, in Clara Bow's last picture in 1929.

Howard Hughes was forced to eat his words. America wasn't going to see HELLS ANGELS for his precious planes but for Harlow's beautiful blonde hair and her wonderful, dream-on-boys, how-about-those-egg-rolls Mr. Goldstone ...

If she was nix, her pix sold tix.

Jean Harlow was well worth the $3500 a week Arthur Landau negotiated for her initial personal appearance tours but after his commission, the balance wasn't for Jean but for the

Caddo Corporation. Them's some tasty words, Howie and some contract, Arthur!

Five Jean Harlow pictures were released in 1931 alone. IRON MAN, PUBLIC ENEMY, THE SECRET SIX. Hughes loathed her but realising she could make his planes fly, kept loaning her out to other studios who, obviously, queued up for her services despite her patent lack of acting talent.

I can hear Mae West's warning to those instant stars who have no foundation of talent or theatre experience ... Oh Mae, where were you? I can hear her reply, *"Paramount, sweetie ... And it's Miss West to you!"*

Jean made GOLDIE at Fox and then two movies at Columbia one of which was THREE WISE GIRLS but the first of which was PLATINUM BLONDE which made of Jean Harlow a national monument. Platinum Blonde clubs were formed all over America and beauty parlours had never been busier.

Arthur Landau finally negotiated better terms from Hughes who still disliked Harlow. He thought her common and vapid and had no time for anything but her receipts. He even loaned her out to Cosmopolitain, the production company which although associated with MGM, was owned and run by William Randolph Hearst for, so t'was said, the sole purpose of providing vehicles in which Hearst's beautiful but decidedly-not-dumb blonde mistress Marion Davies could star. For Hearst, Jean made BEAST OF THE CITY playing, guess what? Another loose-living blonde charmer. If Hughes had really thought Jean common and vapid, he sure didn't do much to help her change.

Jean could not have been unaware of the scorn poured upon her perceived lack of acting ability 'though she seems to have insulated herself from the worst effects of that cruel criticism by immersing herself in her paying public's perception of her as a sex symbol. She revelled in her body, touching her breasts quite publicly, brushing her thighs quite openly when 'answering' questions and devising often chilling ways of making sure her nipples were standing strictly to attention whenever she was out on press parade.

It would seem that she was being expected to be and stay a star with little emotional support. She was still living with Mama Jean and Bello, she seemed to have no close girlfriends and she had no suitor. She was close guarded by agents, studio press representatives and, most of all Bello who it seems not only beat up on her when she tried to control his spending but could have sexually threatened her as well.

The meeting of the most desirable woman in America and MGM's most serious-minded and deep-thinking producer presaged essence of the Monroe/Miller association of some thirty odd years later. The folk tale touched by intellect which begets true art-house culture is one which she thought legitimised her and Jean so wanted to be thought a 'real' actress.

Paul Bern and Jean Harlow were two lonely people both emotionally crippled. When Louis B Mayer heard one of his trusted aides was to marry his most detested star - for Louis B too thought Harlow a tart - the remarks of the man who all but single-handed endowed America with its loving, caring and sharing family values were apparently unprintable. The wedding itself, star-studded and roundly reported by the world's press, was nevertheless graced by the whole Mayer menage.

But why, why Jean Harlow, America's sex goddess, hadn't found out before her wedding night that her husband's physical endowment was so insignificant that it had rendered him impotent from shame, I cannot imagine. Bern's small penis had caused him to grow up through aching years of embarrassment. As a result, he had developed psycho-complexes so convoluted that he could only give vent to the resulting frustration by violently beating up on the object of his thwarted desire. Before meeting Jean, Bern had gone through a permutation of sexual experimentation. He'd thought himself homosexual. He wasn't. He'd had dates, even a mistress, even a wife ... What he'd never had and what he was cursed never to enjoy was any sort of sexual satisfaction.

On his wedding night to Jean, he got drunk and beat up on her. He took a thick cane and beat her across her back, hurting her kidneys and gall bladder, an organ that was later to cause her an insurmountable problem.

Jean fled the house after he collapsed and was only persuaded not to stay fled by the studio and her agent and her devoted step-father all of whom saw their own bright stars in imminent danger of implosion in the aftermath of the unseemly press speculation which would have resulted from a too-swift marital break-down.

Much has been written about these terribly sad circumstances. Much more can be read in detail if so desired. The newly-weds got to hate each other and, suffice it to be said here, in the end, Bern is supposed to have killed himself. Though some say Jean or another did it, Bern is supposed to have shot himself after leaving a note:

"Dearest Dear: Unfortunately this is the only way to make good the frightful wrong I have done you and to wipe out my abject humiliation - Paul. You understand that last night was only a comedy."

I tend to believe the note was genuine. 'Abject' is a word Bern would have had in his vocabulary. Louis B would probably have had to look it up and even then dismiss it as being effete and elite.

The reference to the 'comedy' of the previous night was that having no confidence in medical opinion that he *could* have satisfaction if only he could overcome his fear of coitus, Bern had invested in a strap-on dildo and had appeared in Jean's bedroom so accoutred. Jean apparently became hysterical in the grip of a mixture of uncontrollable mirth and helpless sadness. Bern had, it is alleged, hacked off the offending contraption before leaving her to retire.

Anyway, next morning he was dead.

Next morning the press had the first of many field days through which they would sniff and hunt and chase the possibilities. It transpired that Bern had had a mistress, that he had also been married. His first wife, Dorothy Milette was herself found drowned. Jean also found out that her husband on $1500 a week had left her only debts and bills and a mere $2000 of cash wealth even with his final week's salary check un-spent. What had he spent his money on? The mystery of Bern lingered itchily for decades but at the time it gnawed ravenously at Jean's self-worth.

Following Bern's coffin was the beginning of Jean Harlow's road to her own private Cavalry. She felt not only once again let down and betrayed by a man whom she had thought had properly loved her, she felt wounded and vulnerable when faced with the rabid press speculation on the most intimate of her personal affairs. She felt empty and unfulfilled and, not being the heaviest intellect on campus, utterly confused. Her sanity saw the first cracks appear in its housing.

It is said that bereft of the sexual attention which would have validated her own image of herself as the altar and fount of sex, America's blonde sex siren took to cruising the Hollywood mean streets disguised and in search of men. Any men. She seemed fascinated by the possibility of making herself anonymous and picking up men. Overtaken by this wild freedom, she was later to cut off her hair to a very short bob, darken all her make-up and take off ... To San Bernadino she went alone by train and laid a salesman in a hotel room. In San Francisco, she took a taxi-ride round the streets and laid the taxi-driver. Later she would lose herself sometimes for days in drunken oblivion having casual anonymous sex.

Whether Mayer knew about this and it increased his personal revulsion toward her, I don't know but suffice to say Mr. Mayer knew everything. What Jean confided in Mama Jean must have gone the rounds. Mama Jean was too stupid to stay shtum and be a decent mother to her lonely, frightened daughter. Jean had confided to Mama that she wanted more than anything else to have a baby and that her apparent debauchery was really a search for a father for the baby. If there was ever an unloved soul, justifying her search for love by this painful perception that motherhood would make her loved, Jean's awful predicament bears witness.

The studio circumvented the problem of the absent Harlow tresses by making two perfect blonde Harlow wigs which were always kept dressed and ready and movie-goers never saw Harlow in her own hair again. The first film she made in the wigs was RED DUST and whilst filming, Jean started building a new house for herself, despite her financial embarrassment and despite Bern's mistress surfacing and demanding $50,000 for the journals she had obviously written each time the top MGM executive had sort-of-shagged her and then skedaddled.

Jean went into Irving Thalberg's HOLD THAT MAN with Clark Gable which pleased her ego and which delighted audiences for the movie was a huge hit. Whilst Jean began the slow slide into the nadir, her star, ironically, had never been higher. It was calculated that in 1933 when America's population was one hundred and twenty five million, eighty eight million people went regularly to the movies and that a Harlow picture was guaranteed to pull, throughout its exhibition life, between fifteen and twenty million adult movie-goers.

She made David Selznick's DINNER AT EIGHT, a top-flight property based on an Edna Ferber and George Kaufman play which George Cukor directed, gathering a first rate MGM star cast. It was on this picture she had become close with the cinematographer Harold (Hal) Rosson who had been thought to have coaxed better performances from her by making a little fuss with the camera before her shots. Rosson was therefore scheduled to photograph her on her next movie, BOMBSHELL. The twenty-two year old star and the thirty-eight year old cameraman were married in Yuma on the eighteenth of September 1933.

For the short time the marriage lasted, I have a hunch that she knew what it was to be loved securely and squarely and on a regular meat'n'potatoes basis by the same man. It was what she had always wanted but I also fear it wasn't what she wanted. The Rossons started to do all the right things, like moving away from Jean's new house on Beverly Glen and away from the whingeing, swingeing presence of Mama Jean and Marino. They moved into a third floor apartment in the Chateau Marmont on Sunset.

After falling ill with tremendous pain in her lower back, Jean was operated on for appendicitis. When Mama Jean tried to prevent the hospitalisation on Christian Science grounds, Louis B called up and told her definitely that it was he who owned Harlow not Mama Jean. If only ...

As her marriage to Hal drifted to its conclusion, Jean was making GIRL FROM MISSOURI. When Hal finally moved out, he was replaced on the movie by Ray June and after GIRL FROM MISSOURI wrapped, Jean threw a wobbly and stayed away from the studio when Mayer wouldn't accede to certain of her demands. Another of her mainframe relationships, namely that with her long suffering agent Arthur Landau ruptured although she reluctantly went back to work in Selznick's RECKLESS, a script which she initially loathed as she thought it was a veiled reference to her real life drama with Paul Bern.

With Landau out of the arena, the persistently scheming Marino Bello finally got his hand around the tiller of Jean's career and business life. He boasted of being able to help Mayer with a studio industrial dispute. He failed. He boasted he could make a movie deal for Jean with the Kordas in England. He failed. But he also became even more careless with his extra-marital tricking and Mama Jean was beginning to have had enough.

RECKLESS was not well-received and although it seemed that the Harlow dynamo might be slowing, at MGM Louis B was providing all his major stars, a list which included Jean, with new bungalows and was delighted that TIME Magazine wanted to put Jean on their August 19th cover that year, 1935. Jean had been making CHINA SEAS which was linked to the TIME cover, an auspicious accolade having been accorded to only a handful of movie stars before and which well and truly put out of joint the jealous noses of other MGM mega-belles. Jean then went straight into RIFF RAFF with Spencer Tracy.

Late in 1935, Mama and Marino split, acrimoniously. The cruddy Italian left, gagged with a $50,000 spit-in-the-eye and Jean and Mama moved out of the Beverley Glen house and into a smaller furnished house. RIFF RAFF completed and Jean went into WIFE vs. SECRETARY with Myrna Loy and, once again, with Gable.

By the beginning of 1936, Jean was feeling confident enough to ask more of Louis B, that being a good picture with her longtime friend and probably lover William Powell and she wanted $4000 a week to do it. She got her money and after making SUZY with Cary Grant and Franchot Tone, she was scheduled to make LIBELLED LADY with, apart from Spencer Tracy and Myrna Loy, William Powell. The picture wasn't what she wanted and Jean figured ways of getting the MY MAN GODFREY writers to really team her and Bill Powell together.

But other matters were afoot in the cosmos, namely the destiny of Irving Thalberg, whose death in September 1936 made MGM question its future. The Schencks got to Louis B and economy was in the air.

At home, the vamoosed Marino had left Mama Jean horny and bitter. She was taking her frustrations out on her daughter whom she blamed for the split up, even for Marino's infidelities. Mama Jean pulled out the love rug from Jean's feet. It was the very, very last betrayal the twenty five year old needed.

PERSONAL PROPERTY started shooting in January 1937 with Robert Taylor not William Powell although Powell had given Jean a huge sapphire ring on their unofficial engagement. She travelled by train to Washington for a presidential celebration but fell ill. Feelings of coldness and freezing hands and feet had been plaguing her for several weeks. She returned to Hollywood but was on the sick list for February and March and in April went for a time to Palm Springs contemplating yet another picture with Clark Gable called SARATOGA.

Before the picture had finished shooting, Jean had collapsed and all the studio could discover, even from Clark Gable who called at the house, was that Jean was in bed, sick and being amply tended by the ministrations of Mama Jean as directed by Mary Baker Eddy.

Mama Jean, as evidenced by the witness of Gable, Arthur Landau and other visitors, had plainly gone barking mad. Although doctors were given access and despite Jean's deteriorating condition, Mama Jean refused to allow hospitalisation where surgery could have corrected the inflammation of the gall bladder whose effects were rendering her daughter unconscious. At least Jean became less aware of the acute pain she was in.

Louis B was begged to visit Jean's bedside. He had banished Mama Jean once before. Couldn't he do it again? There is a story that he merely shrugged and turned away.

Her fast failing kidneys were causing uraemia which was poisoning her whole system. She was unable to understand her condition and unable to give her own permission for the treatments which would have saved her life.

When Louis B himself finally called the hospital, people jumped. Jean was transferred by silent ambulance to The Good Samaritan Hospital in Los Angeles. Two total blood transfusions were administered way too late. Jean died at 11.40 in the morning of June 7th 1937, survived by her mother.

She was twenty six for God's sake.

CHAPTER 5

Blonde at Last

Blonde at Last

With the growing influence of the movies and the growing empowerment of women came the growth of the beauty parlour, the spread of the salon de coiffure ...

Peroxides are stringent and powerful disinfectants. Carelessly used in the wrong hands, the stuff can sting! New breeds of professional men and women accompanied the rise of the movie stars. No longer was the monopoly of hair cutting held by the Barber of Seville. Try Charles of the Ritz, Alexandre of Paris or Nestle (pronounced Nesslay) of New York, a salon de coiffure founded by Karl Nessler and who perfected permanent waving in 1904. In London, for example, there was Monsieur Lichtenfeld, coiffeur Français of Oxford Street and of course there was Marcel Grateau.

Songs weren't written with lines about Marcel-waving just because the words rhymed or scanned. The fashion for Marcel's waves was obviously the talk of whole continents and the waves themselves were applied by highly trained professional hairdressers in professional salons who could achieve the changes in 'look' that their clients required.

Shown a picture of Theda Bara or, later, Colleen Moore or Clara Bow, woe betide the hairdresser who could not effect the requisite transformation! The hair that now needed cutting in order to match the couture fashions and cinema-generated images and to be stylish had to be cut and set professionally before the same could be achieved by women themselves less expensively at home. As well as traditional dressing to keep it healthy, along with the new need to be cut, thanks to science, modern hair could also be coloured. Dyed. God's handiwork too could be re-wrought by science and expertise.

"You wanna look like Mae West, lady? Sure. But it'll cost ya!"

So where did a girl go if she wanted to copy her favourite movie star and become a blonde?

Before the First World War, I contend that such a girl was one of a very, very small number, that she was occupied probably in or on the fringes of show-business, the licensed trade or that she was basically a tart. I say this not in a demeaning way but because of certain history and tradition. There wasn't a great call for a bleached blonde in the last days of Oscar Wilde and Queen Victoria.

By the late nineteen twenties, there were blondes akimbo on the silver screen. Esther Ralston, Betty Compson and Mary Nolan being some of the less well-known now, although at the time, they were up there with the best. Who, alive at the time, could have possibly missed Lilian Harvey in MY LIPS BETRAY, made by MGM and hyped as *"Gracious, Vivacious and Gay ..."* or her starring role as the Lalique Glass Statuette in I AM SUZANNE, for Fox.

These blonde careers and many, many more remembered now only by the anorak brigade, probably suffered in the wake of the more brilliant shooting stars who eclipsed and, over time, because of the degeneration of silver nitrate film stock. Like too solid flesh, their movies physically turned to dust.

Traditionally, women had always worn their hair long. True, there had been periods when it had been fashionable for ladies of quality or means to wear wigs and these wigs had often been great exaggerated creations topped with ships and birds of paradise and infested with either lice or mice or both. Wigmaking was a sophisticated art and there were many establishments in big towns and cities throughout the world although it was a form of hairdressing only affordable by the rich. Indeed, it was the poor who kept the wig-makers supplied. The poor and convents of nuns often sold their hair, then covered their heads until a new crop had sprouted. For the wig-wearers, however, natural hair would have still remained in long tresses pinned up beneath the wig.

Before he became assimilated by Minneapolis, Saint Paul himself had decreed that long hair for women was ideologically sound and it had been always so, short hair being considered a badge of some sort of shame. *Nice* girls and *decent* women wore their long hair up. From where else did it arise (and why else, ask yourselves), the expression we still use about 'Letting Your Hair Down' to indicate abandonment of decorous behaviour? And indeed, what sacrifice would it have been (if short hair had been the accepted norm) for a nun to be shorn of her tresses as one of the signs of her renouncement of the world and its wiles?

There had been several periods in history when blonde or lightened hair had been favoured. For the Greeks, blonde was the colour of the hair of gods and heroes. Saffron, henna and a variety of naturally sourced pastes were used to achieve as light a tone possible. Other concoctions used such gruesomely culled ingredients as lizard fat, swallows' droppings and the finely ground bones of bears.

In Ancient Rome, it had long been both tradition and law that ladies of the night should sport either lightened hair or blonde wigs to show that they were where the good times rolled. Whether it was censure or advertisement is not known although the disguise was most helpful to the third wife of the Emperor Claudius, Valeria Messalina, who was apparently given to donning the odd blonde wig and nipping out of the imperial palace to join in the roamin' merriment. Such was her reputation that for a time, a flurry of thicker-skinned Roman easies joined her in lightening their hair and buying blonde wigs and generally getting it on. Girls, and chaps too if the truth be known ...

Later, in the wealthy city state of Venice, ladies after washing their hair in rainwater and chamomile would sit in the direct sun with their long hair spread out over the brim of very wide, crownless hats to lighten their coiffures.

However, other than the puritans disapproving of the revelation of any sort of female hair, whether covered by hats, caps or bonnets, female hair in general remained long and up.

Before the First World War there were obviously hairdressing establishments in the bigger cities for those women who could afford the luxury. It was after all a Parisian hairdresser, M. Alexandre F Godefroy who in 1892 built the first purpose-designed hair-dryer. Apparently, thrifty and innovative Victorian ladies since the invention of the electrically operated vacuum cleaner had been making use of the blowing action of this appliance to dry their hair. Monsieur Godefroy was obviously god-sent.

However, for the vast majority who could indulge in the luxury of having regularly dressed hair, it was the lady's maid who dealt with coiffure and she did so using her own jealously guarded secrets in the privacy of her mistress's dressing room at home.

New styles that the lady's maid observed, such as they were, probably originated in Paris which was the centre of the couture and perfume industry. Paris fashions were avidly followed by women in both the old and new worlds in all classes regardless of wealth. New fashions have traditionally been accompanied by new hairstyles but these, as the gowns, were way outside the pale of possibility for the majority of middle and all working class women. Copies of both were, of course, made for more pressing budgets as the designs were published in the many womens' magazines which were extremely popular.

None of any such new hairstyles emanating from Paris would have openly advocated the colouring of women's hair, or the changing of natural colour. Colouring the hair was not considered 'nice' and when colouring was done at all, it was effected by dyeing to preserve or bolster original natural colour in a private booth at a hairdressing establishment or, indeed at home.

Home hair care and dressing had always been where women gave attention to their hair, often in groups although treatments were seldom either expensive or scientific. A 1928 copy of *Good Housekeeping* warns its readers against the use of chemical colourants as these were toxic and dangerous. Vegetable rinses and herbal washes had, of course, always been popular although the colouring effect of these always washed out, often in the rain.

CHAPTER 6

Marlene Dietrich

Marlene Dietrich

There is little anyone can add to the objective but entirely respectful analysis of Marlene Dietrich's life, times, personality, foibles, whims, idiosyncrasies and impossibilities than the biography recently effected by Marlene's daughter Maria Riva. In it you will find the woman laid bare, warts, bones, seams and all. It's a great write and a riveting read because altogether it's a sort of history of our century. History made flesh. Go ask for it, buy it and read it with as much joy and wonder as I did.

The little I can add, however, is a personal appreciation of Marlene's achievement and the way she managed it for I think Marlene was the star of stars.

Me, you, Maria, her husband, von Sternberg (her mentor)... We might not have liked her sometimes, but Marlene was only ever herself. No phoniness, no trickery, no mirrors, no hype, no pretend. She was as hideous and frightening and incomprehensible and extraordinary as she was glamorous, beguiling, single-minded and ordinary.

She was able to be herself because very few people ever said 'No' to her. A lot of people complained, felt hurt, rejected, badly treated but they could have always said 'No'.

Maria Riva did say 'No', many times, painfully and, honestly and if you ever read this, Maria, it was the best thing you could have ever done for you ultimately reminded your mother that she was herself and that what she was no one else's fault or doing but her own.

Marlene inhabited Marlene Dietrich as truly and as dearly as many a drag queen has since, praise the lord and pass the ammunition, inhabited the same host shell. Marlene lived to

---

create many Marlene Dietrichs but there was only ever really one. In this art-cum-science, Marlene was as post-modern as is Madonna who, I imagine, when she too runs out of the practical possibility of re-inventing herself yet again, like Marlene will freeze herself in time and just be the definitive Madonna.

I saw the definitive Marlene at The Queens Theatre in Shaftesbury Avenue, London. I saw elegance, I saw professionalism, I saw achievement, style. I saw a sort of perfection. I knew it was rehearsed to a millimetre, I knew she was dressed in some horrendous rubberised body corset to keep her straight and proud but even that knowledge added to a feeling of being somehow personally vindicated by the performance I had witnessed. Yes. Witnessed.

The sound of her voice as she sang SAG MIR WO DIE BLUMEN SIND (Where Have All The Flowers Gone)... I could feel the presence of all those dead souls looking back from eternity, glad to be remembered. Witnessed.

This definitive Marlene existed for far longer, decades longer than the brief and not entirely distinguished film career which spawned Marlene's finest creations in the nineteen thirties for this woman was born in 1901, December twenty-seventh. The image of the figure in the beaded gown, the Marilyn-style blonde coiffure atop the chin-up, chin-out ramrod-stiff hauteur defines Marlene Dietrich and it was a Marlene Dietrich that wasn't invented until the woman was almost fifty, her film career long since over.

Very recently, I had the pleasure of meeting Lilly Wolff, a ninety-four years young lady who had been a neighbour and at school with Marlene in Schoneberg, Berlin and who was also at the world premiere in that city of THE BLUE ANGEL, directed by Josef von Sternberg and which was supposed to star Emil Jannings who was Germany's biggest star at the time.

Lilly still remembers how exciting it was to experience the beauty and intrigue radiated by the soon to be discovered young actress who innocently stole Jannings' limelight. Innocently because at that time, Marlene didn't know Marlene

Dietrich at all. She would no more have known how to 'do' or 'be' Marlene Dietrich than fly.

Lilly Wolff believes quite unalterably that the twenties and thirties in Germany, before the Nazis, were the best times to have been alive. I think that Maria Magdalena Dietrich rather thought so too. It was the perfect breeding and the ideal grounding for a future star and Maria Magdalena encased her star creation in that brittle but tough shell, rather stiff, proud and arrogant, garnered from this pedigree. Marlene *expected*.

To experience Marlene Dietrich in the flesh must have been entirely intimidating from the outside and yet headily exciting from within, intoxicating to the point of addiction. That haughty, worldly, rather bored, languidly self-confident loucheness of a completely emancipated woman who's been there, done it and come back.

Lilly Wolff told me it was a great surprise to her that the school age Maria Magdalena with her halo of fine blonde hair even grew up to be an actress, let alone a star. Lilly's family lived opposite the Dietrichs and Lilly confirms that Maria Magdalena was brought up extremely strictly according to the social protocol that befitted a family with aristocratic Prussian connections, protocol which had nothing to do with one of its daughters working, let alone in the theatre. And nothing to do with working with Jews for anti-Semitism was profligate amongst the German social high command. Marlene displayed no aversion to mixing with Jews. Josef von Sternberg taught her everything he knew about the lighting which wreathed her, the image that captured her and the scripts that surrounded her. She loved him.

As so many millions of families did in the carnage of the European War, Marlene, together with her mother and elder sister suffered multiple bereavement. Both Marlene's father's and then her stepfather's names were added to the lists of the slaughtered. Only the Holocaust and now AIDS since the mediaeval plagues have matched the First World War in Europe for this mind-whirling, sense-shredding, logic-defying phenomenon of multiple bereavement. Maria Magdalena had to *be* something for the opportunity to be what she had been brought up to be no longer existed. To *do* nothing would have been to sink into the bitter, regretful no-man's land between the then and the now. It was a lethargy that fell to so many war-bereaved. That was not a fate for Marlene. It would have been alien to her character.

The Germans are great ones for affectionate abbreviations. Tender diminutions: Mutter to Mutti, Vater to Vatti. Maria Magdalena fancied correctly that by creating a synthesis of both her given names, she would create more of an impact upon the world. It was the first device to which she resorted in a long life of making and believing. After several cruder initial attempts at abbreviation, all considered too obvious and unappealing, Maria Magdalena became Marlene and the Dietrich saga was born.

Marlene got up and did and she didn't have much patience for or tolerance of those that didn't. Tales of her scrubbing floors and doing dishes and cooking endless German culinary delights for her loved ones and the guests at her table are at the same time legendary, occasionally apocryphal yet often true. She was mean and she was generous. She was kind and she was cruel. She was selfish and she was selfless. She was every contradiction on every continuum and she was rivetingly fascinating. I love Maria's tales of her mother's appropriation of everything in the wardrobe of a film that wasn't physically nailed down. Marlene looked upon such pillage as her right and she hoarded better than any squirrel. She kept all her costumes, labelled and wrapped and hangered, together with all the necessary accessories similarly filed.

She was a perfectionist to rival God. Any seam on any garment that wasn't just *so* would be unpicked, often by her, and remade. Wigs, hairpieces, trimmings, furs, haberdashery, shoes ... All had to be exactly chosen and perfectly fitting. Because Marlene was only ever Marlene, the costume and the make-up and the lighting spoke more for the substance of the characters she played than ever did the investment of reality which her craft injected into her screen personae. She took endless trouble with designers like Travis Banton who dressed her at Paramount and photographers like Hurrell who photographed her. The 'look' was all important.

BLUE ANGEL caused a bow wave of excitement through the film industry worldwide and Marlene was invited by Bud Shulberg at Paramount Publix Studios to come to Hollywood to make MOROCCO with von Sternberg. Marlene arrived in Hollywood at the time of Alice Faye, Miriam Hopkins, Jean Arthur, the occasionally blonde Joan and Constance Bennett, Ann Harding ... Blondes who didn't really shake sticks at sex. Harlow and West were hard at it but I don't think Mr. Zukor saw Mae as the class act that Marlene was perceived to be and MGM's Harlow had to be rivalled..

At first Marlene didn't like Hollywood in the slightest and was quite prepared to return to what she saw as the civilisation of Europe. However, America saw Europe in an entirely different way. It was the 'naughty' continent. It was where sex came from. The moghuls knew they needed female shoulders round which to drape the stole of sex but they needed it dressed up, they needed it classy. Marlene saw her niche and stayed.

Marlene sold sex and she sold it because to her sex was not the magical commodity it was seen to be by film-makers and audiences alike. For Marlene sex was part of ultimate romance, part of the necessary seduction process by which you hooked, landed and then weighed your catch. Marlene was a huntress, an exciting, venal huntress and she saw no problem in marketing that excitement. She was like a cat, playing with a mouse, a serpent transfixing a rabbit with a stare.

I contend that she single-handedly invented Hollywood glamour as it has come down to us. The characters she played were always larger-than-life, never ordinary, shot through and through with unpredictability. She was the woman whom the nice man meets on a weekend conference; she is the siren who entrances and entraps, dangerously and defiantly. Marlene was the ultimate femme fatale in the perennial fatal attraction. She showed she was in control, even when she lost. She alone was in charge of her desirability. No one could take it without her first granting the boon.

Marlene promised her male audience desire but for the women who watched her films, Marlene was the woman whom each of those rapt faces wanted to be ... for a while. No woman left a Dietrich film feeling that Marlene's current creation was anything less than exciting. She made a trademark of her cigarette and she made the wearing of trousers by women first daring, then possible and finally fashionable. Her films may have been their directors' vehicles but each was tailor-made around her insistence. BLONDE VENUS, DISHON-OURED, THE SCARLET EMPRESS, THE DEVIL IS A WOMAN, DESIRE, THE GARDEN OF ALLAH, SONG OF SONGS ...

About Marlene, Madonna has been reported to have said: *"... I wish I had slept with (Marlene Dietrich). She had a very masculine thing about her but she maintained a sexual allure."*

Marlene's own sexuality was indeed multifaceted. She conducted relationships with women at the same time as she allowed herself to be wooed by a string of endlessly replaceable, fascinating men including von Sternberg, Richard Barthelmess, John Gilbert, Ronald Colman, Maurice Chevalier, Brian Aherne, Yul Brynner and Jean Gabin. Although she had married Rudi Sieber in Berlin in 1923 - she called him Papi - she never divorced him. They remained more like brother and sister even though for much of their marriage he lived in Paris with the woman who started off as her only child Maria's nurse. Poor Tami - doomed never to have a child of her own, she suffered several abortions and ultimately madness as the price of loving Dietrich's husband for Marlene, Prussian aristocrat that she believed herself to be, would brook no scandal or gossip that would harm her career. The tearful, distraught Tami *submitted* to those abortions ... Jesus!

Marlene was earthy and bawdy and yet at the drop of a hat she could be elitist and raffish and superior. She regarded the studio moghuls as common and had as little to do with them or the press barons like Hearst as she could. She had few good words to say about the actresses who were her contemporaries. Mae West amused her but the thought of Mae producing a bosom from her breastworks at Marlene's dinner table rendered their friendship bounded strictly by the Paramount lot.

She studiously eschewed television and sank into a bitter old age, holing up in an apartment in Paris when the inability to carry Marlene Dietrich onto the world's stages overtook her and she wisely let no one see her in either decline, fall or ruin. Canny old girl. She wanted to ensure that we all remember *only* Marlene Dietrich! The reality was painfully unimportant to her and in her latter years she drowned and tempered that reality in alcohol.

There have been many stories about her attitudes to the two Germanys, her's and Hitler's and why she never went back except in death, why she remained in America as an American despite her cultivated German-ness. I repeat the following story, told me by Lilly Wolff of the dilemma that Nazism forced upon Marlene, the absentee Prussian and how she squared up to her German-ness from afar.

Hitler's art department were desperate for the blonde, Aryan Marlene to return to the fatherland's fold from the decadent life she led amongst the Jews of Hollywood.

Lilly and Marlene had mutual friends, the husband of the family of father, mother and young son being a solicitor and who acted in an occasional capacity for Marlene. He was an intellectual. His crime was being a social democrat and merely to have been heard speaking a word out of turn against Hitler would have incurred Nazi wrath. Oppression and tyranny threatened this family for years but was impossible to ignore any longer when the son came home from school wanting a Hitler Youth uniform just like all the other boys. When he returned home bearing swastikas for his mother to sew onto his clothes, the parents could no longer just wait the situation out. For the son to have gone back to school saying that his parents had refused to allow him to wear the swastika would have been grounds for the parents to have been incarcerated in a concentration camp and the child either similarly dispatched or taken under the thrall of the Nazi state.

Marlene did not hesitate in arranging first for the removal of the young son to a Swiss boarding school and then, secondly, for helping to facilitate the parents' escape from Germany, immigration into the United States, the establishment of a legal practice in New York where they were later joined by their son.

It's not Schindler's List but it's more than a lot did and I'd bet there's more. Marlene herself died in Paris in 1992, aged ninety-one and was finally borne home to Germany to be buried beside her mother.

Hail Marlene, star of stars!

CHAPTER 7

New Looks, New Dreams

New Looks,
New Dreams

As I have already emphasised, the First World War was indeed a watershed both in its physical and political effect. The Armistice co-incided with the accelerated growth of the movies as both entertainment and education and attending these performances were women of all classes who had a) been widowed and who, in middle and working class contexts likely needed employment, who had b) decided that a life in service as a lady's maid was no longer for them and who had, probably most importantly, c) the chance to dream *major* dreams. As Don Black's apt lyrics impart in SUNSET BOULEVARD, referring to the early careers of Norma Desmond and Cecil B de Mille, *"We gave the world new ways to dream ..."*

The ex-lady's maids saw new ways not only to dream but to earn and those middle class widows and wives of men perhaps involved themselves in trade and thus endowed with a little capital, saw an opening to found a career in 'beauty'. It only required one lady capitalist to join up with two ex-ladies' maids for beauty salons to take root and prosper in every city neighbourhood, suburb, small town and village.

Needless to say there was a ready clientele at all prices. It also seemed that men, smelling the profit and being at an economic advantage, were quick and ready to capitalise on women's aspirations.

My mother remembers her childhood in Great Malvern, a

then highly fashionable Spa and residential, moneyed town of some thirty thousand souls. It was not untypical of many regional towns throughout Europe and the United States though its population included a proportion of fashionable ladies of quality who would arrive and depart with the seasons. In the late 1920's, the two main centres for women's hairdressing in Great Malvern were in the rear of shops originally opened in the nineteenth century as gentlemen's barbers. Messrs. Burley and Messrs. Tite had such establishments *both* of which were fronted by a retail store dispensing home-care hair and beauty products.

This observation is highlighted by the writer James Stevens Cox' own archives regarding his grandparents Mr. and Mrs. John Stevens who maintained hairdressing establishments in Clifton, the fashionable area of Bristol, for the last decades of the Victorian age.

After the First World War, the industry boomed and there appeared the salons which had been opened by the single or widowed ladies; in Great Malvern, it had been Gwen Ferris who had paved the way, the succession of her assistants usually leaving to found their own businesses, thus expanding the industry in second generation terms. Apprenticeships in beauty and hair salons became a sought-after occupation for women whose only other employment alternatives would have been factory, land, domestic or shop work.

To spend money at the beauty parlour signified a disposable income which validated a woman's standing in her community and amongst her peers *as well as* endorsing - after he had been persuaded - the status of her husband.

As it became acceptable to be seen at the new, luxurious movie palaces which the studios and theatre owners rushed to build, so it was deemed mete to sport the hairstyles and fashions as popularised by the heroines of the films which were so eagerly watched. Because it was never thought 'not nice' for a woman to be seen alone or with other women at the cinema as it would have been thought of a single woman in a public house for example, women also found themselves dressing and creating an appearance for other women too.

In Berlin and Birmingham, Paris and Philadelphia, London and Los Angeles, the twentieth century's women celebrated the revolution in fashions dedicated by the movie industry's launch of the good ship Beauty which set out, like the Mayflower, to found not one but many empires. The debt that Wella, Redken, L' Oréal and Sassoon as well as Revlon and Fabergé owes to Hollywood is enormous. One of the most famous names, Max Factor, began life as a manufactory of make-up in Hollywood specifically for the film industry and went public after having developed a particular type of pancake foundation. Its products were for years branded as 'Max Factor of Hollywood'.

To not only cut off her hair but to have it styled and coloured was social derring-do indeed for the woman of the early 1920's. Such a gesture, at least, matched the abandonment of the restrictive long skirts, the reading of Marie Stopes' publications about family planning and, as far as families, fathers and finances would allow, the assertion of the potential of a new womanhood to facilitate the modern age of ultimate democracy.

The early hairdressers and salon proprietors had a lot to learn as colouring came out of the closet and bleaching and blonding became more and more acceptable for the principle of bleaching is involved to some extent in all modern colouring.

In the nineteenth century, it had in fact been men who had had the most immediate and respectable access to hair colouring. Chemical surface dyes such as silver nitrate and gold chloride were used by barbers to re-colour beards and moustaches. However, such ingredients were only of limited and patchy success for in all cases, after a while, the re-colouring faded to horrible and unpredictable shades.

In 1859, William Henry Perkins, whilst working for Professor Wilhelm Hofman at the Royal College of Chemistry in London, discovered a purple dye from synthesised quinine mixed with alcohol which saw the birth of a whole industry based on the chemical engineering of dyes for fabrics. Relatives of these dyes were those which emerged in hair colouring although it would appear that the first temporary colour rinse, the most sophisticated form of dyeing, was not invented until sometime in the 1920's when a Monsieur LeMur obliged the ladies and movie studios of the world.

The hair's natural colour is the result of the presence of a combination, or lack of, three varieties of the pigment melanin; eumelanin, pheomelanin and trichosiderin. Eumelanin determines brown to black hair, pheolmelanin is responsible for yellows to just red shades and trichosiderin accounts for redheads. The presence of large amounts of trichosiderin in certain African and Asian follicles accounts for the frequent inability of the hair to be bleached to white but fetching up a dazzling orange.

Lightening of the hair can be achieved to an extent by the application of any tartaric or citric acid ingredients, such as lemon juice. The matt 'curd' residue remaining on the hair after washing with any soap is removed by the acid and the hair shines. Exposure to the natural oxidisation process of the sun's ultraviolet rays accelerates the effect of baywatch blonding.

However, in order to introduce chemical dye to the hair, the natural colour has first to be eradicated and this is done by bleaching. The pigmentation is neutralised by the process of oxidisation. A naturally sourced sunray process would take too long and so an oxidising agent is used to speed the plough. Hydrogen peroxide was discovered by Louis Thenard in 1818 and is the most often used oxidiser. The peroxide has to be made alkaline, however, and this was achieved initially by adding an oil or powder bleach containing ammonia.

As Patricia Spencer points out, in the early days of this century, bleaching was literally a haphazard mixing of pure hydrogen peroxide and a few drops of ammonia. Some of the results must have been tragic for although oxidisation works fairly successfully on eumelanin to reduce dark browns to very light, pheomelanin has a greater resistance to oxidisation and takes longer to be neutralised and often the platinum, white blonde effect cannot be achieved at all. There would have been bitterly wept tears if Marilyn's hair had failed to react to the bleach. She just wouldn't have been the same as brunette Norma Jean Baker, aka Marilyn Monroe, would she?

Later, powder bleaches, adapted for the continuing home use which all hair product companies acknowledge in their huge profits, were adapted by the addition of magnesium carbonate (white henna) together with a powder detergent like sodium lauryl sulphate.

The bleaching preparation, once applied to the hair, begins to be absorbed between each hair's cuticle scales and works to affect the molecular structure of the pigment granules in the hair's cortex. The destroyed pigments leave the hair whitened or blonded ready have another colour applied or to be ultimately, as in the case of our un-natural blondes, platinumised by the application of a final silver rinse to achieve that special shining platinum effect.

It has to be said that whatever compensatory techniques have been developed, the hair is always damaged after these onslaughts of chemicals either for bleaching or for permanent waving as many stars found out to their cost and to the great profit of the wig-makers. Nowadays, Vidal Sassoon's regime forbids the perming of bleached hair and the bleaching of permed hair to obviate any disasters.

It seems probably that it was from the ranks of wig-makers and those already versed in the area of theatrical hairstyles and make-up who were siphoned off by Hollywood and who founded those indispensable studio departments which ultimately bore resounding names like Guillaroff and Westmore. The hair and beauty industries must have had a hot line to those men and women of the hairdressers' and make-up artists unions. Whilst attending their charges on set with brushes, pencils, paints and pansticks, they must have also been eagerly awaiting any news of a change of hair colour or make-up style of the current stars. If Harlow had even been allowed to decide to go brunette, the production lines would have been working overtime to supply the home demand for brown dyes.

The time for blondes was nigh. Hollywood and The Talkies and the huge audiences and the hair technology and the beauty parlours were pretty well-established by the time the first of our blondes came West and hit the silver screen.

CHAPTER 8

Ginger Rogers

Ginger Rogers

Other than Harlow, our blondes so far, and most of them hereafter share an atavistic need to perform. Marlene was a bit player in random theatre projects all over Berlin before she arrived at UFA Film Studios. Mae, like polish, was all over the vaudeville boards from the off. They *had* to get up, get out there and strut their stuff ... Forever.

Is it something in the gut that flicks a switch in the developing child and turns them on, making them seek out the spotlight? It's true that most children seem to have an un-repressed ability to perform, an innocent desire to either individually or communally take their place as the centre of attention in a gathering of grown-ups. But most lose this desire as social pressures build, as webs of taboo net their once free spirits and as their own psychological profile clouds and complicates.

The few who emerge from childhood with their need to stand before us and be applauded, validated, loved ... These are disproportionately few. As we grow older, some call it maturing, the majority of us rely on these relative few to do our public appearing for us. These people, the non-mature perhaps, are our entertainers, our religieux, our politicians. These people are often our leaders. Like children, they often need to be indulged, forgiven and granted endless second chances to prove themselves once again.

But what about this *need* of theirs for us to grant them licence to lie to try and get us to believe? Could there be a common formula of circumstance which engenders the child who stands up and performs? Might it, maybe, be genetic? Sadly, in all my reading about these performing blondes, I have detected no hint of a formula worth even a penny of research funding.

Some of them even have that rogue element in the performing gene which commutes the desire to show-off into such a state of terror and self-doubt in later life that performance is no longer possible? Where does *THAT* come from? What factor *slakes* the need to stand up and be shot down?

These ultimate refugees who flee the limelight altogether are very few. For work is not work to the actor, the writer, the director. Read 'any artist'. Work is life. There are no tidy, nine-to-five compartments, no overtime. *you* are your *work* which is *your life* which is *you.* They are one and the same.

What appears to happen to careers is that having conquered one field, the fires of ambition are rekindled to conquer even further fields. Would anyone have believed the prediction in 1935 that one day an actor would be President of the United States? Would people have found it even mildly credible that a mere blonde actress could have shaken the institutions of the most powerful state on this planet to their foundations?

But there are too few stages and screens and so most performers will never be satisfied. Some wanting one thing, end up with another. And some people, as the actor and writer Rupert Everett reminds us, get what they want but in the form they deserve ... Some, go back to what they started to do but do it more advantageously.

Ginger Rogers is one such person.

In her autobiography, GINGER, MY STORY she takes pains on many occasions to remind us that, '... she acted, who also danced'. Quantifying it, she points out that she made only ten films with Fred Astaire and seventy three in all. She is an actress, therefore, more than a dancer. But then, what *we* think we've done with our lives is not necessarily what *others* are prepared to validate. What was that about getting what we want in the form we deserve ...? Could it be that Ginger has been a far and away better dancer than she was ever an actress?

That she is a star, is not for a second in question and one of influence and importance to the lineage of our glamour blondes. But somehow, the very stardom that her dancing and her partnership with Astaire bestowed on her prevented her from becoming what she patently desperately wanted to be. An actress. And not just any old summer stock, repertory-in-Hampshire actress. She wanted to be considered by her peers as a 'proper' actress and told so. Harlow too wanted that. So did Marilyn. They all thought that what they were recognised for wasn't somehow quite nice. All of them like children needed other validation.

But whichever way you look at Ginger's cards, to have had your niche in eternity created based on a mere seven point three percent of your performance output is having been dealt a truly great hand.

She was born Virginia Katherine McMath on July sixteenth, 1911 in Independence, Missouri. Her mother Lela Owens McMath, had already left her husband Eddins McMath in Kansas City and until she married John Rogers eight years later remained on her own. Perhaps lonely, certainly somewhat besieged by her single parenthood and fighting the absentee Eddins for custody of Virgina whom Eddins once kidnapped, Lela found both comfort and strength in Christian Science and, in due time, passed it on to Ginger.

Uh oh ... Behind you, Ginger ... Look behind you! Thankfully, it seems that Lela and Ginger enjoyed rude health. Lela also passed on her ambition.

Lela had always wanted to write and armed with hope and a prize-winning short story she set off for Hollywood leaving her tiny daughter with her parents. This smacks of Harlow's story although the two could not have grown up more different except for one huge irony which comes later.

Lela Rogers' story has a great deal to do with Virginia's success for, being otherwise, so many childhood and teenage experiences on and to do with the stage and its denizens would have been denied the little girl whom we shall henceforth call by the name which her young cousin Helen bestowed on her. The child was unable to pronounce 'Virginia' which became 'Badinda' and then - hoopla! - Ginger.

Show-business is more than anything about meeting people. Each meeting is a signpost. It points your way to your next meeting. They like to call each of the acting and dancing and muzo performance arts a profession but for them that's been there, it's a question of following the signs, for each is a clue. Show-business is more like a treasure hunt. It's not about bits of paper with beautiful writing saying you're a this major or a that graduate. That comes later. *Much* later.

Lela Owens McMath was the best meeter and follower and in Hollywood, she was to meet Raoul Walsh, Henry King at Fox, Theda Bara for whom she wrote a script and one of the very few women screen-writers, Hettie Gray Baker. In New York, a mecca of movie-making then, Lela was close with movie star Mae Marsh, her sister Lovey and the Broadway star Jane Cawl with whom the eight year old Ginger once appeared on stage selling War Bonds in 1917. First World War Bonds ...

More than any of our blondes, Ginger Rogers' career truly spans the century in *all* its media in *all* colours and sizes of screen.

Having met and married John Rogers, whom Ginger calls the kindest man and the best father, Lela and her new family settled in Fort Worth, Texas. At home, Rogers loved to write and compose songs in which Ginger was co-opted and, continuing her work, Lela wrote the theatre and movie reviews for the Fort Worth Record, saw all the movies and got to know all the theatre owners on the local Interstate and Orpheum vaudeville circuits. It was better than money in the bank for later. Ginger and Lela met many headliners, Jack Benny, Sophie Tucker an eminent blonde in vaudeville who to an extent made an impact in music in the early days. They saw movie stars Gloria Swanson and Rudolf Valentino in personal appearances at the Majestic, Fort Worth. Seeing the stars in the flesh made the screen magic seem tangibly real.

Appearing locally when Ginger was about thirteen were the

Foy Brothers and from Eddie Foy, himself merely waiting to be dubbed by the sword of fame, Ginger learned to dance the Charleston and appeared on-stage with the Foy act when one of the brothers went sick. By 1925, ignoring an invitation to be schooled in ballet in New York by Adolf Baum, Ginger won the Texas State Charleston competition. Lela arranged an act for her with two supporting, red-headed dancers and Ginger started to work on the Interstate circuit. She was fourteen and not yet, of course, a blonde. Lela was right behind her. Wish fulfilment do I hear someone whisper? I wish, I wish.

The act, now with Earl Leach and Josephine Butler, was being booked as the vaudeville support to the movies being shown in the theatres and the kids worked the Paramount Publix route doing four shows a day. The Skouras Brothers, one of whom late became president of Twentieth Century Fox Studios, booked Ginger's troupe in her first four week engagement in Chicago. The act was making anywhere between two hundred and twenty five and three hundred and fifty dollars a week although Ginger had solo designs and in Chicago began singing with bands, first Ed Lowry's and then Paul Ash's with whom she arrived in New York, solo, in August 1928.

Could it have been a detrimental effect of growing up without fathers which made at least four of our blondes - Harlow, Marlene, Doris Day and Ginger - marry at very young ages? But then so did Mae and her old dad, Battling Jack West, was always around. Ginger was only seventeen in 1928 when in New Orleans she married Jack Culpepper, a former beau of her Aunt's. Lela was furious and the marriage was over before it had begun although they were not divorced until July 1931. No longer lousy with virginity, Ginger dusted her skinned knees and was off again.

She must have been pretty damn good because the momentum of her career didn't take long to accelerate. She secured agency representation with William Morris - not bad for starters - and they got her a deal doing two reelers, probably silents, in the New York film studios. Her first movie was with Rudy

Vallee. She was meeting some pretty influential people. Remember she already had the powerful Schencks under her belt and securing the part of Babs Green in the Kalmar/Ruby Broadway show TOP SPEED brought her friendship with one of the male chorus who'd changed his name to Hermes Pan. This friendship with the talented terpsichorean who became Hollywood's legendary dancing master lasted for over sixty years until Pan's death in 1990.

All our blondes had their 'moment' and Ginger's eventually came in 1930 when Walter Wanger brought Adolf Zukor, the founder of Paramount to see TOP SPEED and offered her a screen test for YOUNG MAN OF MANHATTAN with Claudette Colbert, Norman Foster and Charles Ruggles. She tested (with cigarette) for the part of Puff Randolph at the Paramount Studio then functioning on Long Island and in July signed a seven year contract. The movie came out and her Mae Westian line, *"Cigarette me, big boy! ... Well, light it!"* got her noticed.

She was still in TOP SPEED at night and was wanted by Eddie Cantor to star opposite Al Jolson in a Florenz Ziegfeld show. She failed to get it because Jolson was all but engaged to Ruby Keeler whom he wanted to play the part. Keeler got it and Ginger admits she learned a basic showbiz lesson! Connections, my dear. Careers are based on *who* not *what* you know!

In quick succession she made QUEEN HIGH, THE SAP FROM SYRACUSE and FOLLOW MY LEADER with the young Ethel Zimmerman (no, not Bob Dylan's granny), the fresh-from-the-chorus Ethel Merman.

Paramount agreed that Ginger be released for a time at a thousand dollars a week to play Molly Gray in GIRL CRAZY in 1930, the George and Ira Gershwin musical which gave us EMBRACEABLE YOU and BUT NOT FOR ME. Gee! Our Ginger was sure in at the beginning of some legendary work and with some pretty legendary artists. In the GIRL CRAZY orchestra were Gene Krupa, Benny Goodman, Jimmy Dorsey on sax, Glen Miller and Jack Teagarden on trombones but not, I hasten to add, all at the same time! Also in 1930 she made her fifth Paramount movie HONOUR AMONG LOVERS directed by Dorothy Arzner, one of the scant band of women directors then working.

The success of GIRL CRAZY introduced her to the New York theatre and literary elite including the celebrated members of the Algonguin round table, Dorothy Parker, Robert Benchley, George S. Kaufman, Moss Hart, Marc Connelly, Donald Ogden Stewart, Alexander Woolcott and Lela's friend Harold Ross of THE NEW YORKER who Ginger dated along, it must be said, with quite a few other comely chaps. She made friends with column-ist Walter Winchell and got to know Dave Chasen who was later to open Hollywood's famous chili restaurant and tem-porary Oscar repository.

And in 1930, she first got to dance with Fred Astaire al-though professionally he was still partnered by his sister Adele who had not yet married Lord Charles Cavendish. Ginger and Fred dated too. They even *could* have been lovers but ... A kiss in the car wasn't that fundamental ... It wasn't to pan out like that.

Many who were later to become stars had initial movie studio contracts which were deemed not worth continuing. Paramount, surely from their goodness of their bottomless hearts, thought it right to let Ginger go and waved her off to the pastures new she had espied in the golden west. In June 1931, Ginger left New York by train with Lela and Harold Ross and crossed America to the sunset with the Lunts, Alfred and his wife Lynn Fontanne, America's first couple of the theatre who were en route for MGM to make THE GUARDSMAN. That was some piece of networking.

Whether Paramount had known of her plans, I know not but Ginger was en route for RKO where she was due to make THE TIP OFF. Ginger and Lela put up at a cottage in The Garden of Allah, the exclusive hotel/residence which had been built on the Sunset Strip site of the former home of silent movie queen Alla Nazimova. Nazimova had used the proceeds to settle the debts of her failed movie production company.

Utterly ignorant of all this ruinous financial history, the

dark-haired Miss Ginger Rogers set off from the Garden of Allah on her first day of work at RKO. But even before she'd stepped in front of a camera, the blonding of Ginger had taken place on the instructions of studio boss Charles Rogers. She and Lela were absolutely furious but Ginger's been blonde for sixty four years.

Her contract was at $1000 a week but she was making 'B' pictures and after she had fulfilled her obligation to make three, all directed by Al Rogell she returned to New York for a brief spell in the theatre before signing with Warners at the instigation of the director Mervyn Le Roy who was another of her many dates. Ginger's career is traceable by joining up the studio dots. She covered Hollywood and found herself next at Fox, prior to this studio merging with Twentieth Century Pictures, where she made HAT CHECK GIRL and THE THIR-TEENTH GUEST for their Monogram subdivision.

Broadway themes as well as Broadway performers were the stuff of Hollywood throughout its heyday. 'The Show', be it on Broadway or in a humble barn, was the building block of Hollywood's DNA. Ginger next appeared in FORTY SECOND STREET for Warner Brothers, with former rival Ruby Keeler, playing Anytime Annie (I *love* that name) and ended up mak-ing GOLD DIGGERS OF 1933 for her 'date' Mervyn LeRoy also at Warners. But she didn't make any of the other subsequent five GOLD DIGGERS. As if she didn't know, she'd been called to higher things and she'd never doubted it.

The name of Ginger Rogers became synonymous with the creation of a new art form. No longer was the film musical a filmed musical. Whereas Hollywood had aped its Broadway counterpart when it came to making shows for the screen, the Hollywood Musical evolved as the thirties progressed as a genre conceived entirely for screen production and perform-ance. The results were far more lavish than their theatrical cousins and available to more people for a fraction of the cost. They also made far more money. However, the down-side put concert hall-based music even further into the shade. There was no need for grand opera to popularise those parts of itself which would fill the cheaper seats. Those audiences were now humming along to Nelson Eddy and Jeanette MacDonald and fantasising about the light fantastic created by Ginger and Fred. Cinema committed the concert form forever to minority interest.

So 1933 was a pretty hectic year for our Ginger. Her agent, Leland Hayward, who was Myron Selznick's partner, must have been working overtime. The connections Ginger was making out of office hours though weren't quite good enough because against all Ginger's ding-dong-bells expectations, LeRoy went off and married Doris Warner, the studio boss's daughter. Ouch!

Not to be down-hearted, Ginger went out on the town to the most famous of all Hollywood Nightclubs, the Cocoanut Grove where she met and started to date Howard Hughes instead - this was some busy little social butterfly here - and continued her ceaseless scurrying and skittling round the studios. She and her mother also quit the bungalow in the Garden of Allah and moved into a proper house on Dundee Drive.

She screen-tested at Columbia for Harry Cohn who passed on her talents and she ended up at RKO again for PROFESSIONAL SWEETHEART and then, loaned out, made DON'T BET ON LOVE at Universal where she finally met up with heart-throb actor Lew Ayres with whom she says she had been in love since seeing ALL QUIET ON THE WESTERN FRONT.

Having her hair done at Oddie's, just down the street from Schwab's famous Sunset drugstore, Ayres arrived as un- announced as the accompanying earthquake. They kissed, the earth obviously moved but RKO merely continued to loan her out, this time to Paramount for SITTING PRETTY. But love *was* in the Ayres.

And so, at last - Dammit! You're late! - was Dame Fortune, because, in 1933, Ginger also made FLYING DOWN TO RIO where her career was re-united with Hermes Pan's. The picture starred Dolores del Rio but its scenes were indisputably stolen by Miss Rogers and the Hoofer King of the Great White Way, Mr. Fred Astaire, making only his second movie.

She referred to her partnership with Astaire as a 'two-sided blessing' - presumably because whilst he had several dancing partners there was only ever one Astaire - and whilst planning to further this blessing with him in the GAY DIVORCEE, the film of Astaire's Broadway triumph THE GAY DIVORCE, she set herself up for a proper divorce by marrying Lew Ayres in November 1934. Her maid of honour was Janet Gaynor. There was a big reception at the Ambassador and the luvvies honeymooned in Carmel before returning to a new house on Roxbury Drive. But ... Ginge was the teetotal Queen of the Day whilst Lew liked to party. What do they say about oil and water?

Lela Rogers was not letting the grass grow either. She was running a small talent theatre on the RKO backlot and claims influence over the teaching of Betty Grable and Lucille Ball. Lela Rogers must have been a pretty - how can I put it - pushy teacher because Joan Fontaine was only one who rather forcefully declined the gift Lela had to give.

Ayres was a 'proper' actor, an intellectual even, so Ginger tells us in her autobiography but whilst he went on making his 'proper' films, Ginger continued with ROBERTA and then TOP HAT with Astaire, who apparently acted up and stamped his foot a lot but still gave us wonderful songs like ISN'T IT A LOVELY DAY and CHEEK TO CHEEK.

IN PERSON was followed by another Astaire movie FOLLOW THE FLEET which included Irving Berlin's LET'S FACE THE MUSIC AND DANCE. In 1936, as well as making SWING TIME, Ginger's star status was validated by an invitation to go to Washington and appear at Franklin Delano Roosevelt's birthday ball. I wonder if she sang THE WAY YOU LOOK TONIGHT, the hit from SWINGTIME?

1936 didn't sing as sweetly for Ginger at home. She decided to leave Lew Ayres and she moved to a house on Gilcrest which had a tennis court. Presumably she pounded her frustration out on those balls and 'though she started dating Jimmy

Stewart, she felt herself to be not above listening to a proposal of marriage from the relentless Howard Hughes on which she took a rain check for some three years.

She was, after all, still a married lady and one, by all accounts, with a heavy heart that wasn't as free as Ayres'.

George and Ira Gershwin's SHALL WE DANCE gave her LET'S CALL THE WHOLE THING OFF and THEY CAN'T TAKE THAT AWAY FROM ME whilst 1937 brought STAGE DOOR, the movie taken from Edna Ferber's and George S. Kaufman's script.

Renegotiation with RKO came around. Female stars were usually compensated for equal work far less than men, who ran the show. Ginger herself points out that women were allowed to write stories, but to direct them, produce them and be represented other than as actresses was unusual. Famous exceptions do *not* prove the rule - Dorothy Arzner directed and Margaret Booth was a renowned editor at MGM but apart from them ... And of course, there was Elinor Glynn.

As a leading moneyspinner for RKO, Ginger's contract rewarded her $3000 a week before renegotiation and $4000 afterwards. She is at pains to point out the comparatively small weekly salary but, with the perspective of hindsight admittedly, I in turn have to point out that salaries were paid to contract artists whether they worked or not. Of course the studios were protecting their interests by maintaining their stars' availability but it was, to a great extent a two-way street only blocked when one side saw a greater reward in another direction.

Ginger is also very sensitive to the spectre of residuals, payments made to actors performing in films which are later screened either on television, video or in sound recordings. All of the 1930's and 1940's performers, all of the black and white stars and most in Technicolor until the sixties, do not receive any payments. Ginger maintains that at the point of her successfully renegotiating her RKO contract in 1937, that Lela's raising the question of residuals was laughed roundly off the table. I have to say, in fairness to Ginger although most agents wouldn't have dreamed of raising the point, the phenomenon of television was generating about the same reaction from the 'men' that talkies elicited when seen as possible competition to silents. Most didn't believe either sound or television stood a chance until their pay checks were forfeit.

So, good try Ginger and Lela and to you, Leland Heyward, I hope you made enough commission off the first screenings because residuals work great for agents too, you know.

The years 1938 and 1939 saw CAREFREE and THE STORY OF VERNON AND IRENE CASTLE as the Rogers/Astaire output. They were not to work again until 1949 when they made THE BARCLAYS OF BROADWAY.

When it ended, it had been a terrific run. Ginger may not have had the elegance and cool of Cyd Charisse, and she was less animal than Rita Hayworth but as a dancer she did bring the character she was playing into her choreography. Her assets as a comedienne stood her in good stead and her facial acting was always more accessible to audiences than others'.

But still footloose and still working, she and Lucille Ball apparently dated room-mates Jimmy Stewart and Henry Fonda although it was Howard Hughes who piloted out of the wide blue yonder again in 1940 with a five carat emerald engagement ring. She wore both it and all the other jewellery he gave her but when she found out what a two-timing, two-bit cheater he was and, bridling at his growing obsession with control, she sent all the baubles back and sent him on his way, bidding a final adieu as he lay crocked and cracked in a hospital bed after an auto wreck. Take that, you ... you ... millionaire, you!

She comforted herself by dating Jean Gabin, much, so 't was said, to Marlene's fury. I can almost hear the star of stars mumbling a careless, *"Well, skwoo you!"*. Ginger Rogers was someone Marlene would have dismissed with a tip.

In 1941, they gave Ginger an Oscar for KITTY FOYLE which she oh-so-humbly accepted from the gracious hands of Lynn Fontanne whose career, Ginger notes to remind us, had remained firmly planted in 'the theatah'. She bought land in the

San Fernando valley making her one of the first valley girls and about half Oregon, a place to which she was occasionally to repair in the ensuing war years during which she was married to the younger-than-she marine soldier Jack Briggs whom she converted to Christian Science by helping his bleeding foot warts heal. He was hooked. Must have been kosher because all the other American troops in the fighting used her name as a password: 'Who goes there?' 'Ginger Rogers' ... 'Ginger Rogers Who?'

Life as a marine's wife was good until Jack got back from the war and wanted to 'be someone', which was fine but it wasn't going to be on Ginger's back so after stoutly defending her unimpeachable mother who was dragged in front of one of the myriad Un-American Activities Committees which were to mark the freedom of that fair land from the threat of fascist oppression, Ginger ditched the marine.

She dated Greg Bautzer the celebrated Hollywood lawyer and Lana Turner's friend - she had taste this lady - and then Cary Grant. Whoops!

Husband number - where are we? Oh, yes, four - was to come in the shape of Jacques Bergerac a young French lawyer whom she met on a trip to France - her first outside the USA. He called her Pinkie and she couldn't for the life of her see what was so terrible about older women having, sorry, *marrying* younger men.

Bautzer was still hanging in there but, not young enough, I suppose, and in 1952 Ginger and Jacques married in Palm Springs. Unfortunately he didn't want to keep his steady job and left the law to become a film actor, a career which was not furthered particularly by being Mr. Ginger Rogers. He also had a nasty case of the boils which of course Ginge cured with a sensible poultice of Christian Science. Whilst in Rio de Janeiro, she also claims to have been sent to a certain Elaine Stewart's hospital bedside by an angel and that it was she, Ginger, and not the angel who cured Ms. Stewart of a nasty attack of peritonitis.

Ginger's work was patchy in the early fifties. Appearing in Coward's TONIGHT AT 8.30 on live television in 1954 didn't help her career and life at home was itchy. Why, I beseech you, can an attractive, horny, self-obsessed young unsuccessful Frenchmen not be content with an utterly slavish monogamous relationship with an older, self-absorbed successful lady? What possesses such a man to want to shag anything that's younger that's breathing? Naughty Jacques. But he'd blotted his copybook by speaking French to Noel Coward all through a Swiss lunch once - can you believe, French! The impertinence! - and he and Ginger were divorced in 1959. She did met him some years later, though, and had a very nice lunch a deux 'as though nothing had happened'. That's what I call most civilised.

In 1960 she met an actor G. William Marshall, 'Bill' whom she married in 1961 but he drank and he abused her and he borrowed money because he too wanted to be 'someone'. She admits to being somewhat, shall we say, financially challenged after her spree with Bergerac and went back to the theatre, touring for much of the early nineteen sixties. She and Bill tried working together in THE CONFESSION but Ginger already was 'someone'.

She made her last film for the independent Magna Pictures in 1965 - couldn't you tell the studio system was all but dead? - when she played, for some reason entirely unknown to anyone except herself and, presumably her Christian Science practitioner buddies, the part of Mama Jean, Jean Harlow's mother in HARLOW. Ginger obviously was steeped in the rectitude of her faith and must have believed that what Mama Jean did to her sick and terrified daughter was in some way behaviour with which her (Ginger's) fans would identify. Ginger would never have let her fans see her ugly. Why should she want them to see her as a virtual accessory to what I shall kindly call euthanasia? Her acceptance of the role is incomprehensible.

The movie sucked anyway. Carol Lynley held no candle to Harlow and the whole thing was a sorry end to the movie career of Ginger Rogers which had been blighted only by her perception of her stardom.

Her recording career didn't prosper either. Way back, there were tales of Decca recordings that 'hadn't gone very well' and they and the contract were scrapped. Her future didn't lie in the recording studio and neither did she become a 'proper' actress, I'm sad to say. I'm afraid that in order to have and exercise control over your circumstances, you have to have a faultless foundation of true transferable talent. But Ginger knew one thing infallibly. She knew how to be a star and within the parameters of the freedom that allowed her, she hoofed and tapped and mugged and hammed for a jolly good few years more.

She appeared for David Merrick and then toured successively in HELLO DOLLY and MAME but she created neither part and audiences flocked to see Ginger Rogers hoping, beyond hope of course, for a bit of magic. Further theatre tours and television guest appearances followed but, well ... I saw her London MAME. It was quite the most frightening thing other than having Auntie Mame Dennis for your real Aunt.

God bless her, she was divorced again in 1970 although she didn't make *that* much of a bid for more movie parts because she didn't like the permissiveness that was creeping into Hollywood. God forbid, ma'am. Marriage is after all, sacred, isn't it and one must set an example? I love stars. They write their own rules, you see and when they break one, they merely rewrite it.

When other people's tours weren't available, she created her own, THE GINGER ROGERS SHOW in which she and four male dancers tickled the fancies of the world with ostrich feathers and bias-cut swirly frocks for many a year, from Las Vegas to gay (that word again) Paris. She too did what Mae and Marlene did. She froze herself in time and, thank you Mary Baker Eddy, she's still there as I write in 1995, a mammoth amongst legends, safe in the permafrost. Her name still conjures up the effortlessness, the lightness and the precision elegance with which we all move in our dreams.

Without this lady, folks, I'd like to wager that we wouldn't have had Doris Day either.

25th April 1995.

We had just returned from the third funeral we had attended in three weeks. I was making dinner when through the open kitchen door I heard the BBC newscaster. " *... and Ginger Rogers who danced her way to stardom in Hollywood's golden age has died."* Thank you, Ginger. From all of us. God speed.

CHAPTER 9

The Lady
is a Blonde

The Lady
is a Blonde

When faced with potential competition from an outstand-
ingly beautiful woman, other women, most women, do not
necessarily freak out with jealousy or envy or immediately
think that said siren is about to compromise their life and loves,
lay claim to and/or ravish all their nearest and dearest.

That is usually what a man does.

Women are not only generally more tolerant of other fe-
males, they are also blessed with the propensity to want to care
for and protect their own sex. Forced to choose, I'd take the gal
for a buddy any day.

During the war, the First World variety, women had been up
there with the men, not at the front line but in the fields, the
farms and the factories, the front lines of supply. They'd made
bombs and bullets, guns and ships. They'd been without, gone
without, put up and shut up but there'd come a point ...
Armistices had been signed on all fronts except the ones left
behind at home. Women all over wanted a better deal. They'd
been to the future; most of them had seen it; the first movie stars
may have been silent but, God! Were they glamorous! Did they
not live and love and strut and fret in gorgeous gowns and
fabulous furs and did they not always get the better of the
villain, were they not always rescued by the hero, did they not
always live happily ever after? Of course they did because
that's what the men who made these things *knew* their pre-

dominantly female audiences wanted to see.

Maybe a little chicken and egg but, an effective partnership between entertainer and entertained, gratifying the entertainer with money and the entertained with the thought that maybe the drunken husband's philandering and abuse need not be put up with but that women did have the right to expect, nay demand, better. No matter where or what or who the woman, everyone deserved to be rescued in the end.

Maybe that's all a bit simplistic but ... I have a horrible feeling it's not. Women came out of the nineteen teens with the knowledge that if they didn't like the way things were, things could be changed. And that included their appearance. Traditionally long-grown hair was chopped off. Defiance? No. Assertion. Along with what was possible, it emerged that women were no longer prepared to meekly accept the fact that what the rich did was not for them, that it wasn't 'the place' of the poor to ape their 'betters'. The war had wiped that smug smile from the face of the western world's 'ladies'.

The movies demonstrated that anyone could be a lady and that although bad girls could have good times with good boys, good girls had even better times when they had shown the bad boys the error of their ways.

Confused? You're obviously not a good girl.

Involved in war work, some women had begun to cut their hair short although there was no rush to adopt the 'bob' as the short cut was generically known and made famous by Colleen Moore and Clara Bow. However, by 1924, it was the full fashion. Shingled hair also appeared around 1923 and began to give the bob a run for its money. In 1926, the *very* short Eton Crop began to be adopted, validating the very nature of fashion's only real stock-in-trade which is constant change, perpetual evolution, natural derivation.

By the end of the twenties, women were in the thrall of the influence of the cinema as far as fashions were concerned. Couture, as Marlene Dietrich was observed by her daughter to realise, was a greater art and higher craft in Hollywood than in

Paris and, concomitantly, the standard of hairdressing was entirely complementary. The length of the current bob went up and down as did Garbo's. When Harlow's blonde tresses were revealed to an eager world, that world took look-alike to new peaks.

Their female audience stayed with the wayward West, the good-hearted not-a-harlot-really Harlow, the mixed-up Monroe, the nubile Novak because they were redeemable, forgivable victims ... These stars were perceived as people who didn't really *want* to be 'that way' and if they did, there must be a good reason. Most women, I would suggest, recognise that there but for the grace of God goes another victim.

That their menfolk also drooled and fantasised and dreamed about these women as objects of sexual desire mattered not a jot. If a woman goes to the movies with her husband, lover, beau, they watch the *same* woman on the screen. They maybe hold hands and steal a kiss and rub up during the course of the picture so the woman has no reason to think that her male partner sees the female star on the screen in any other light than her own empathy and sympathy.

It seems that even the most outrageous blondes only ever *attracted* female audiences. They could not have repelled punters. If they had done, it would have shown in the box office and another blonde sacrifice would have been made.

And so what? What did it really matter if the women knew their boyfriends fancied a bit of Mae West or a clinch with Betty Grable or a grapple with Dolly Parton? What better way to ensure that such betrayal never occurred than to do your best to look most like that object of desire? To the 'modern' woman, their movie stars and then the singing stars and, lately, the MTV idolettes are also role models, life-leaders. They have re-transcended reality to be once again *real* people of emulative worth and comparable value. The stars and the parts they sang and played became interchangeable. Type-casting re-inforced the female fans' perception of the 'We-could-be-best-friends-if-not-sisters' ruse which usefully concreted the star's image which was, after all, the basic constituent of the studio star-makers' tool chest.

So, if a woman wanted to change herself in another's image, let her change. If alterations were necessary, let her make 'em as long as you have to buy something to do it with.. " ... *So, go fix your hair, fix your face ... After all, it's no one else's but yours to fix and if' n' he don' like it, fix him too. Mae did, Harlow did, Marilyn did, Grace did and Madonna certainly does. If she can hire and fire an industry, you, girl, can surely hire and fire a mere man!"*

CHAPTER 10

Lana Turner

Lana Turner

Some film smarts find it rather easy to be glib, nay snide about Lana Turner and such thinking is entirely unjustified. As a star, she is unique and as an individual she was thoroughly professional. Comparison is usually an invidious occupation and as questionable as biography but I am not about to compare her and I am neither hagiographer nor character assassin. And it was whilst studying the available material on Miss Turner that I came across the first of what could be a significant link between a significant number of our blondes to date and to come.

Lana too started out with a daddy but lost him and, I believe, lost out. She was mainly brought up under the influence of one parent as were all our girls. Even Mae's relationship with Battling Jack was as nought when compared to that with her adored mother.

There exists time-mauled folkspeak about daughters and their fathers. Whilst it is patently an important relationship, it can never be as important as the relationship between the two parents. A loving friendship is a great umbrella under which a child can shelter, no one in the nuclear triangle loving anyone else any more. Differently, perhaps but more? Never.

What a child sees, it copies. Seeing nothing, it registers nothing in that part of its arsenal of social ammunition. Not having happily, stably married parents makes for a pretty strong instinct to find a partner and be what your own parents weren't. I suggest that whilst marrying early was more the norm in the twenties, thirties and forties, all our blondes made first and often subsequent marriages that were NOT approved of and which seemed in a large measure to destroy their ability to cohabit in a mutually rewarding give-and-take perspective.

And something made them terrible choosers.

So, shoot me down but hear me out and read on. I know Lana missed her daddy. She was born in Wallace, Idaho on February 8th 1921, to Mildred Frances née Cowan and John Virgil Turner. Mildred was sixteen, John Virgil was twenty four. Their child was named Julia Jean Turner. They were so young to have such responsibilities so early in lives which they hadn't planned but into which they had fallen because being married was the thing to be. What hope was there for such bruisable characters?

Going away to the war had unsettled many a young blood throughout the world and made a return to normal life difficult to the point of impossible. The men had seen things and done things they were unable to speak about and the women who had remained at home had no idea of the gravity of the psychological effects that leaving home, risking life and limb and surviving when so many others died had on tender teenage souls.

Julia Jean's daddy had returned from the First War decorated for gallantry, feted as a hero. Working in the mines didn't therefore have any appeal to a hero who was also handsome, witty, sang and danced and played cards.

Well, we all play a little cards ... John V. Turner however gambled. He also boot-legged for it was the era of prohibition and the family probably skipped more bills by changing its name from week to week than surely was healthy or legal.

Heroes often return to fanfares which fall cruelly silent the next day. Mildred always had to work, initially in beauty parlours. The marriage was not to last after the Turners moved to San Francisco and John Virgil moved out. Mildred took Julia Jean to Sacramento but money was so tight that they returned to San Francisco where Mildred boarded her daughter and visited her only once every two weeks. John Virgil too would arrive occasionally bearing and promising gifts like first bicycles the way that absent daddies or mummies have a knack of fouling up.

Turner didn't live long enough to fulfil the first bicycle promise. He was found murdered on a street corner in San Francisco after winning a fair sockful of dosh in a travelling crap game. His murder was never solved. For your father to die is one thing. For him to be taken forcibly from you and coshed to death by a person or persons unknown becomes baggage that a child doesn't need to carry. For a further year, Julia Jean was not even to have the comfort of living with her mother.

Mildred and Julia Jean finally moved in with another family and the little girl started to go to the Saturday movies. She loved Kay Francis whom she thought looked like Mildred who had copied her hairstyle. Norma Shearer, (Mrs. Irving Thalberg), Julia Jean also rated. At around fourteen, egged on by those who liked her 'little' singing voice, Julia Jean didn't make much of a hit on a radio talent hour broadcast and retired mortified. Her teenage talents, however, provided her first ambition which was to be a clothes designer. Julia Jean, who was still dark-haired as nature had intended, and her beautician mother Mildred loved the movies as much for the clothes, the hairstyles and the fashions as the acting and the storylines and Julia Jean whose school grades were no more than average, took to sketching out fashion ideas with definite thoughts of fashion as a career.

At fifteen, Mildred moved to Los Angeles to stay in the house of her friend Gladys Taylor on Glencoe Way. Ostensibly, this latest move was because of Mildred's poor health exacerbated by the arguably damp Bay Area climate. It was 1936, the height of The Depression. So far Mildred had managed to keep the wolf from the door and was indeed at least moving to a job in another beauty parlour, the Lois Williams Beauty Salon in Los Angeles. But throughout California there was real misery. Over four hundred thousand unemployed. The Turners' accident-cursed four hundred mile trip south from San Francisco with baggage piled in a shared and borrowed old car sounds like a scene from THE GRAPES OF WRATH. It was just how millions arrived in California. Still do...

Julia Jean's first impressions of Los Angeles were of Hollywood for that is where she and her mother were dropped, on the corner of Highland and Sunset not a stone's throw from Julia Jean's new school, Hollywood High. It was a far cry from other L. A. high schools since made famous by their rich-kid registers. She skipped a lot of school by her own account and at fifteen was having a soda one day in the Top Hat Cafe on Highland and Sunset when an older gentlemen was introduced via the soda jerk. The soon-to-be Lana Turner *was* discovered in a soda fountain but she was drinking a nickel Coke and it absolutely wasn't in Schwab's.

Her admirer, not of course a nasty old lecher in any way, was Billy Wilkerson, the proprietor of THE HOLLYWOOD REPORTER. It was Julia Jean's day although strictly it was Judy Turner's day for the child had already re-christened herself once she turned teenager.

Wilkerson, bless him, obviously had at least one good eye although the fifteen year old claims that she hadn't really appreciated how much of a man's eye's apple she had become. Billy Wilkerson also had connections. He must have had integrity too because he was as good as his word and within the week, he had written and introduced her to the retired movie star Zeppo Marx who had turned talent agent. After making Judy swear to never reveal her underage - she was supposed to be eighteen - Marx agreed to take her on although for a good twelve months neither he nor his colleague Henry Willson could get her started.

It was left to a third agent, Solly Biano to be the one who took her to Warner Brothers and introduced her to writer/director/producer Mervyn §who had, if your memories recall, borne more than a passing interest in another blonde, Miss Ginger Rogers.

LeRoy, who had changed his name from Levy, (because, it is protested for some reason, his famous uncle Jesse Lasky had refused to employ him), was impressed with the impressionable teenager and gave her the part of Mary Clay in THEY WON'T FORGET, based on Ward Green's novel DEATH IN THE DEEP SOUTH. Judy Turner's was to be the death. LeRoy signed her personally to a $50 a week contract rather than a studio contract, a future salvation of which the ingenue was unaware. LeRoy renamed her yet again and she left his office that day as Lana Turner. She had a lot to learn but Lana was to prove a great little learner.

Her part in the movie was small but - *very* important, this one - featured. Lana's name would therefore be on all the handouts and publicity material. The role was squelch, literally, involving her walking down a street in a tightish blue sweater before she got murdered. The publicity department worked overtime when stills of her in the sweater reached the back office. The word was out. Lana Turner was *sexy*.

Mr. LeRoy's protégée was photographed in an assortment of sweaters and was tagged by those illustrious wordsmiths of the publicity department, 'the sweater girl'. She hated the label then and she hated it for all the years she tried to shake off the well-deserved appellation. As Mae West or was it Dame Savvie Getsmart said, *"Tis better to be looked over than overlooked."*

The movie came out and Lana was definitely noticed. Her next outing was in THE GREAT GARRICK and then Leroy loaned her out to Sam Goldwyn for THE ADVENTURES OF MARCO POLO with Gary Cooper after which her eyebrows, plucked and shaved as ordered, never regrew.

A word about being loaned out ... Of course, you still got your weekly salary - gee, thanks, boss. A whole fifty bucks! - but whoever held your contract got to keep the change between your salary and the amount they were charging the subcontractor. Some really big stars were getting their four and five grand a week whilst being loaned out for many tens of thousands of dollars per picture to rival studios. But a contract's a contract even though many signings bore more the hallmark of the press gang than the notary ... Shoot! I knew I should have been a lawyer as should everyone thinking of making a stab at startime.

Lana was still not a blonde. But she was developing into a transferable asset and LeRoy, at $6000 a week one of the highest paid directors in the business, took her with him when he moved to MGM. It was 1937 and the recent death of Jean Harlow had left a slot vacant notice up on the MGM lot. LeRoy must have sensed Lana Turner could fill the vacancy just as she had filled his sweater. LeRoy must also have known he could place her in LOVE FINDS ANDY HARDY with Mickey Rooney and Judy Garland and on February 20th 1938, just turned seventeen, she signed a studio contract at $100 a week.

The agent sure wasn't working overtime but Lana was assured by her reception at the studio that she wasn't a 'six month option girl to be passed around the executive offices ...' Gracious, what does Miss Turner mean in her autobiography, LANA, THE LADY, THE LEGEND, THE TRUTH!! Anyway, the hike in salary enabled the Turners to move into a proper house of their own. $100 went a long way in 1938.

And, with Mickey Rooney and Judy Garland and Freddie Bartholomew amongst others, she had to go to the MGM school run by Carol Horn as per California law, a fate escaped presumably by the 'six month option girls' whatever their age as they'd have been far too busy in the executive offices bent over, as the English actress Jill Bennett once observed, 'a little low dusting'.

Lana then made DRAMATIC SCHOOL directed by Robert Sinclair with some really hefty stars - Luise Rainer who played up and Paulette Goddard whom Lana set up as a role model. She tested for Scarlett in GONE WITH THE WIND along with everything with female apparatus who could wear a pair of curtains and, failing to convince as a putative Scarlett O'Hara then appeared in CALLING DOCTOR KILDARE. By the time the Kildare situation had been taken up by television, Lana had been a star long enough to have regretted being too old to be considered.

Making IDIOT'S DELIGHT with Clark Gable in late 'thirty eight turned her from darkly auburn into a blonde. She hated it but, like Ginger, stayed that way for the best part of sixty years.

The beginning of the war in Europe heralded an upturn in California's - and America's - fortunes and Roosevelt was able to buttress the new infrastructure created by his New Deal and use it for real national prosperity. The second world war put the boom into an America which could have gone bust and gilded California youth partied on the proceeds. Lana and her girlfriends and their dates had the best time, cruising the boulevards in big convertibles, wearing glamorous clothes and being provocative. L. B. Mayer himself has occasion to reprimand Lana's high jinks in front of Mildred, accusing her in a dirty-minded jibe of sexual promiscuity. L. B. talked to his gentile contract girls in a way that I rather fancied he would have shied from had he been faced with a nice Jewish girl and her mother!

Lana must have been learning because she moved from the Marx Agency to the William Morris office who renegotiated her MGM contract at the end of its first year and got her $250 a week. And she got to meet Greg Bautzer.

Man-about-town, lawyer-about-lot ... Bautzer was the Warren Beatty of his day. He was a product of Hollywood and they still haven't broken the mould. Lana fell deeply in love with the thirty year old Bautzer, thirteen years her senior and whilst she admits it was he who disabused her of her virginity, he was practising for that moment with a lot of other women including the much more mature Joan Crawford. Though heartbroken, Lana's career proceeded with her receiving co-star's billing on THESE GLAMOUR GIRLS with Lew Ayres, another cast-off of Miss Rogers - what a small world - and then made DANCING CO-ED with twenty-eight year old band-leader Artie Shaw.

It seems to have been hate at first sight although invited by

Artie later on a date, Lana admits to have been drawn to the highly intelligent Shaw who revealed himself as what she interpreted to be just another guy who wanted a picket-fence and family kinda life. The kinda guy she could marry and give the kinda life her poppa never had ...

So marry was indeed what they did in Las Vegas. She was nineteen and almost immediately realised that it was a revenge marriage, grasped at on the rebound from her shabby treatment by Bautzer for whom she obviously still held more than a candle.

Lana had absolutely no idea who or why she had married. They returned from Las Vegas to be greeted by a press pack which had been alerted presumably by Bautzer to whom Mildred had immediately referred after receiving Lana's telegram from Vegas which omitted to name the groom. Like Bautzer, Shaw hadn't been exactly celibate and it seems both Judy Garland and Betty Grable were shedding unrequited tears.

Shaw refused to talk to the reporters himself and forbade Lana who passed the whole thing over to MGM's head of publicity Howard Strickling who alerted a very unhappy Louis Mayer to the news. He needn't have been that worried. The egotistical, chauvinistic and entirely repellent Shaw cooked his own goose well enough. Within a very few months, he'd managed to make a sweet young girl, who only wanted a partnership, hysterical with his insensitive treatment of a woman who was also a movie star.

When he told her that shining his shoes was more important than finishing WE WHO ARE YOUNG, just like the newly weds in the movie, Lana knew her marriage was in the toilet. Ironically she called Greg Bautzer who arranged for her to exit the unhappy home. But the marriage was far from over because Lana discovered she was pregnant. Shaw displayed a callous lack of interest and didn't even believe the child was his. Her agent at William Morris, Johnny Hyde, advised on an abortion and for the huge sum of $500, Lana submitted to the hit-and-miss technique of a back street hack and after pain, degradation and humiliation, as a married woman for heaven's sake, terminated the pregnancy. Hyde also later represented another focal blonde, Marilyn Monroe. Tell me, Mr. Hyde, was it also on your advice that Marilyn's feet were no strangers to the quack gynaecologist's stirrups? Silence. Anyway ... When told the news of his lost child, Shaw, Lana reports, merely sniffed, *"I might have been consulted ..."*.

So, boys and girls, repeat after me, 'Don't ever do anything on the rebound ...' For every nice Doctor Jekyll, there's always a Mr. Hyde.

She rested awhile but went back to work to make ZIEGFELD GIRL, directed by Robert 'Pop' Leonard. Her part of Sheila Regan was rewritten and built up and she admits that she realised that she discovered what acting was all about which wasn't just merely being herself, just walking, just being Lana Turner ...

I told you. Lana Turner was a good little learner. It's as great a talent as being a good listener.

By her twentieth birthday in 1941, Lana was a forces' sweetheart and America's pin-up. She was invited along with a bevy of Hollywood-folk to toast Franklin Delano Roosevelt on his birthday in Washington. She remembers the occasion with pride and sadness and was much affected by the paralysis which rendered powerless the most powerful man on earth.

She was slated to appear as the barmaid Ivy opposite Spencer Tracy in the fictional DOCTOR JEKYLL AND MR. HYDE but she claims she asked not to be so cast because she felt that she wouldn't be able to do justice to the emotional depths the part required. After having claimed to have found out what acting was all about, this seems an odd motivation, to *not* want to act. But Ivy was also a part-time prostitute and general good-time girl and although I'm *sure* that must have been entirely incidental to the desperately image conscious Miss Turner, it was Ingrid Bergman who got to act the knickers off Ivy leaving

Lana, after L. B. Mayer's 'understanding', to play the prim, buttoned-up daughter Beatrix.

Image, dears. Image.

Also in her twenty-first year, she re-signed yet again into the 'family' of MGM at $1500 a week and got to play opposite Clark Gable in HONKY TONK. She claims she didn't fall for 'the King' who was otherwise involved with his bride of a few months Carole Lombard. However, she did claim to have fallen for Robert Taylor who was cast opposite her in JOHNNY EAGER, again directed by Mervyn LeRoy, who was now married to Barbara Stanwyck. Apparently, Lana cooled his ardour but Barbara Stanwyck sure wouldn't be votin' for no Oscar for no Lana Turner, not 'til hell froze over!

In the year that the Japanese crowded America into the world war, Lana almost broke through the Bel Air barrier, settling instead for a new house in Westwood, the closest thing. She made several sorties into greater America though, selling kisses for $50,000 a throw on a War Bond Rally. Many Hollywood stars 'served' in this way, especially the women. The men were conspicuously receiving draft papers.

But, watch out, Lana, bandits again at ten o'clock. Is it a bird, is a plane? No, it's that Howard Hughes again. I wonder if Lana and Ginger Rogers ever met? They sure had a lotta guys in common over the years. Mister Hughes, who Lana tells us never wore underwear, was much taken with Lana apparently and also with Mildred Turner with whom he used to talk 'for hours' (Why?) and who sewed strategic rips in his torn pants as expertly as other ladies were sewing parachutes to save the pilots who fell out of his planes. He didn't last long with our Lana, though. She thought him grubby, late and - ouch - boring. She also, she tells us, thought even less of his preference for blow-jobs. So, on your way, you ... you ... millionaire, you! What do you think I am? A six month option girl?

In the middle of Lana Turner's story, in 1942 in fact, we have to pause to dedicate a paragraph to another blonde whose career the faraway fighting at the various fronts was to terminate. I know Lana would not mind Carole Lombard being mentioned because I have a feeling that Lana would have certainly respected her work. More than any other major star, for major star she was, Carole Lombard worked for just about every studio in Hollywood. For Paramount she had made RUMBA with George Raft, as a redhead she made LOVE BEFORE BREAKFAST for Universal. For Columbia in 1932 she had made NO MORE ORCHIDS and for RKO, MR. AND MRS. SMITH with Robert Montgomery directed by Alfred Hitchcock and, completing the litany, THE GAY BRIDE with Chester Morris for MGM. There were many, many more, probably one for Fox and one for Warners if I was an assiduous researcher.

But on with the story. Lana found herself teamed again in SOMEWHERE I'LL FIND YOU with 'the King', Clark Gable. Half way through production, MGM received the news that returning home from a War Bond Rally, Carole had decided to fly instead of taking the train and that her plane had crashed. Gable, who was an outdoorsy, rough 'n' ready man's sorta man had finally fallen for Lombard who matched his love of the open air and huntin', shootin' and fishin'. He was devastated. Mourning did not become Gable, who was stoically magnificent and yet, they all knew, aching with his loss. L.B. Mayer apparently asked Lana to pitch in like everyone at the studio was doing to ensure he wasn't alone, even go home with him for dinner if he asked ... Although she protested and although nothing ever happened when he did ask her, can I really believe Mayer's sincere concern? He'd sacrificed other women before to keep his male team happy.

Lana too was to make other War Bond sales drives, one taking her back to her birthplace in Wallace Idaho where the small town closed down in her honour and she realised just how far she'd come in the fifteen short years since she'd left and just how long she'd been without a man in her life.

She was not to wait long for Steve Crane to throw his horse shoe. She always called him Stephan. What he called her is not recorded but he saw the future and it spelled Lana Turner in very big letters. Three weeks after they met, they were married in Vegas - second time lucky? No. That's not right, surely - and Lana very soon fell pregnant. As if there weren't problems enough with her inherent Rhesus blood status, the 'forgetful' Crane told Lana that it was just *possible* , because he'd lost the damned piece of paper, honey, that he wasn't exactly divorced which meant ... you got it. They weren't married at all. The ceremony in Vegas was annulled and Lana was once again shattered and technically single and facing the dilemma of being an unwed movie star mom.

Thank heavens this time there was no question about abortion and she eventually remarried Crane who, since being called to the draft and was doing basic training at nearby Fort Arthur, courted her constantly and passionately. They were remarried in Tijuana, Mexico in February 1943.

Baby Cheryl was born six weeks premature and struggled for life. It was in the days when received wisdom was for mother and baby to be separated until the child was considered well enough and it was an agony of some days before Lana, who had developed serious anaemia herself, insisted and finally got to hold her baby.

She went back to work because she had to in MARRIAGE IS A PRIVATE AFFAIR. She was discovering that Steve Crane was a mañana man, didn't know what he wanted and yet knew what he didn't want which was to work. He'd been discharged from the military medically unfit and just hung around the house all day. He gambled and spent her money and ... Sounds a little like what her daddy might have been, to me. Anyway, she ended it by telling him she was in love with someone else and to skedaddle. When he asked her the name of his rival, she rather foolishly told him it was John Hodiak, her entirely innocent current co-star. Ummm. Silly, Lana. Forgivable in the young Judy Turner but not anymore. It was actually rather a common thing to have stooped to.

In 1943, Lana also made SLIGHTLY DANGEROUS in which she plays the part of Peggy Evans, a shop-girl who claims the life of the long-missing daughter of a wealthy family. Somewhere in a cinema somewhere in California, there was a young girl called Norma Jean Baker watching that movie. I just know it. When Norma Jean became Marilyn Monroe, looking at Lana Turner had already been the greatest and only acting course she'd ever had.

1945 began with another renewed contract at MGM which initially brought her $4000 a week, making her one of the highest paid movie stars in the world and so she moved her menage across Sunset Boulevard and made her entrance into Bel Air proper.

She made many other entrances in this period, dating frequently, notably actor Turhan Bey who had a stand-up knock-down drag-out bout one night with the still jealous Stephan Crane who wanted his three carat engagement ring back. You cad, sir! Take that ...!

In 1945 she made KEEP YOUR POWDER DRY during which the costume designer Irene hurled herself to her death for want of Gary Cooper. Sans Irene's expertise, Lana found herself in THE POSTMAN ALWAYS RINGS TWICE directed by the alcoholic Tay Garnett and co-starring John Garfield. A difficult filming schedule due to Garnett's excesses still bore a movie in which Lana appears in white halter top and turban to create a fashion impact of seismic implication and brands herself indelibly into the minds of a whole generation of cinema goers. 'Just wrap a towel around your head and you could be Lana Turner, love.'

Called away to South America accompanied by the perfidious Sarah Hamilton, Lana stooped to another rather silly charade she reveals for some reason in having Greg Bautzer sell her house while she was away and buy another smaller one because it was the only way she could get rid of her dear, darling, wonderful mother whom she felt was cramping her style. The dear, darling, wonderful Mildred must have been pretty put out when the lack of room in the new house in Brentwood was made apparent and she was posted to a smaller billet.

Lana notes that relations between them improved. Case of being cruel to be kind, I suppose. Mildred wasn't exactly helpless and surely, deserved better? It also appears in the light of later days of reckoning that perhaps Lana also needed the profit from the sale of the house. She had developed a costly penchant for good jewellery, having noted Mervyn LeRoy's very early advice to her to 'never wear anything imitation, dear' when he saw her at a party wearing a five 'n' dimestore fake ring.

Whilst in Buenos Aires, Lana met Eva Peron and was delighted to notice that the famous-once-actress quite una-shamedly copied the Lana Turner style. So, those Argies must have wondered exactly what kind of goddess had come amongst them, mustn't they?

She made one of her worst choices in the love department when she fell for the still-married Tyrone Power. Lana says she never detected the homosexual side of Mister Power's charac-ter but then she also admits to not really liking sex that much, far preferring the kissy-kissy holdy-hands bits which, of course, is all grist to a gay boy's mill, one half of which had wheels that had to be seen to grind real corn.

Mister Zanuck, Ty's boss and Mr. Mayer, Lana's boss didn't like the set-up at all and nor, understandably, did Annabella Power who Lord knows had enough to contend with from the wings. But Lana loved Ty to the point where, having made GREEN DOLPHIN STREET, she flew a thousand miles to be with the rather miffed Ty on New Years Eve in Mexico, 1947. She says it was a night never to be forgotten although Ty hadn't initially been too pleased to see her. Probably things from the wings again.

Back in Hollywood and into making CASS TIMBERLANE, Lana developed for the part of Marianne her most invaluable tool, one which all stars need. She changed her voice. To play the British girl, Lana engendered within herself a sort of mid-Atlantic hauteur which, rather like the grafting of a special rose onto a common stock, when mixed with her rather undistinguished but respectably workaday tones created a Lana Turner voice. It is as unmistakeable now as Marilyn's or Kate Hepburn's or Bette Davies's.

Trust Lana, though. One of her little eggs met up with one of Ty's infrequently deposited wayward little wriggly things and once again she was pregnant, unmarried and faced with a putative father who was still married to a woman from whom he didn't ultimately want a divorce. Lana submitted to yet another humiliating abortion and will always wonder if, like the previous, the foetus would have ever gone full term, an agonising conjecture for any woman.

She started HOMECOMING, once again with Gable, directed by Mervyn LeRoy and waited for Ty to be nice to her. He never was. He actually took up with another woman, actress - well, kinda - Linda Christian.

Poor Lana. Probably even more than Greg Bautzer, she loved Ty Power for he recognised and validated the real Lana Turner like only a gay boy can. Not the supposed sex machine, not the *woman* who red-bloods think they should hit on but the *real* Lana Turner.

I wish I could have set Madonna on him, Lana. They can be rats in the sewers of faithfulness, darling, these sensitive souls. Rats.

But other rats turn up just as propitiously and Lana's next laboratory of love experiment came just when the IRS decided she'd not raised enough War Bond Income for Uncle Sam but instead owed him a dowry in back taxes. The rat arrived in a package labelled multi-millionaire Henry Topping and in my humble opinion, I find it sad that from this point on, despite an Academy Award, Lana became too famous for her love-life and under-assessed for her work. I fancy for a time, she was taken aboard by the roller-coaster too.

The much-married Topping came from a back-east industrial barony and basically was a wastrel. Sure, people who spend all their loot benefit the existing economy a bit but they don't *do* much to expand it. Topping bought a lotta jewels and lived like the grand seigneur he'd been bred to be but the guy knew jackshit about working women with careers to look out for.

Whilst the stars and Hollywood's front offices worried about morality, each seemed determined to push the envelope as far as possible to accommodate both the box office and the bedroom. The whole climate was governed by the insidious heat of censure and the dubious light of tolerance spawned by a dozen conflicting religions. It seems ironic that for a nation created by people escaping being told what to do, how to behave and how to live, the United States - though not alone - ended up being judged by the very refugees who had found haven. Freedom too is a moveable feast.

Translated into media lingo, it has always struck me that the behaviour of the stars themselves was a very useful litmus test for the front office to judge levels of audience moral tolerance and therefore of what content could be injected into movie properties to tempt that audience into the theatres. Basically, the message had to be: You want sex? Marry first. They forgot the second half of the proverb, 'Act in haste ...' The end bit goes, '... Repent at leisure.'

But the twentieth century didn't allow people time to repent at leisure. They had to have instant out. Society (the law, religion) had to accommodate the results and thus the dodgem car divorce climate was developed - 'You don't like this car, sir? Well you can just get right in this one.'

The I-will-I-do-Oh-hell-I-won't marriage charades in which the stars were indulged and which the studios endorsed in their movie output made a mockery of marriage for many ordinary people. Fine. If an institution is useless, junk it. But they didn't and marriage remained the mainstay of the legal and social institutions of the nation buttressed by the Dream Factory. Meet 'em, marry 'em and mug 'em in the divorce courts.

Lana is not alone in admitting in her later years that if *only* affianced people could have lived together first ... So much heartache would have been avoided, so many unloved children, so many abortions prevented. Marriage by the fifties was becoming the only way 'respectable' people could have sex!

It is easy to see why Lana married Topping. Although his track record was appalling and he gambled and drank, his was a glamorous life and his social standing vindicated the girl from Wallace, Idaho. He appeared to have money which meant the pressure on her to earn was relieved ... But Lana was a big star now, surrounded no doubt by 'yes' people and unprepared to listen to the 'no' people even if there'd been any. I can sense her enthusiasm now, convincing everyone including herself that *this* one was *the* one. It wasn't.

She had to work. Topping's trust income wasn't sufficient for their lavishly silly lifestyle and she made THE THREE MUSKETEERS in the newly-introduced Technicolor after a showdown with L. B. Mayer when she demanded the part of Lady de Winter be written up for her. It was. She starred opposite Gene Kelly and Vincent Price from whom, she acknowledges she learned about camp and timing.

But there was a lot of quite vicious gossip surrounding the run-up to her marriage to Topping. She was outraged but what did she *really* expect? It was plain she was now cocooned by her stardom, intolerant and impatient and I-am-Lana-Turner!

She lost two babies during the course of her marriage to Topping before realising that she already had one child who was perhaps not benefiting as much as she could from her attention. Cheryl was growing up with her nanny and with Mildred, her grandmother of whom Lana was obviously jealous. Of *course* you can't be a mother and movie star at the *same* time *all* the time, Lana. No one can. It's like politics and the impossibility of fooling all the people all the time.

In 1950 she made A LIFE OF HER OWN directed by George Cukor whose own star was somewhat on the wane. She reportedly had her co-star Wendell Corey fired and was obviously in a full foot-stamping star-snit, behaving not as a creative artist, interested in 'testing' with another actor to effect the best chemistry but only as a movie star determined to have her own way. She cannot have been pleasant during these years.

The Topping marriage ended as his drinking and mood swings became intolerable and he started fooling around with other gals. The final indignity came when this super-rich brat asked for some of his family's jewellery back. It's all too unhappy. She was devastated by her own failure yet again and tried her hand at a messy suicide.

But she wasn't a girl to stay down 'til the count and she went back to work in THE MERRY WIDOW in 1951 and had a really crazy love affair with her co-star, Argentinian Fernando Lamas. The passionate affair, tutted and tusked over and yet endorsed by the likes of socially prominent retired star Marion Davies, teased the nation as well as her fans. But Turner and Lamas fought and others fought over her. She ended up ditching Lamas and, in 1953, marrying the lovable, huggable Tarzan-with-East-Coast-blue-blood Lex Barker.

Was life about to get really good? She'd made THE BAD AND THE BEAUTIFUL for Vincente Minelli which itself won five Academy Awards but must have hurt her tremendously, despite her apparent phlegm, that she was not personally nominated for Best Actress.

It seemed that love and Lex Barker were working out. They'd first settled in Paris because of working commitments but on return, Lana extended her house on Mapleton Drive to accommodate his two children and made THE FLAME AND THE FLESH again with Clark Gable, the last of his MGM pictures. It got her out of the house and him out of the studio which had been his home for a quarter of a century.

Did he get a gold watch? Diddle-'e-squat!

Teevee loomed. Change was in the air. Life was really good for most Americans. Audiences, perverse as they are, now didn't need escapist, star-oriented glamour vehicles to transport themselves into a land of plenty and feel-good. They could drive there themselves. A tougher, grittier vein of production arrived through the cracks that were appearing in the studio/

star system. The cracks very rapidly rendered the institution a ruin. Old faces left and went independent as MGM failed to adapt quickly enough. Musicals were *not* the diet of the day.

Lana was loaned out - the first time in years - to Warners to make THE SEA CHASE with John Wayne, not a happy experience. Except for her last contracted picture for which she was loaned out, Lana's last picture for MGM was DIANE and she left the lot without looking back. She formed Lanturn Productions to foster her movie interests and expand her arena into production but unlike Madonna with her Slutco Inc. and Boy Toy corporations later in the century, Lana didn't really run the show herself.

In 1955, she made THE RAINS OF RANCHIPUR with Richard Burton for Twentieth Century Fox with whom she didn't get on and she wasn't getting on with Lex either. They lost another child, a girl at seven months and the imbalance in their incomes exacerbated Lana's irritation at Lex's little flings - *why* is sex *so* damned important? In 1957, they parted. She sold the Mapleton Drive house and the adolescent Cheryl went to boarding school at The Sacred Heart.

She ran away. Did Lana even realise then, *really* realise, what kind of a childhood she had given that little girl? Cheryls's nightmare upbringing was not over.

In 1957, Lana made THE LADY TAKES A FLYER at Universal when she started to receive flowers and calls from John Steele, a name unknown to her. The mystery man introduced himself as a friend of her old chum Ava Gardner and finally turned up at Lana's house one night. Whilst she was playing what she didn't consider was a particularly good part in PEYTON PLACE, she dated other men. But Steele kept sharp.

He knew a great deal about her and wore down Lana's initial apprehension and froideur - *why* did she never obey her instincts? - by strategic gift-giving and revealing himself ultimately to be the kind of lover she liked, a kissy-kissy sorta guy. John Steele's real name was revealed to her by a friend - thank God she still had some - and when she confronted Johnny 'John

Steele' Stompanato he admitted the deceit but protested his motives were of the best. He hadn't wanted her to be deterred because of what she may have heard or what 'friends' may have told her about his gangland connections. Turned off? Uh uh. Discovering that his own father had been killed, Lana was turned on. But she was also off to England to shoot ANOTHER TIME ANOTHER PLACE and the relentless Stompanato joined her there. Life was not easy. He had a boredom threshold a toddler would have tripped over and a patently unstable, vicious personality. Bye bye, Johnny? Bye bye my eye! No way was he letting go.

As she was fighting him off in Mexico whence he had followed her, shadowing her all the way from the draughts of Hampstead Heath, Lana was nominated for the Academy Award for her role as a teenager's mother in PEYTON PLACE. It was a brave role to essay for one of the queens of glamsex who hadn't turned forty.

But the queen of glamsex had been turned into just another frightened, abused woman by the violent, threatening Stompanato. Her own daughter couldn't understand why the man who made her momma so miserable was in her bed each night. To lie awake and hear through muffled walls your mother being threatened and attacked must have been purgatory.

Why she didn't ... Why didn't she ... Why, why, why? Well, Lana didn't and Johnny just kept on ringing her bells. Joanne Woodward got Lana's Oscar and April 4th 1958 got nearer and nearer. There was a final row and the frightened, hysterical Cheryl stabbed her film star mother's gangster lover with a newly-bought - but not for the purpose - kitchen knife.

No one could have written a better script.

It was a great role for a mother of a teenager.

Mildred came, Doctor McDonald came, Jerry Geisler the lawyer came and the chief of Beverly Hills Police came but at the end of the grilling Stompanato was still steak and Cheryl was taken away. For three weeks she was jailed before being allowed out after a jury in juvenile court ruled the killing was justifiable homicide. The court remanded the teenager to her mother's supervised supervision. The whole must have been the best and worst medicine for Lana. It should have been.

Did 'the Mob' want her so badly? People like Stompanato never act on their own. They are part of a pack of conspirators. Who the rest of the pack were, we can but wonder. Hollywood and The Mob and Las Vegas ... The three were mutually attractive, they each supplied either money or the means to attract money to the other. Mob money was cleaned up by being paid to stars who attracted the punters onto the gaming tables to make even more money for the mob. The sort of sexually explicit photographic material found by Lana and her helpers in Stompanato's possession and destroyed after his death would have co-erced the proudest star or the feistiest studio boss into complying with a Mob 'request'.

To save her professional ass and her checking account's bacon, fate supplied Lana with Ross Hunter who arrived with a draft of IMITATION OF LIFE tucked under his arm; it was a proposed remake of the 1934 Claudette Colbert original and of course any similarity in the roles of the actress and the es- tranged teenage daughter to any persons living in 1959 in Hollywood, California was entirely incidental.

Anyway, it was Universal's highest grossing picture to date and also introduced the world to Sandra Dee. More important to Lana Turner, it enabled her to have a mid-life career. Many of those with whom she had started out, even some of the 'six month option girls' now only appeared on grand charity committees, playing the role that the Lana Turners of the world were denied. Married to rich men. With children. And stable homes, their reel lives long commuted into respectability. Would Lana have been happy?

She wasn't happy for long with Fred May, a race horse owning ranch-dwelling chap who was at least nice to her when he wasn't timing her and making her nervous. Fred was also nice to Cheryl who had blown her probation deal and had, at the Court's instruction, been sent to El Retiro, a school in the San Fernando valley for girls with problems.

Unfortunately for Cheryl there weren't similar schools for parents with problems nor will there ever be until the human race finally sees sense and makes all potential parents take out a licence to procreate. Most would fall, thankfully, far short of even the minimum requirements. But don't watch this space ...

PORTRAIT IN BLACK and POSSESSED were followed by WHO'S GOT THE ACTION. She needed, apparently, the money. So did Fred May and after a monumental row about a Cadillac and $5000 they were divorced in Juarez, only to remain very good friends when Lana moved to Malibu.

Marriage ... I ask you ... No, don't tell me.

And Lana *certainly* didn't hear you. She did it again. After shooting the remake of MADAME X, again for Ross Hunter, she married Bob Eaton, an ex-forces wannabee producer ten years her junior who had surprise, surprise, once a little something to do with Ginger Rogers! It was probably more than a little something for Lana admits he was the first man to make her really know what sex was all about ... It sure had been a long time coming. And it was rather quick going because the younger Eaton couldn't resist all the good times that the mature Lana had already had and so blew his passport to producerland.

A bruising encounter with television and a Harold Robbins-scripted series THE SURVIVORS was not a happy time that also saw the exit of Eaton and the entrance of hypnotist Ronald Dante. The woman's incorrigible. Talk about crying wolf, my lambs. In her autobiography, even the lady herself says rather bleatingly, *"Why? Oh, why?"*

In 1971, after Dante had robbed her blind, she gamely went off to work in the theatre. She played in FORTY CARATS to great success and the theatre became her new employer. Later productions included THE PLEASURE OF HIS COMPANY and BELL, BOOK and CANDLE and her dinner theatre work such as MURDER AMONG FRIENDS where she really could write her own ticket has been also bolstered by occasional appearances in television series. A latecomer to drink, she abandoned it in favour of God who hadn't apparently minded waiting a long time to see Lana Turner.

She is still Lana Turner, even to God. As she said herself, *"People pay to see Lana Turner ... They're gonna see Lana Turner."*

June 29th 1995

And people did see the public Lana Turner. The private version was, I'm sure, as dignified and stalwart and brave as the movie star who played countless women thwarted and betrayed by life. The public obviously knew little of the private Lana. She was a mistress of publicity and had she wished us to know more about her, believe me, we would have known.

So she suffered her years of battling throat cancer privately with her close friends and with her daughter Cheryl whom time had seen grow as close to Lana in latter years as the two had been strangers as mother and growing daughter.

Lana died today. She was seventy-five.

CHAPTER 11

Pioneer Blondes

GUS JORDAN'S DIAMOND PALACE RAIDED!

Sa...

SPECIAL ★ ★ THE Bowery News ★ ★ EXTRA

★ A ROARING, HOT PAGEANT OF THE BOWERY'S SCARLET DAYS ★

MAE WEST BARES
SECRETS OF NOTORIOUS DANCE DEN

'HAWK' SWOOPS DOWN ON JORDAN'S JOINT, CLAMPING LID ON BOWERY SIN SPOT

Gus Jordan's famed Diamond Palace, suicide club of the Bowery, fell last night before the relentless nightsticks of police led by the "Hawk," who placed the bracelets on Gus himself after an unceasing six-months' vigil to apprehend the Bowery's leading light.

The "Hawk" had watched Jordan's Palace until his opportunity last night when he caught the rising political power in his ascendency and smashed the nefarious traffic Jordan had been operating in girls and narcotics.

Diamond-decked Lou, said to be consort of Jordan's, and toast of the town, was taken into personal custody by Captain Cummings, popular young mission worker. Rumor has it the handsome Captain has effected a reform in Lady Lou's will o' wisp career, and the Bowery may hear of wedding bells soon for the reigning queen of Gotham's unholy street.

"I won't say anything," said Lou late last night, almost blinding this reporter with her brilliant diamond array and her gorgeous beauty. "Gus was a swell guy,

but whatever he got himself mixed up in, ain't none of my business.

"And as for Captain Cummings —well, he's a man, ain't he? And he can be had!"

Cummings refused to comment on the last statement.

Lady Lou, stunning beauty of the Bowery, whose picture has graced more brewery and bank calendars than any other of our town's famous sirens, is alleged, according to the handsome Captain, to be innocent of implication in Jordan's evil business.

"I'll stake my life this girl is unsullied by Jordan's unholy transactions," said the Captain heatedly.

"You bet I am," said Lou, when informed of this. "I'm the

finest woman that ever walked, and I want you to know it!"

"Jordan's arrest smashes another link in the net of dance and drink dens that have made our fair Bowery a satanic byword in the

mouths of our people. Gotham has no place for the organized vice political lobbygow like Jordan foist on our respectable city," said Mr. Lexton, head of the famous vice investigating committee.

"ME A GOLD-DIGGER? I SHOULD SAY NOT! I'LL TAKE DIAMONDS... THIS COUNTRY MAY BE OFF THE GOLD STANDARD ANY DAY." SAYS LOU.

Story Inside

TO-NIGHT !   TO-NIGHT !!   TO-NIGHT !!!

CHILDREN UNDER TWELVE NOT ALLOWED.

The Sensational and the Biggest Show of the Year.

—A T—

THE CAPITOL

(Leading Talkie House of the Town)

Comm. Friday 24th November.

6-15 p.m.   (Twice Nightly)   9-30 p.m.

MAE WEST

THE DARLING OF BROADWAY

IN

She Done Him Wrong

WITH

Cary Grant, Owen Moore, Noah Beery, Gilbert Roland.

THE PEAK PRODUCTION OF 1933.

Comm. Tuesday 28th Nov.

Most Glowing Romance of the Year.

"PICK UP"

WITH

**SYLVIA   GEORGE
SIDNEY   RAFT**

SCREEN'S GREATEST TEAM.

Matched in human and heart touching drama!

Comm. Friday 1st December.

THEY ARE HERE AGAIN

The word's foremost funster's in a dizzy riot of laughs that eclipses all previous efforts !

GEORGE   CHARLIE
SIDNEY   MURRAY

IN

"THE COHENS & KELLYS

IN

TROUBLE"

WITH

MAUREEN O'SULLIVAN.

Rattan Printing Press, 6, McLeod, Road, Lahore.

PRINTED IN U.S.A.

"If he were mine, I'd love him . . . and no woman would have a chance of getting him away from me!"

"I know you're as important to him —downtown—as I am—uptown!"

Clark **GABLE** Jean **HARLOW** Myrna **LOY**

A CLARENCE BROWN'S PRODUCTION

of **WIFE** *Versus* **SECRETARY**

with May ROBSON George BARBIER
James STEWART Hobart CAVANAUGH

A Metro-Goldwyn-Mayer Picture

DIRECTED BY

CLARENCE BROWN

Produced by Hunt Stromberg

Here's no story of "frowsy wife versus snappy secretary". . . it's a story of two beautiful and attractive women . . . and one man. Get ready for a grand battle of hearts spiced with laughter, rollicking with fun.

Faith Baldwin's deliciously racy Cosmopolitan Magazine triangle romance played by three of your greatest favorites!

It sparkles like champagne— and it's twice as intoxicating.

It was like a dream come true . . . but there she was in Havana!

EMIL JANNINGS

MARLENE DIETRICH

BLUE ANGEL

DIRECTED BY
JOSEPH VON STERNBERG

UFATONE PRODUCTION

Marlene Dietrich . . . . . the new *thrill* of the screen! Exotic . . . . beautiful. . . . clever — a new motion picture star sweeping the country like wild-fire!

"Dishonored" — a story of the cunning — daring and charm of one woman pitted against a horde of scheming men!

"Dishonored"

a Paramount Picture

Country of Origin, U. S. A.

Starring

VICTOR McLAGLEN

MARLENE DIETRICH

THE NEW THRILL OF THE SCREEN

VICTOR McLAGLEN

MARLENE DIETRICH

IN "Dishonored"

NEVER BEFORE
IN ALL THIS
WORLD....

A MUSICAL EXTRAVAGANZA STAGED IN THE CLOUDS!

Thrilling stars, teasing tunes, delirious fun and gorgeous girls in scenes of ravishing beauty...the year's most exciting revel!

COME, TAKE A JOY RIDE THROUGH THE SKY!

See this grand, breath taking climax of all screen musical entertainments!

Heart racing romance...so daring, so different...that even your wildest dreams of a "music show" will come to stunning fulfillment!

Hear these tantalizing songs....
"Music Makes Me"..."Flying Down to Rio"..."Orchids in the Moonlight"...and the new dance sensation that will soon be sweeping America...the hypnotising, compromising "Carioka"!

MELODY THAT SWEEPS
DOWN HEAVEN'S
TWINKLING PATHWAY!
Music by
Vincent Youmans
greatest living composer of heart catching tunes whose hits include "Tea for Two", "Halleluja", "Hit the Deck", and "No, No, Nannette."
Lyrics by Edward Eliscu and Gus Kohn

FLYING DOWN TO RIO

DOLORES DEL RIO

GENE RAYMOND · RAUL ROULIEN
GINGER ROGERS · FRED ASTAIRE

Directed by
Thornton Freeland
MERIAN C. COOPER
Executive Producer
Louis Brock
Associate Producer

RKO
Radio
PICTURES

LADIES AND GENTLEMEN, here's a SHOW!

See them dance the "Piccolino," this gay nation's new ballroom adventure! reckless

PLAZA

(Direction: Empire Talkies Distributor)

Comm. THUR. 6th FEB.

RKO Radio

TOP HAT

TOP HAT

FEATURING

FRED ASTAIRE

GINGER ROGERS

RELEASED BY

EMPIRE TALKIE DISTRIBUTORS

LAHORE : BOMBAY : CALCUTTA : DELHI : KARACHI

Irene DUNNE
Fred ASTAIRE
Ginger ROGERS
JEROME KERN'S
amazing musical stage success . . . ten times as tantalizing on the screen!
A dream-drenched story of Paris at love time . . . with heart-breaking beauties in gasping gowns!
All your life you'll TINGLE to its heart-disturbing tunes!
SO WONDERFUL YOU CAN'T BE-LIEVE IT'S REAL!
RANDOLPH SCOTT ★ HELEN WESTLEY
VICTOR VARCONI ★ CLAIRE DODD
FROM THE PLAY, "ROBERTA"
Books & Lyrics by OTTO HARBACH
Directed by William A. Seiter
A PANDRO S. BERMAN PRODUCTION
RKO Radio

TO-NIGHT !   TO-NIGHT !!   TO-NIGHT !!!

THE PLAZA

From TUESDAY, 19th May

6.45 P.M.   (Twice Nightly)   9.45 P.M

FOR THREE NIGHTS ONLY

GLORIOUS REVIVAL

"ROBERTA"

WITH

FRED ASTAIRE—GINGER ROGERS

NO WOMAN EVER LOVED...WITH MORE TO LOSE!

With her lips she erased from his...the brand of dishonor!

JACK H. SKIRBALL and BRUCE MANNING present

GINGER ROGERS DAVID NIVEN

Magnificent Doll

and BURGESS MEREDITH

with PEGGY WOOD HORACE McNALLY ROBERT H. BARRAT

A UNIVERSAL-INTERNATIONAL RELEASE

Director of Photography JOSEPH VALENTINE, A.S.C. Copyright by Hallmark Productions, Inc. 46/870

Directed by FRANK BORZAGE

Produced by JACK H. SKIRBALL Original Story and Screenplay by IRVING STONE

"Rocking America with laughter!"

"NEW LAUGH-AND-LOVE TEAM TAKES NATION BY STORM!"

ANOTHER GREAT
FRANK CAPRA
PRODUCTION

A COLUMBIA PICTURE

Screen play by
ROBERT
RISKIN
Story by Clarence
Budington Kelland

GARY COOPER

MR. DEEDS
GOES TO TOWN

JEAN ARTHUR

GEORGE BANCROFT ★ LIONEL STANDER
DOUGLASS DUMBRILLE ★ H. B. WARNER

Her Lips Made "FOREVER" Seem Too Short
and "ALWAYS" Seem But A Single Day!

Timeless romance and breath-taking beauty will hold you spellbound as glamorous Marion—and an all-star cast who are all real stars—bring you the best picture in years. Don't miss it!

WARNER BROS. PRESENT

Marion DAVIES in

"Hearts Divided"

WITH DICK POWELL · CHARLIE RUGGLES
CLAUDE RAINS · EDW. EVERETT HORTON

ARTHUR TREACHER · HALL JOHNSON CHOIR · A FRANK BORZAGE PRODUCTION

A Cosmopolitan Production   Released by First National Productions Corp.

Hear Marion and Dick sing: "Hearts Divided" and "My Kingdom For A Kiss", by Harry Warren & Al Dubin

CHAPTER 12

Doris Day

Doris Day

Doris Day is famous for many songs but I'm picking up on QUE SERA not because I think it's very dangerous, which I do, but because it best sums up Doris's life and career. In QUE SERA, life kinda just happens. And that's just what seems to have happened with Doris. She appeared never to really *do* anything to *get* anywhere and she resolutely maintains that she never *wanted* to get anywhere except into an apron and stand in a kitchen waiting for *him* and *them* to come home to *her*. I find this QUE SERA thing not very inspirational and, as I said, a dangerous philosophy for millions to have been tempted to follow.

In what little of her candid self she displays in her 'autobiography' as 'revealed' to A. E. Hotchner, she seems to have had the ability to conveniently ignore anything inconvenient. If she had to call black white for a quiet life, then white black was and if there was anything she didn't want to know, she simply didn't know it.

She was America's number one box office star for five years on the trot and she sold millions of records and it's perhaps no co-incidence that America itself, nay the Western world even, was going through a similar delusory era. After the war, the Second World variety, America ignored what it found unpalatable and called whatever colour happened to be on the 'opposing' team, red. It was a sanitised time to be American and Miss Day served her country well. She fulfilled the current need of both her own country and the rest of the world serviced by Hollywood to be lulled and charmed and convinced that boy still met girl and that marriage came before babies and that it was okay for women to have a career *before* they married. America especially went very coy on both glamour and sex in the Doris Day era. But, hey ... I can't complain. It was why we in Britain and Europe could export the shocking and the sexy in such huge quantities westwards in the wave of insanitary which followed *The Beatles* and which turned into the immensely lucrative sixties.

Doris's was the swan-song which heralded the decline and ultimate fall of the studio system which could not withstand the tide of domestic consumerism which made sure that televisions were bought to be watched in the privacy and non-social fight ring of the American home. Doris's career came with the death rattle of the studios, several of which she saved with her pictures, and went with the triumphant roar of television in which chorus her voice was also heard.

Doris's place in the blonde pantheon is immutable. She was an extremely talented interpreter of lyrics and she was an unrivalled singer of a certain sort of song. She was a bridge between then and now, between the big band and the four piece, between Edna Ferber's new world of post-1918 and the newer-still world heralded by Joni Mitchell and Janis Joplin, two relatively unsung blondes whose relevance has paled with time. Doris Day's ticket and record sales helped finance the more adventurous record companies whose coffers became used to being full. Make no mistake; Doris Day was mega. Big. Big. Big.

She was, thank heavens, however, born small. Usual poundage, she emerged in 1924 in Cincinatti, the daughter of William and Alma Kappelhoff and named for Doris Kenyon, a silent screen actress whose star Alma Kappelhoff followed at that time. Both her parents' families were obviously German although of her father's she admits knowing very little. Her mother's, the Welzes, who proved to be stalwarts in the future of the Kappelhoff children, were bakers and, one intuits, perhaps not as highbrow as their Kappelhoff son-in-law. Doris' birth was preceded by the arrival of Richard who died at age two and Paul, a fine healthy boy who was some years older than she.

Their father taught piano and music and was organist and choral master at a local Catholic church. Though catholic by form, the Kappelhoffs weren't too seriously religious. Then.

Alma and William were not merely ill-suited, they were mis-matched. By explaining that Alma disliked classical music and opera to the extent that she would interrupt her husband's listening and switch to a hillbilly station on the radio speaks volumes. Really important issues like musical tastes have often dictated divorces it seems and the Kappelhoffs were no different then. William understandably began an affair with a similarly serious-minded woman and left when Doris was eleven. She saw her father once a week on Wednesdays for a while and then never saw him again for years.

As a separated and then divorced working woman, supporting her children, Alma decided against dating and seemed to devote herself to raising Paul and Doris. Though her father had encouraged Doris to learn piano, her child's faulty attention span thwarted his hopes but instead, later, she went to dancing classes. She loved, she asserts positively, to perform and she ended up at the Hessler Academy in the Mount Adams suburb of Cincinatti where not only dancing was taught but acting too.

Doris was not a happy pupil at the catholic high schools she attended but excelled at dancing. She tapped her way to the top of Hessler's Academy with the twelve year old Jerry Doherty. It doesn't seem to have been a romance as Doris later dated his elder brother Larry but good ol' pals they must surely have been.

With their song-and-dance routines, the Doris/Jerry duo won many local competitions culminating in a $500 win which their respective mothers decided they would invest in a trip to Hollywood to visit the famous dance academy of Fanchon and Marco. Hollywood was at the peak of its influence and Doris and her mother were under it. It was the Schubert and the Albee chains which had cinemas in Cincinnati with the Evanston showing the horror movies. Doris's second favourite was Betty Grable, an up-and-coming little blonde but her first fave and all time rave was Ginger Rogers. Of course, in those days the stars of the movies made personal appearances where the movies were playing. It was grist for dreams for Doris saw both her heroines live.

The four week trip to Hollywood was a roaring success and the Kappelhoff/Doherty team impressed at Fanchon and Marco and were booked out to perform at events in the Hollywood area. It was decided by the mothers that they would move to Hollywood. For the sake of their children, of course. What was to be done for the sake of the putative stars' siblings is not clear.

Plans were laid and on Friday 13th October 1937, friends of Alma's gave a bon voyage party. Doris, dating Jerry's elder brother, and a couple of friends went out after the party and on the way home their car was hit by a train on a crossing point. Left with her right leg shattered and the prognosis of at least a four month recovery period, Doris was on the one hand lucky to be alive but on the other destined not to return to Hollywood for some years. The ensuing apprenticeship was probably the making of her.

And poor old Jerry Doherty, too. Let's hear some for Jerry, guys!

During her invalidity, Doris didn't go to school for some strange reason, which omission didn't stand her in good stead later. Whilst her mother was presumably out at work, Doris instead listened to the radio constantly and, unable to dance, sang along with all types of songs. Still in plaster, her mother decided the patently ambulant Doris could benefit from singing lessons rather than school and Doris was sent to study with Cincinnati's Grace Raine. According to Doris, Alma was never a 'stage mother' although it would seem that her ambitions for her daughter knew no bounds. Presumably she was similarly proud and propelling of her son Paul who was making waves as a potential professional baseball player.

Grace Raine was much impressed by Doris who has accorded her old teacher the ultimate accolade - "*... without whom all this would never have been possible ...*" Grace's teaching was obviously good but even better were her contacts. Life's a non-starter without the letters of introduction. Grace's husband Ferde was a publisher's song plugger and his time spent at radio stations furnished Doris with the opportunity to sing on WLW Radio for showman André Carlin. The resulting broadcast enabled Grace to teach Doris more about microphone technique and vocal delivery. Apparently, the radio-virginal Doris popped her *p*'s. Puh-puh-puh ... Mercy me.

A domestic terpsichorean performance of her own re-fractured the broken leg and Doris' next career move was made hobbling up to the microphone at Charlie Lee's Shanghai House Chinese restaurant where Doris sang for her supper whilst other people ate theirs.

Again due to Grace Raine's networking, Doris got a call from Barney Rapp who fronted a big band with a big band sound. Off the road and now based at his club The Sign of The Drum, Barney was convinced and hired peg-leg Kappelhoff at $25 a week. He thought he was paying her $50 but the band's manager was hiving off the rest, she notes with wry hindsight. It was the first of many rip-offs she suffered. I suppose it just wasn't 'nice' for a young girl in those days to ask awkward questions about contracts and money.

It was also Barney who re-christened her. Kappelhoff certainly was some mouthful although Doris hated the 'Day' with which Barney landed her. Me? I'd've been pretty cross about Doris but there you are.

She was driven to and from work by the grumpy and ungracious Al Jorden, one of the Rapp band's trombone players. Obviously not just any old trombone player, Jorden had two reputations, one as a musician of some consideration and the other patently unmentionable. Doris had actually wound up in a milieu which, entirely unbeknownst to her, was a pool of the créme of American musicianhood. When Jorden started dating the almost sixteen years old Doris, she found that the acerbic crosspatch turned into a beau and their juices mingled.

They made plans, entirely rejected by Jorden's jealous mother. Coincidental to Al Jorden leaving Cincinatti to play for Gene Krupa, The Sign of the Drum folded and Barney Rapp took his band back on the road. It was sans Doris. She maintains that she didn't want to entertain the travelling and, once again thanks to Grace and Ferde Raine, auditioned for Bob Crosby and his Bobcats who were appearing at The Black Hawk in Chicago.

Now this outfit *was* a touring band but they were paying $75 a week. The money was useful as brother Paul had by this time sustained head injuries in a baseball accident which was causing him epileptic seizures. Alma was thrilled with Doris's break and herself occasionally travelled with the band as the virtuous Doris one-nightered with the equally virtuous Bobcats. Her heart still belonged to Al Jorden who had since left the Krupa band to play for Jimmy Dorsey.

For this time in the history of the twentieth century, guys, this is pretty serious muzo lore we're talking here.

But, in its turn, The Bobcats' style became dated and Doris must have been shaken when Gil Rodin, Crosby's band manager informed her that Bonnie, the band's other singer, was being kept on for a series of one nighters in New York and not Doris. She must have been equally thrilled to know that Les Brown, the leader of a very happening band, had asked her to join him. Now sixteen, Doris signed on. It was 1940. I have to say 'sixteen' once again because I think it's an extraordinary feat for a sixteen year old girl to be hacking it with the best of the big bands. Think about it.

It seems that some bands then certainly got their share of the excess of the sex-drugs-and-rock'n'roll sort that later characterised the lives of touring musicians. It seems that Les Brown's band, however, wasn't one of them. They were apparently known as the milk shake band. *All* of them?

Al Jorden was also playing in New York with the Dorsey band and, away from momma, asked Doris to marry him. So, marry they did, too early too quickly and against the advice of anyone who knew Jorden. Sure! So maybe he was the greatest lay in the world. But why not a single one of the people who made with all the advice ever spelled out the fact in plain language that Jorden beat up on women and whose violent jealousy was embarrassing, even indictable, I don't know. Doris says she loved him and, believing Madonna loved Sean Penn, one can only believe her.

It is quite humbling to learn of the number of women in times gone by whom society somehow convinced into enduring marital violence. When Doris became pregnant, Jorden insisted she undergo an abortion. Doris seems to have had sufficient of Jorden's bullying that she wanted the baby more than she wanted him but she still endured life with him and produced Terry, her son, on the eighth of February, 1942. Jorden was conspicuously absent.

Doris returned to Cincinatti with her baby son and Jorden quit his band and came too. Finally, driven to the limit by his mental cruelty, Doris changed all the locks on the little house she'd rented and Jorden was out of her life. He occasionally reappeared but after a while, he joined the Air Force and served as a bandsman at the Great Lakes base.

Doris went back to work at WLW where she was one of the resident singers assigned to sing backing for sponsored commercials. She felt deeply betrayed by her marital experience. Being a wife, mother and homemaker had been her only avowed ambition although being the father as well was something she hadn't figured on. She needed something to lean on. There was Alma, sure but at times like these, a person needs a little stroking. Thus her tentative re-exploration of her inherent Catholicism which brought her head-to-head with a priest who wanted her to confess her sins left her decidedly un-stroked. The idea that she may have sinned, that any of her situation was perhaps her fault, left her un-desirous of re-entering the Catholic fold. And now she was a working mother. And it was wartime. She wasn't even twenty.

Answering Les Brown's third call, she left Terry with Alma and went back on the road and had her first hit records, the most notable being SENTIMENTAL JOURNEY, a song which had first seen life in New York's Brill Building song fountain. All seemed to be going well except ... These musicians ... George Weidler, the sax player in the band, caught Doris's eye and, once again in 1946, she found herself mangled in the maw of the marriage machine.

As Mrs. George Weidler, Doris moved to California and lived in a trailer, keeping house but, what will be ... was. And because she had to sing to earn, she sang. First on a local CBS Radio station. But the joy and the thrill had gone out of live performance. She now found it frightening and the nervousness too draining. However, her past apprenticeships singing live paid dividends in the shape of Al Levy one of the founding agents of Century Artists along with Dick Dorso and Marty Melcher, who had seen her singing in New York. Levy had become not only a fan but an admirer.

Though Levy introduced Doris to his colleagues at Century, neither Melcher nor Dorso could get her going in Hollywood and so after some months, Doris made the trip back East once again to appear with Billy Reed at his Little Club opening in New York.

Whilst she was away, George Weidler wrote her that he was going to leave her. Not for anyone else but just leaving. She returned to California feeling she'd once again failed miserably as a woman. They talked but there was no reconciliation. But at least Doris seems to have learned and swore she would never marry again until she had thoroughly explored her future husband by living with him.

Al Levy invited her to a party at Jule Styne's house where she sang for the director Michael Curtiz whose production of ROMANCE ON THE HIGH SEAS at Warner Brothers, which was to have starred Judy Garland and then Betty Hutton, was acutely leading-lady-less. They needed a cute blonde and so Doris found herself in the proverbial right place at the proverbial right time although she resonantly maintained she was not sure whether she wanted to be or even could be an actress.

Doris screen-tested and ROMANCE started shooting and she got herself a contract at Warners in 1948. It was for seven years and lasted until 1955. She found the process of making all seventeen of the subsequent pictures she made at Warners, greatly to her liking.

On the love stakes, as well as dating Jack Carson, she maintained a loving as well as liking relationship with ex-husband George who introduced her to Christian Science. The influence of Mary Baker Eddy was certainly hugely powerful in those middle years of our century. Remember Jean Harlow? Oh, Doris ... Do be careful!

Look behind any successful career and there is a staircase made of the efforts and help of many other people who through inconvenience but mostly through politics and the greed of yet more people have long since either been elbowed or whose further contributions were found expediently expendable. Doris had completed STORM WARNING, a good straight role, co-starring with Ginger Rogers and there was no doubt her career was really on the up.

But it was Al Levy's turn to be a stair tread. Having secured her career, loyal old Al disgraced himself by becoming obsessed with our Miss Day who had been, as we know all women are, oblivious to the reasons underlying his faith in her and his beyond-the-call-of-duty efforts on her behalf. Like it's okay to admire from a distance but don't love the lady close to. He was removed from the arena of her operations and shipped back East. His embarrassment and shame and rejection must have been mortifying for him. You can obviously love someone too much and Doris and those around her didn't want no Al Levy lovin' no Doris Day.

The agent vacant situation in her life was duly assumed by Martin Melcher, one of the other partners at Century Artists.

As we shall see, Doris found that she *did* want Marty to love her and, boy, did he love her. Sadly, to love her he had to shaft her for the six foot three, good-looking Melcher loved money more and, as we all now know of course, the love of money brooks no rival.

Again we have one of those "So why didn't anyone *tell* her?" scenarios. This lady was *not* a good chooser. She hated choosing but she chose someone who everyone else in town appears to have known as a bad news booboo since the year dot and carry.

Melcher was married to Patty Andrews, one of the hugely influential and successful Andrews Sister of close harmony fame. Patty's star was not in the ascendant. Doris's was. Que Sera, Patty ... Funny how that song has a decidedly different ring when applied to the loser ...

Marty and Doris married on her birthday, April third, 1951. Doris had bought Martha Raye's house in Toluca Lake and they moved with Doris's mother Alma and Terry. Later Alma moved to her own apartment and Martin Melcher officially adopted Doris's son Terry who admitted later that their meeting when he was seven was his first memory of his mother at all.

But Doris really thought life had brought her the happy family which had always eluded her and, obviously, nothing could have convinced her differently. Later, momma Alma revealed that she had known Melcher ill-treated the young Terry from the off. But Doris, apparently, saw nothing.

By 1952, Doris had made it into the top ten box office ratings in a poll of the theatre managers of America. In 1953, SECRET LOVE from CALAMITY JANE sold over a million copies, her third platinum song. She was working like crazy and, having no yardsticks by which to budget her energy, Doris was becoming exhausted.

The creeping influence of Mary Baker Eddy had been adopted by Marty, even more fervently it would seem than by Doris. Born a Jew, religion also played second fiddle to Marty's money love. Taken so to heart by his wife, Marty was not about to allow her religious tenets to come between him and his golden goose. Better to convert and convert he did.

Doris dealt with her developing ill-health as a Christian Scientist. She found swallowing painful and breathing difficult and also had found a lump in her breast. Which came first, who can tell but she was riddled with worry and fear and yet, true to what she *thought* was right Christian Science thinking, didn't go to a doctor. Her health continued to deteriorate despite all the while consulting Martin Broones, a Christian Science practitioner.

Finally, thank Sanity, a doctor was called who diagnosed hyperventilation and chronic stress syndrome. After due R and R, Doris was able to return to work but still held true to her Christian Science disciplines. She seemed to honestly believe that nothing in life was either good or bad but, as Shakespeare apparently reminded her, thinking makes so. Well, Doris, honey, believe me ... There *is* bad and it's always made worse by not recognising it.

Bad was Arwin Productions, the company formed by Marty Melcher for Doris's services to the industry and whose first outing was in conjunction with Warner Brothers and her last contractual film for that studio entitled YOUNG AT HEART co-starring Frank Sinatra whom she had known in her radio days. Frank was so sweet and dear, especially when being kind to old lady actresses like Ethel Barrymore - with whom they all had their photos taken by the world's press to celebrate the lady's millionth birthday - and he was even sweet and dear when threatening people with instant unemployment and personally disciplining ill-mannered louts who creep into lowly, menial positions on films sets.

And Marty, of course, was now the producer. The producer is the man who is in control and who handles not only the money but also the volatile temperaments of the artists he employs for the good of the picture.

Sinatra had Melcher thrown off the set.

What did Doris do? She kept knitting apparently. Sure, Marty wasn't the only one thrown off the set but ... The Producer? Doris must have been a little bit hip to the dude, though, because in a few months, Arthur Park would be brought in as her agent, to handle all the tricky situations in Doris's dollar-generating life like work.

How she got to do the good movies she did in the business circumstances which Marty Melcher was about to establish, I haven't the faintest clue. She admitted that leaving Warners and having to *choose* scripts was very difficult and as she told us, to choose means that one choice is better than the other which means kinda good and bad and, of course, nothing is really good or bad so ... See? Tricky thing, choice.

If I didn't know better, I'd think that choice seemed to have singled Doris out above other mortals on the planet. But, hell ... Someone chose something somewhere along the line and she made LOVE ME OR LEAVE ME, the biopic centred on the life of Ruth Etting and that 'thirties torch singer's relationship with the manipulative and deceitful Marty Snyder, played by Jimmy Cagney. The earthy character of Ruth Etting brought Doris some adverse fan reaction. She explained to us in HER OWN STORY that some people in her audiences were easily confused. Though it's Ruth Etting on screen, Doris elaborates, all *they* see is Doris Day. Get it? Sure, we get it, but ... like, compounding that confusion, ought we not also better check on just *who* in *that* scenario might Doris Day be? We gotta be sure about that because if we're not sure who Doris Day is, how can we be sure of what America itself is? And who are we? And who, I ask even more importantly, am I???

The decidedly un-travelled Melchers travelled to Europe on the Queen Elizabeth to do the French scenes for Hitchcock's THE MAN WHO KNEW TOO MUCH. Doris was adulated by clamouring mobs in London and liked that as much as she liked the sea crossing although in France life seems to have been plagued by Americans, especially at the Cannes Film Festival. Yuk! However, Morocco was the *real* bummer 'cos in Morocco they aren't kind to animals like they are in America and Doris was so appalled that she wanted to go right home and have Grace Kelly do the picture for Mr. Hitchcock. But Grace had another destiny and Doris made another wonderful movie completing the interiors in Hollywood where no one, man nor beast, wants for anything. I don't know if Doris ever saw the need to leave the USA again. I have a friend like Doris in Laguna Beach who says he has everything he ever needs right there in Laguna and sees no need to go anywhere else. It's an interesting concept on which to base a life.

All these movies. All that money. The name Jerome Rosenthal was being mentioned more and more in the house at Toluca Lake for it was Mr. Rosenthal who was handling all the Day-Melcher moolah, putting it into sensible investments like hotels and oil wells and bonds. To keep Mr. Rosenthal's bottom-less requirements for new investment funds satisfied, Marty sprang JULIE on Doris to earn the necessary but forbade her to spend anything herself on her own passion, 'art'. In California, they have 'art' on the walls like the rest of the world has paintings.

About to film JULIE, Doris at last started asking questions about Mr. Rosenthal and she did so after visiting one of the hotels built with her money to find that it was in a location which any right-thinking potential guest would have avoided like the pox. Doris was also detecting a zoning problem in her relationship with Marty. I think she concluded that the fulsome sex life they had been enjoying had gone on the blink. At the same time, two weeks into JULIE, Doris also started haemor-rhaging one day. Marty agreed completely with the Christian Science practitioner Mr. Broones that there was no need for medical input and that Doris carry on working and finish her work on JULIE with Louis Jourdan. No work meant no money and a cross Mr. Rosenthal.

Melcher and whoever-else let Doris get so ill that she herself went to see her gynaecologist who diagnosed a huge intestinal tumour and had her immediately operated on. At the same time they took away her womb and all her womanly necessaries. Poor soul. She was only thirty two.

But the Melchers got to move from Toluca Lake to Crescent Drive in Beverly Hills and Doris got to sign with Columbia Records the biggest record deal ever done for $1,050,000. That was a lotta money then. She was a very big star.

Promoting JULIE, she got to Cincinatti to find her father still living there. He owned and ran a bar in a black neighbourhood, assisted by Luvenia Williams whom he was to marry. Doris only saw William Kappelhoff once again before he died. But shucks, if you don't control these extraneous emotional demands on your time, who the hell would ever get any work done? Like your kids ... Suddenly they're teenagers and can be real disruptive if, like their stepfather tells you, they fall in with the wrong crowd ... Terry was sent off to Military School. Que sera ...

Doris's brother Paul, who had been continuously ill and according to every testimony was the sweetest guy, had come out to California with his family and worked for Doris and Marty. His baseball injuries finally killed him and Doris was much shaken. She was making PAJAMA GAME with Clark Gable whose simplicity she just adored and over 1958 and 1959 made two pictures which dipped at the box office somewhat alarmingly.

To compensate, her favourite producer/agent, Destiny, arrived in the person of Ross Hunter who handed her PILLOW TALK which she made in 1959 with Rock Hudson and which cemented her into her niche in eternity. Ross Hunter, if you remember, also performed a life-saving salvage job on the career of Lana Turner. In 1960 Doris and her movie were number one at the box office and she personally remained in that position, America's favourite, for five years, making a succession of clone movies, two more - LOVER COME BACK and SEND ME NO FLOWERS - with Rock, then two with James Garner, THRILL OF IT ALL and MOVE OVER DARLING and ultimately A TOUCH OF

MINK with Cary Grant. She loved them all although Cary she found tough to get to know. Gee.

Ultimately too she got Marty's number when she finally realised he was beating up on Terry to the extent that Terry moved out. The extent that Marty was beating up on her bank balance was not, however, apparent although Doris did decide that they should part. The separation, like the marriage, didn't work out because Marty informed her that they couldn't get divorced because of poor, hungry Mr. Rosenthal; he moved back in although they both led separate lives. Pretty advanced stuff in the moral climate of America at that time though I doubt many knew about the heavily rumour-mongered 'indiscretions'. The Melchers' arrangement would have been pretty civilised too if the understanding hadn't been based on such a sordid subtext. 'I don't want to be with you but I can't afford not to be ... darling'. It's hardly a line from PILLOW TALK now, is it?

Purely on his own account of course, Terry Melcher found his own success as a record producer at - go on, guess? - Columbia where he did very well with THE BYRDS. Marty really hated this success and became even more eaten up with jealousy and a lot of negative stuff ... And Doris wasn't on his team any more and hated the bad scripts he persisted in setting up for her. Nature took over where a lot of people would have liked, it seems, to have placed the dagger and Marty Melcher, terrified of doctors and of knowing and admitting to anything approaching the truth, succumbed to a condition which resulted in an inflammation of the heart muscle rendering the organ useless. Too late was he finally admitted to the hospital and duly died.

The aftermath of his death brought Doris the realisation that she had no money whatsoever and that she was tied into starting a television series she had no desire to do, a regressive step in her eyes which took her back to all the terror and fears she experienced performing before a live audience. I don't know if it was the difference in the size of the two screens or the difference in the distance between us and our stars but instead of being remote and afar, television sapped not only the strength of the movie as a star vehicle but made the stars more intimately and immediately accessible. Almost tangible. Being so close, it was no longer viable for a star to project an image that their audience could only dream of being. From a deferential distance, the audience was happy with that state of affairs.

However, in the privacy of their own laundry-strewn, kids-trashed, bills-waiting living rooms, the world's audiences didn't want their stars glamorous and giddy lives grandly perched high on dizzying pedestals. They wanted to see their stars with hands deep in the same figurative shit that they shifted every day.

The blondes won out hands down in these new stakes in the new game of television. Many people's first memories of television will be of the situation comedy starring Gracie Allen, the dizzy giddy blonde wife of the laconic, wry, patronising George Burns. Far from dizzy and giddy, Grace was a clever lady. Always kept her own name. Her own identity. And for this bit of media pioneering, red-headed former movie star at MGM, Lucille Ball, must have been infinitely grateful for when she turned to teevee, the black and white made her look like a blonde.

Doris Day and Dinah Shore escaped the worst of the indignities of dizziness in their own highly rated teevee variety shows but the non-glamour principle was the same. Homey, folksy, accessible ... The image of the television blonde as somewhat loopy was of course continued as teevee developed throughout the sixties and seventies passing its stars onto the big screen only when the teevee shows which brought them to fortune had waned. Farrah Fawcett, Elizabeth Montgomery, Angie Dickinson ... I name but three.

But as with all the blondes I have just mentioned, Doris Day's television audience was to be her largest, one of several tens of millions. Somehow, I feel this number ought to have been one which also reflected the health of Doris's finances.

However, instead of being quantifiable in terms of six zeros, Doris's life was reduced to a single fat one.

But, true to her lights, she didn't fade away or buckle or bow; she got on with it and persevered and triumphed. Following on from the pioneering Dinah Shore, the two years of Doris's THE DORIS DAY SHOW set the standards and the television format which every 'big' male and female singing star would utilise in the sixties and seventies to capitalise on their record success.

A sort of pop vaudeville was resurrected on the small screen.

But it was Doris's showbiz apotheosis. She couldn't go on and she couldn't go back. Her movie career was shot and her personal life, especially with Terry gettin' into drugs and thoughtlessly not being at his old address the day the Manson family came to call ... And then being left half-dead after a motorcycle accident. And still she sought the way out in the form of spiritual guidance. Doris still needed to be *told* what to do.

Dead Marty's legacy was as insidious as his betrayal alive. It was a two year plus nightmare for Doris and Terry, fearing rabid hippy/loony/zealot reprisal and revenge until Manson was found guilty and sentenced and it took two more years plus and a lot of money until Jerome Rosenthal and his associates were found guilty on March fourth 1974 and for Doris to get her ... wait for it ... Twenty two million eight hundred and thirty five thousand six hundred and forty six dollar settlement.

She hasn't worked significantly since.

I probably wouldn't have either.

She loves dogs and cats and lives in Carmel, California. According to an interview on British television in 1994, she says she does all her own supermarketing and is very domestic. So, if you wanna catch the only Doris Day movie still to be in perpetual production, go loiter at the Carmel supermarket check-outs with a camcorder and make it yourselves. It's the only one she ever wanted to be in.

CHAPTER 13

Marilyn Monroe

Marilyn Monroe

It fell to Doris Day to be the ultimate replacement for Marilyn Monroe in the Twentieth Century Fox movie SOME-THING'S GOT TO GIVE. Marilyn never completed work on the last Fox film she was ever to undertake and, in truth, Marilyn was irreplaceable. The casting of Doris, a woman herself devoid of scandal and entirely wholesome, was the final sanitised coat of whitewash that the rotten and imploding Hollywood studio system applied in their vain attempt to both erase the inconvenient memory of Marilyn Monroe and to abet one of the most glaring political sleaze cover-ups of all time.

Very early in the morning of the fifth of September 1962, employees of the Twentieth Century Fox Film corporation and as yet unidentifiable agents of the state of California and Federal US bureaux acting illegally and unconstitutionally - but on the highest authority - removed or destroyed most documentary traces of the last weeks of the life of Marilyn Monroe, arguably the world's most popular actress.

Why?

These same persons also ensured in the days following Marilyn's demise that those who might talk carelessly about the nefarious goings-on would be wiser to decide against doing so.

Why?

When these sinister, shadowy persons were first summoned to their grisly task that day in the City of the Angels, Marilyn was, of course, quite dead. But so quickly was the scouring and bleaching and disinfecting operation mounted, it might seem to the cynical hind-sighted interested observer that her demise had been expected. However ...

Marilyn would have still been warm, only the merest breath on the wrong side of death. They worked around her corpse, removing papers and pills, diaries and documents first from her bedroom and then systematically from the other rooms in the Brentwood house, burning much of the material in the drawing room hearth. Others arrived at the offices of the telephone company and removed all paper records of her recent telephone calls. (I wonder if her estate was later billed for these and if so, how did anyone know what amounts to bill?)

Even her corpse was violated. It seems Marilyn was removed from the bed upon which she is supposed to have died, probably to a local hospital before finally being brought home again. She appeared to have been dumped back on her bed just as though her now-redundant body might have been lifted from a gurney and left, as straightened and as un-naturally posed in death as she herself had been sinuous and at ease with the same body in life.

Oh! It's just a hairline border, the flutter of moment's moment, a whisper in the gale and ... goodbye.

The intelligence operatives who must have all but touched her terrified ghost in her only half-made home did not fulfil the letter of the law and telephone the police authorities for fully six hours after Marilyn's death at ten thirty on the night of September 4th. They allowed themselves six hours to complete their fascist task. Six hours is a long time; almost a full working day. One of the most inconvenient women of all time was being expunged. It was a big job. Oh that this so Californian a girl had had so many willing hands to help her up the ladder of her career up which she had clawed her way, rung by slippery rung, all by herself.

Thank heavens ninety nine percent of the human race could not have abetted in those deeds that day or we would have no civilisation at all. There would be no plot to lose.

Them, thee to which we sing, even ... The tippy tip-top of the pyramid of power, the political and social elite, those who reign over us, happy and glorious ... Whoever, whatever, the powers-that-be had perceived that this thirty-six year old, platinum blonde, Californian film star and actress, appeared to threaten the very foundations of the federal state of what was vaunted the greatest nation on earth. It had been deemed that something indeed had to give in the over-stressed and over-strained machinery which maintains national and governmental credibility and the most expedient was Marilyn.

You see, one faction was out to get another which was out to get another and these factional interests which ran America like a racket saw that the whole caboodle pivoted for an untimely couple of weeks on the entirely unwarranted person of Marilyn Monroe. The politicians had wanted her as a symbol, shadowy organisations and rich corporations wanted her as a bargaining chip, the wealthy had wanted her as a plaything, media moguls wanted her to sell their newspapers, intellectuals had wanted to educate her, teachers wanted to teach her, mothers wanted to mother her ... She was perfect, yet how much more perfect she would have been, they thought, if only they could have gotten their hands on her for a moment ...

Weird though all this may sound but in a country, nay a world, that still had not undergone Watergate, politics and government as much as the life of any movie star was being juggled and counter-balanced for the advantage of the few. Some might now, with the wisdom of over thirty years hindsight, opine that Marilyn's was an un-necessary death warrant. Others might add that someone, the following year, finished the job properly in Dallas, Texas, when the FBI and the CIA and all other agencies of intelligence could not prevent the assassination of the President of the United States, John Fitzgerald Kennedy, who had been Marilyn's lover.

Make no mistake ... Marilyn's was a state execution. Whether she ultimately executed herself at the end of the course of the roller-coaster events of the last several weeks of her life or whether there had indeed been one lethally administered injection of nembutal and other narcotic sleeping drugs on the night of September 4th 1962, it matters not. Wheels turned within wheels which turned within wheels and Marilyn was systematically manipulated into death by men and women who could have saved her. It was conspiracy and it was murder; murder most foul and murder most definitely but to prosecute the conspiracy would have meant putting America both in the dock and on the witness stand. Much easier to turn the victim into the criminal. It is the most often-used excuse by male rapists - *"But she was asking for it!"*

If indeed offence it was, sex was Marilyn Monroe's only crime. She had slept with a married man. Sorry, two married men. Actually, probably hundreds in the course of her eventful thirty-six year old life. Though she didn't know it, Marilyn had knelt down at her execution block the day she knelt to fellate the first man she decided could help the 'six month option girl' whom Twentieth Century Fox knew as Norma Jean Baker, to become the movie star the world and immortality would know as Marilyn Monroe. Strange to think how recently in recorded time it was deemed that one human being's marital infidelity could jeopardise state security.

But Norma Jean was never hot on timing and she went down on a time in history when healthy sex could only ever rear itself as ugly head. The very men who had obviously enjoyed the pleasures Marilyn could prove had been so conditioned that they were unable to look upon the pupating Norma Jean as anything other than a tart, a slut, even a whore. The butterfly that was Marilyn had not yet displayed the box office talents which would have made a afternoon dalliance with her re-spectable. The leg-up which she sought in return for the leg-over which she granted was never the right yield of interest on the principles with which she gambled. Marilyn deduced that by allowing herself to be used in the short term, she would, long term, end up in command. Such mattress tactics proved mistaken strategy as the casting couch gave way to the psychiatrist's. She had come from nowhere. It was presumed that to nowhere she could therefore be returned.

However, those isolated and remote studio heads and the Washington-bound political brass figured their figurings oblivious of a glaring omission. Us. We, the people. That irksome ingredient in the loftily proclaimed democratic process that is so often forgotten. The people *loved* Marilyn Monroe. We noticed when she was no longer there.

In her turn, Marilyn knew we loved her but what *she* didn't figure was this blindness that the movers and shakers had to her incredible fame. A true child of democracy, truth and the American way, she failed to realise that constitutional and human rights fail to apply to individuals. Even Princes, Popes and Presidents are not immune to political erasure.

In September 1962, having irrefutably become Marilyn Monroe and having long ago commuted back-lot blow-jobs into the full whiteknuckle real McCoy, Marilyn suddenly found that she had no one else to sleep with. She had just finished servicing the President, the most powerful man in America for whom she had substituted the then Attorney General, perhaps the second most powerful. But in September 1962 neither President Jack Kennedy nor his brother Attorney General Robert even wanted to recognise her existence. They and their minions wanted only to forget that Marilyn Monroe ever existed. In the mad game of spin-the-bottle she had started, there remained only one other player greater than the President of the United States, that 'one nation under God'. That player was God himself. The bottle was spun for her and Marilyn had no alternative but to end up with God.

But what was Marilyn like alive, before she was worth more dead? She paid a terrible price for merely wanting to make something of herself in a world where the odds were stacked against her even being fleetingly fulfilled.

In the theory of blondes, she emerges most well-qualified of all. Abandoned by her putative father, Stanley Gifford, before she had even been born on June first 1926, Marilyn's mother Gladys Baker, who would later suffer from incapacitating mental illness, brought up her little daughter Norma Jean more by accident than design. The mental illness was also suffered by Della Monroe, Marilyn's grandmother. That the same illness might occur in her own middle years was a spectre which haunted Marilyn all her short life. Marilyn did not know for years that she also had two half-siblings, a brother and a sister but the three children were never together. Gladys had married twice, first to Jack Baker, her elder children's father who removed them from her dubious maternal capability and then Ed Mortensen who was later killed. Mr. Gifford, apparently, happened to live across the street. Even the Fox front office would have trouble doctoring this wrong-side-of-the blanket family history.

Luck had everything to do with Norma Jean(e) Monroe Baker Mortensen (Gifford) and ill-luck at that; judgement weighed in on her side rarely and with very little effect. She was shunted from foster home to foster home and when not being fostered, was housed in a Los Angeles Orphans' facility. She herself told interviewers of being sexually abused by at least one foster-parent and although there were women whom she called 'Aunt' and who undoubtedly cared for her, there was never regular love from one dependable source. Love was where she could find it and, discovered like that, love always looks like sex.

The young Norma Jean had physically matured wondrous early. Wolf-whistled by boys even from pre-pubescent years, no wonder Norma Jean emerged from puberty assuming that boys make you happy and that she had what made boys happy in abundance. Women, however superficially pleasant must, after all, have come a distant second in Norma Jean's priority. Women had only ever deserted her, abandoned her and chastised her.

Born, bred and brought-up in movie land, it was not surprising that Norma Jean was an enormous fan of the movies themselves. In fact, California itself is a major player in the story of the making of Marilyn Monroe. California is so huge it's easy to forget. There are millions and millions of people in it, so many that one person seems as significant as a single ant. It is easy to get lost in California. Easy to be anonymous. Easy not to be cared about and easy not to care. Norma Jean grew up never having left the state.

There is an unreality about California even now. It often proves hard to keep a grip on the few shreds of reality which do exist when surrounded by its limitless horizons of geography and ambition. What it must have been like in the mid-thirties is unimaginable except in terms of the unreality engendered there by the movie makers whose flickering images of faraway places and distant stars devoured in the dark by the poor and the ill-educated hardly made for a solid foundation on which one little ordinary person could get a life.

But everything's relative when you have no relatives. The distant stars were more constant to young impressionable minds than distant parents, irretrievably installed in institutions for the insane. And stars there were a-plenty. Jean Harlow was still making movies when Norma Jean was ten and it was with Harlow whom Marilyn later admitted to identifying most. Ginger Rogers too provided solace and inspiration in the 'gay', frothy musicals through whose doors escape was offered from the uneasy world of 'thirties unemployment and poverty. Later, Lana Turner must have been a huge influence. In SLIGHTLY DANGEROUS made in 1943, it could be Marilyn up there on the screen at times. She must have seen the movie at least once. Could the young Norma Jean really have imagined that in a few short years, Harlow's own hairdresser Pearl Porterfield who invented the 'hot platinum' for Jean Harlow in PLATINUM BLONDE would be applying sparkling peroxide and laundry 'blueing' to turn Marilyn née Norma Jean into an even more famous blonde than Harlow?

At Grauman's Chinese Theatre, Norma Jean's local movie house, a child could get in for a dime. And you could sit through the programme more than once on really bad days and a lotta days were bad days then. In the dark, scrunched down in your seat, however bleak life was out on the side-walk, inside there was hope. Its mesmeric light shone like a beacon from the movie screen and heaven was Twentieth Century Fox.

In June 1942, as soon as Norma Jean was legally free, the emotionally-deprived and psychologically-challenged teenager was off-loaded by her patchy, run-down so-called-family into the arms of Jim Dougherty, a twenty year old sailor-lad who seemed willing to take her on as his child-bride.

It was Over-the-Rainbow time.

As all her three marriages were to prove, Marilyn's first was a doomed affair and after its end, Norma Jean was left knowing she really was on her own. As an English blonde, Yaz, was to sing much, much later, *"... the only way is up."* But however rinkydink, Norma Jean's family was a family. From the day she married Dougherty, she never had a family again. It is a cruel irony to reflect that through all the pain of her later troubles, Marilyn Monroe still had a mother and a father living. But her memories of them proved as distressingly ineradicable as our memories of her.

Dougherty joined the marines and Norma Jean went into war work in the Radio Plane Company defence plant in Burbank. Marilyn was photographed by a visiting war photographer who showed his photographs of the brown-haired teenager in a sweater to a Miss Emmeline Snively who ran the largest modelling agency in Los Angeles. The one hundred dollar fee for the 'read-the-small-print' modelling lessons which new signings with the Dickensianly named Snively were obliged to take were paid for out of Norma Jean's first modelling assignments. Despite Snively's instructions, Norma Jean refused to become a blonde.

Meantime, Mr. Conover's original photos of Norma Jean in work clothes inspecting parachutes and applying glue to aeroplane fuselages had found a home in magazines. Girlie ones.

Other, sexier photos were taken of her and she became quite a regular. She also gave in and became a blonde.

There are as many sides to the 'I-discovered-Marilyn Monroe' story as there are holes in a waffle. I like mine best and it's yet another Howard Hughes story? Can you believe it? It actually doesn't matter a hoot who found her so let's shoot the stork!

The as-yet-undiscovered Marilyn Monroe must have still been exuding the perfume of the aeroplane factory because when Howard Hughes saw Norma Jean in a girlie mag he must have smelled his own glue. Norma Jean and her aeroplane pedigree obviously gave him a double hard-on because it was the indefatigable Howard who some say started the ball rolling for Norma Jean. As the owner of RKO studios at the time, he issued instructions that he wanted the aeroplane girl to screen test.

Things don't 'just happen' in *ANY* branch of show business. People give orders, then things happen.

The magazine was contacted, then the photographer, then dear Miss Snively who must have smelled money as stickily as Howard Hughes could smell aeroplane glue. Miss Snively rang her friend the agent Helen Ainsworth who chaperoned Norma Jean and secured her, it appears, not the RKO test originally on offer but one with Twentieth Century Fox. Ben Lyon, Fox's casting director, wasn't entirely convinced but when he heard that RKO was hot to trot ... Lyon too could give orders.

Ominously, for Marilyn would later unwittingly supplant her as Queen of the Lot, Norma Jean screen-tested at five-thirty in the morning on the set of Betty Grable's picture MOTHER WORE TIGHTS. The test was photographed by Leon Shamroy. Lyon and Shamroy saw the young brunette in the borrowed sequined dress on the screen, " ...*radiating sex*". Shamroy also described what he saw, equally euphemistically as 'flesh appeal'.

What the hell did they mean by 'radiating sex'? Are they saying beneath that quilt of euphemism that they wanted to fuck her? I suppose they saw what later decades would call 'a sex object', a fleshly vessel available to sop up their spilled fantasies. Procurable, exploitable, manipulable, bribable, temptable... A pawn in the power game, a mountable, stuffable trophy. A scalp for a man to hang with his boy scout knife on his belt. From the men at Fox and from the front office suits and stuffed-shirts who grudgingly depended on her for their livelihoods and careers, there was never any dignity allowed Marilyn Monroe. Ever. Say thank you to a tart? No way. You pay tarts precisely so that they won't bother you afterwards.

Sex is not a sin. The sin is seeing sex as sin. That's what makes it dirty. That's what made sex objects. Marilyn Monroe was only ever a glamorous woman to *us*. To the men of power, to the great and the good who made her and who broke her, Marilyn Monroe was never anything more than a commodity, a side of beef hanging from a meat-hook in a butcher's chiller.

Anyway, now we can dispense with Norma Jean because along with her new name of Marilyn Monroe, (Marilyn donated by the studio and Monroe being her mother's family name), Marilyn got herself a six month option contract at $75 a week, a mere half of what she was earning as a model.

Remember the MGM six month option girl that Lana Turner would have hated to have been? Marilyn joined a stable of them; it was indeed a collective, a chattering of starlets, two hundred women of whom the majority would never ever become movie stars, of whom the majority weren't then and would never be actresses, of whom the majority would be dropped as Marilyn was after six months, maybe a year when they'd done the rounds of those dangerous executive offices that Miss Turner was so suspicious of two hundred women of whom only a very few would see anything happy at all come from the high hopes that they *all* had of their initial dreams-come-true.

It was the same for Marilyn; being a six month option girl was a dream come true because she had been vindicated for the first time in her life. She was at last 'somebody' and a somebody in the film studio of her dreams, Twentieth Century Fox. She foolishly mistook the studio for a replacement family. Families suffocate as well as succour.

To keep her dream alive and to ensure that the father figures who gave the orders kept right on giving orders about *her*, Marilyn patently became the best six month option girl on the lot. She had a lot of love to give and there was heavy competition from the indentured lines of whinnying blondes in the Fox looseboxes through whose ranks she knew she had to scythe for most of these women were ultimately prepared to use the same tactics to get to be the baby on the daddy's lap. Blonde Betty Grable was already a star and certainly no filly but Marilyn studied her like a set text; June Haver and Vivian Blane were blondes far further up the starry ladder than Marilyn and had to be overtaken. But she had what it would take. She always had it and she knew it. Luminescence. Magnetism. An aura.

Marilyn posed for photographs and signed autographs and posed yet more as Fox's representative in carnival parades and pageants but movies? Uh uh. She went to screenings, studied other actresses, attended acting, singing and dancing classes but ... Movies? Uh uh.

Denied parts in Fox pictures, Marilyn set to work on the parts of Fox executives. President Joe Schenck would fall to her charms as later President Spyros Skouras would also be ensnared. Meeting the super-agent Johnny Hyde from the William Morris office, thirty years her senior, didn't do too much damage to her either although she virtuously declined his marriage proposals. She was the least avaricious woman in Hollywood. Money came her way but it never intrinsically interested her. Being validated interested Marilyn. The late-developer with a bad case of arrested development yearned for the recognition of her peers.

Marilyn was developing an early predilection for Presidents. What she didn't develop was any notion that life isn't what other people give you its what you get for yourself. She knew what control was but the only way Marilyn learned to exercise control was through the power sited between her breasts and her thighs. There was no one close enough or dear enough, no one, at least to whom she would have listened who could have told her, *"Marilyn, sweetheart ... Presidents come and presidents go. And they're accountable, sweetie. Not to actresses but to their electors and to all the others who're after their job. Honey, to a married man, a shag's a shag. It doesn't come boxed with a Tiffany ring ..."*

And there were, unbelievably, the healthy, straight men who were immune to her charms. Fox's President at the time was Darryl Zanuck. He not only had no respect for Marilyn but, like her final nemesis, the director George Cukor, he didn't even like her. Zanuck loathed her, although at the end, he felt very sorry for her.

Her influential 'daddy' figures secured her a part in SCUDDA HOO! SCUDDA HAY! This, believe it or not, was not a long lost poem from Robbie Burns but a Fox musical and in it Marilyn was ultimately seen to utter only one word, *"Hello"*.

But it was hello and goodbye because Zanuck cancelled her contract. The later nineteen forties saw her freelancing and picking up fifty bucks here, fifty bucks there ... Once she picked up fifty bucks for posing nude for photographer Tom Kelley, pictures which later formed the hard core of a calendar which graced the garages of grease-monkeys all over America. Instead of provoking scandal in 1952 when she admitted posing nude as the calendar girl, letters of support inundated Fox offices.

Ultimately, agent Johnny Hyde got John Huston to cast Marilyn in THE ASPHALT JUNGLE which won her plaudits but no other contract with any studio. Marilyn badly wanted to go to MGM. Instead, Johnny Hyde somehow persuaded Zanuck to relent and Fox took her back on the most minimal contract and for that studio between 1950 and 1953, Marilyn appeared in small, mindless parts in seven movies. Other than in ALL ABOUT EVE, she achieved absolutely zip. Darryl Zanuck may have relented but it didn't cost him much. He seemed purposefully to drag his feet as far as Marilyn was concerned. She took more acting lessons from Natasha Lytess and studied hard the art of motion picture performance. She got absolutely nowhere.

Enter Spyros Skouras and enter he did with more than a bang. As a result, Marilyn got to be in MONKEY BUSINESS much to the undisguised fury of Zanuck and his hench-people.

Then came NIAGARA which was released in 1953 with its accompanying publicity poster of Marilyn apparently lying temptingly across the foaming falls themselves. It and the movie finally made Marilyn a star. In it, she appeared with Jean Peters, co-incidentally later to become Mrs. Howard Hughes.

But Zanuck couldn't argue with public reaction, nor her mountain of fan-mail and nor with nominations from magazines like *Photoplay* who dubbed the new Fox phenomenon 'the fastest rising star of 1953'. GENTLEMEN PREFER BLONDES and HOW TO MARRY A MILLIONAIRE followed and then RIVER OF NO RETURN and THERE'S NO BUSINESS LIKE SHOW-BUSINESS. Once Skouras gave the order, the Monroe bandwagon rolled and was soon commuted into a juggernaut.

However, although she started off by being pretty good-natured about it, her casting was of the dimbo-bimbo variety and her roles were, on the whole, pretty much lightweight. For a while she hacked it but hacking it can never properly assuage platinum ambition. Her original deal with Fox was desultory under the circumstances of the box office profits she was generating. It was the Harlow situation at MGM all over again. Harlow's was a tired and disgraceful script twenty years previously and it seemed the parent/master conspiracy which was, after all the studio/agent/vulnerable-star dialectic hadn't changed. It was of the ilk of what a British prime minister was later to dub 'the unacceptable face of capitalism.' Sure, speed the plough and turn a buck but manure the ground you harvest afterwards. Marilyn was earning a mere $1500 a week. Stars of her calibre were then earning $10,000 a week. Elizabeth Taylor ten years later would earn that as a per diem.

In Hollywood it was to be the time of the instant blonde. Anyone and everyone it seemed was for a while pressed into peroxide service. Shake, add bleach and stir. All the other studios were on the qui vive for their own Marilyns and yet others had their own, already successful tamer varieties who were equally as ambitious as Marilyn.

Doris Day twinkled prettily as the girl-next-door type as did Sandra Dee, Sandra Dee, cursed with that virginity. On television, red-headed and once-upon-a-time movie star Lucille Ball had made it to the screen and looked like a blonde and there was, of course, also Dinah Shore. Then out there in the wider world, there was Shelley Winters, Shirley Schrift that was ... But Shelley was much more an actress with a reputable New York theatrical pedigree. Someone at Fox even invented Sheree North, specifically to keep Miss Monroe on her toes. Marilyn must have really dug that one. The musical star Dolores Gray threatened to be another Betty Grable for a minute. Eve Marie Saint was being noble. She became nobler as her gracious career went on from strength to strength. Some studio Frankensteins somehow came up with Joy Lansing, Barbara Nichols, Beverly Michaels, Cleo Moore and Mamie van Doren. Kim Novak was not only a vaunted and spirited contender but a very big star indeed at Harry Cohn's Columbia Studios. Jayne Mansfield, another Fox girl and another blonde come-lately-previously-brunette, decided to become famous rather than become an actress and thus travelled the thoracic route to glory. Carroll Baker was in there waiting to pack her punch and, of course MGM had Grace Kelly who was so much more ladylike about her business than Marilyn. Fox too had the cool, collected and highly intelligent Lee Remick who was in yet a different league altogether but had no LCD appeal. That's lowest common denominator. Remick was a piece of class. Marilyn was a piece of ass.

Some people don't know from ass. Gotcha, guys! Marilyn was like America itself. She could only be discovered, invaded, colonised, settled and developed before her plentiful resources wore thin and finally depleted because no one had ever thought to conserve along the way.

Marilyn's marriage to Joe diMaggio, the baseball star, united Mr. USA and Miss America in what should have been a publicist's dream-ticket. But even the rah-rah Fox men weren't humbled by the husky diMaggio gentlemanliness and I hasard that Marilyn soon found this kindly but unchallenging giant to be somewhat dull. Anyway, she chose doing acting over doing dishes and she was soon back at work in the SEVEN YEAR ITCH. The famous white dress flew up in scandal and hubby diMaggio flew off his handle. They divorced although they remained friends throughout her life. He loved her, but selfishly and just couldn't accept that he had married every other man's fantasy but his own. Blondes *are* babies. They don't *have* babies. Marilyn lost many babies as a consequence.

Oh, Baby, Baby, it's a wild world ...

On *her* own again, Marilyn decided to go the whole hog and throw in the towel with Fox who were intent on keeping her as the bimbo that time forgot. She fled Hollywood for New York where she was introduced by Shelley Winters to Lee Strasberg's Actors' Studio and to a layer of her life which instead of sorting her out, in my assessment, confused her even more. As in addiction, the Strasbergs, Lee and his actress wife Paula, became Marilyn's co-dependants, hooking her up to a regime of living for which her life had not equipped her. She was always conscious of her lack of education, of her frustrating inability often to comprehend simple instructions, of her propensity, perhaps dyslexic, to confuse and jumble memorised lines ... Her past and her upbringing had bequeathed her a total lack of any solid fundament to her life. Because she was a film-star, the Strasbergs treated her as a child which is how she would not have been treated had she *not* been film-star. As surrogate parents, the Strasbergs gave her false hope.

They told her that she could be an actress. Film-stars don't have to be actresses. Being a film-star was the *only* solid reality Marilyn had. I think they took that away from her and, set adrift, sacrificed her to their own regime. It was a gross betrayal. Worse, really, than the behaviour of the Fox people for their motives were as crystal clear as the ringing of cash register bells.

It was the mid-fifties. As well as being the age of the cutesey, kookie, innocent but naughty, giggly dumb blonde it was also the age of beatniks and existentialism and beautiful girls wearing horn-rimmed glasses and being frightfully serious and earnest. Although her public was far from slaked, Marilyn herself was understandably tired of the dumb blonde thing. However, she took the whole intellectual thing so seriously that she married the dramatist and literary authority Arthur Miller, arguably as great a star in America's shallower halls of letters as diMaggio had been in the halloweder halls of sport. For four iffy years whilst she tried desperately to play Mrs. Miller to Arthur's Mr. Monroe, the horn-rimmed marriage lasted but it was to be Marilyn's last. It seems she gave up trying after Arthur. She was, after Arthur and all, Marilyn Monroe, the most famous woman in the world. Why shouldn't she marry a President? Grace Kelly had married a Prince. On hearing the nuptial news, Marilyn is supposed to have telephoned Grace: " ... *I'm so glad you've found a way out of this business.*"

Relations with Fox were patched up and a reasonably decent contract was negotiated with Marilyn Monroe Productions which gave Marilyn at least the semblance of a degree of control over her destiny for the first time in her life. But she'd never be asked to play Edith Cavell or Marie Curie or Marguerite Gauthier, would she? Did she ever think she would?

Instead she made BUS STOP directed by Joshua Logan. Then, THE PRINCE AND THE SHOWGIRL brought Monroe to England to co-star with and to be directed by Laurence Olivier. Olivier, the ultimate thespian, unlike Mr. Strasberg in New York failed to be impressed by the Monroe acting talent. It has to be said that Strasberg's wife Paula was pulling in something like three grand a week as Marilyn's on-set drama coach. To the consummate Olivier, acting was acting. It was what actors knew how to do. It was what they were paid to do, on cue, on schedule and within budget. His Olivieriness was not amused.

The Ruritanian romp was a desperately unhappy experience, far away from home territory. The nerves and shakes and terror before filming which Marilyn had always experienced to a greater or lesser extent were getting worse the more famous she became and the larger became her entourage of interested parties. She was being systematically de-stabilised, not necessarily with malice aforethought but with others' self-interest paramount.

Each movie brought her more to lose. The burden of being Marilyn Monroe was being ever further shored up by a buttress of chemical helpmates. Her lifelong battle against insomnia, probably born of a fear of going to sleep, was lost. Nembutal, Seconal and the other barbiturates became as essential to her sleep as the bed itself. Pill-taking had never been considered unusual in Hollywood. Studios maintained doctors to administer pills to stars who were expected to work exhausted and run-down and frazzled. In whatever mental state they were, stars were expected to work period.

But what if you were one of those stars? Who or what were the pills turning you into? Marilyn Monroe began to become someone that Marilyn loathed but there was nowhere else to go but onward and upward, up, up and up for Norma Jean had been allowed to float far, far away, irretrievable in her bubble of time past. Norma Jean was no anchor, no tether to the unsteerable, uncontrollable vehicle that was Marilyn Monroe.

In 1958, whilst still married to Arthur Miller, Marilyn made SOME LIKE IT HOT mainly, friends aver, because Miller told her to because they needed the money. The movie made tons of money. In 1960, as Arthur Miller metamorphosed further into the lion of American literature and drama, Marilyn was thrown to the lions in LET'S MAKE LOVE. She was seriously shafted by a bad script and also by Yves Montand who in his turn seriously shafted his beautiful blonde wife, Oscar-winning French actress

Simone Signoret. Marilyn's sexuality scythed through marriages like Boadicea's chariots cut swathes through Romans good and true. She was also to rub hackles with the homosexual director George Cukor. Famed director of women though he was, Cukor was used to sure and savvy women like Katharine Hepburn who knew their trade and plied it with the sureties of a merchant bank. Bonking blondes who showed up late and who took take after take to deliver a simple line were not only beyond Cukor; they were anathema. Though Marilyn was fascinated by Cukor, he was entirely un-fascinated by her. After twenty years at the top, the tide of his own career was on the ebb and he didn't want to risk being shown up by someone he deemed unprofessional. Her Regal Cukoriness was as un-amused as His Royal Olivieriness had been a couple of years earlier.

Then came THE MISFITS which His Arthur Milleriness had written for the screen in which there was a convenient part it was thought Marilyn would be able to play. The movie should have been entitled THE MISCASTS. It was Clark Gable's last film, it was Montgomery Clift's last film and it was Marilyn Monroe's last film and for such an auspicious milestone it was a rather silly film, based on intellectual conceits far too lofty for the average movie-goer who was fascinated that their favourite scatty blonde had married the boffin but about the boffin they cared not a bum nickel.

It ought to have worked out for Marilyn so much better by the time SOMETHING'S GOT TO GIVE was mooted than it had done. Marilyn was by now thirty six years old and the times, well ... The times they were a-changin' as Bob Dylan was starting to warble. Fox knew they had to somehow upgrade Marilyn to maintain her box office status in the same way that Lana Turner at MGM had weathered the storm of approaching middle-age. What better ruse than to get her to play a wife and mother and a middle-class mother dressed in Jean Louis couture to boot rather than the enchantingly daffy dimbo from the five 'n' dime whom Marilyn had made her own. I often wonder if anything would have happened to Marilyn if Judy Holliday had lived. Judy Holliday won Oscars for her dimbos. Marilyn was all for this change. What work she was able to complete on the unfinished picture shows her at her best. But America was never to know Marilyn as nice and middle class.

The Twentieth Century Fox Film Corporation also knew that their particular writing was on the wall. Their future as a capitalist industrial institution was at stake. The studio had suffered major financial losses and continued to suffer from the lack of a firm single-hand on its tiller. With the move in movie-making to location-based shooting, vast areas of Fox's now redundant back-lot had been sold off to be redeveloped as real estate into what we know now as the Century City complex.

The studio was pulling in all directions at once, just keeping ahead of the yelping pack of New York-centred shareholders to whom the executives owed their fancy lifestyles. Peter Levathes had been recruited from Fox television to represent Spyros Skouras' interests on the coast although Levathes had men like Philip Feldman and Darryl Zanuck to shuffle into his wild pack. He was neither experienced nor talented enough to take on the Thalbergian task that Fox required for there were also the livid, dollar-dripping jaws of CLEOPATRA to feed. The Taylor-Burton epic was costing Fox dearly, not only in money terms but in terms of lost prestige; the world's press were having a field day parading the grosser immoralities of the Taylor-Burton romance in front of a nation which was infinitely more at home in Sandra Dee's white gloves than the mire of married people's infidelities. Skouras and the other Fox Pharisees, as Louis B before them, may have been venal but they were also prudes and as far as shareholders were concerned, they were kiss-asses to a man for there wasn't a woman to be seen on the board.

Being a mere employee, Cukor would kiss any ass as long as he knew he was the only Empress on his own sound stage. Marilyn had acquired too many vetoes. Cukor loathed the idea of working with her again. Nunally Johnson's script was rewritten and tinkered with and then tampered with some more. Dean Martin and Cyd Charisse seemed oddly cast and felt just as awkwardly when it became obvious that Marilyn had decided to make SOMETHING'S GOT TO GIVE the occasion for yet another showdown with Fox. The studio she had once dreamed of joining, she now no longer even wanted to be associated with. There was an ill-starred aspect to the whole project which culminated in Marilyn's contracting a serious virus which rendered it impossible for her to work. Male Fox executives had had their egos bumped by the uppity blonde broad who was starting to call the shots and they reacted both out of pique but also out of deference to their shareholders who, terrified at the ruinous haemorrhaging of money that CLEOPATRA was causing were aghast when they read in the sullied press of Monroe's absences from the set of the comparatively minutely-budgeted SOMETHING'S GOT TO GIVE. Heads had to roll. Something had to be done. It was too late to do anything about CLEOPATRA but, as with all the Hollywood studios at this time, a climate of economies and cuts allowed for precious little atmosphere of creativity. In 1946 there were four thousand people working at Fox. In 1962, there were nine hundred.

As calculatingly as the services of the other three thousand one hundred employees had been dispensed with over the years, Fox fired Marilyn Monroe and engineered a press campaign against her. However, firing her was to backfire. They couldn't even attempt a claim on the $10,000,000 policy they had taken out in production insurance. Fox were desperate for SOMETHING'S GOT TO GIVE to be made.

They wanted Kim Novak to replace Marilyn, then they wanted Lee Remick. Lee Remick didn't want the part and she was saved from having to do so when Dean Martin walked off the picture. He maintained he had been contracted to appear with Marilyn Monroe and he was *only* going to appear with Marilyn Monroe. He would brook no substitutes. Law suits and counter-suits fluttered down like cold comfort confetti from the smog-laden California skies.

As one of her final, defiant power-plays, right under Cukor's nose, Marilyn flew from the sound stage in a Howard Hughes helicopter and sang 'Happy Birthday' to her presidential lover at his Madison Square Garden birthday party in New York. Pearl Porterfield had done an extra-special dye-job on Marilyn's hair, creating a shade which the papers would later dub 'pillow slip white'. Her ten thousand dollar Jean Louis flesh-coloured beaded and sequined evening gown had had to be sewn on her. Naked beneath its gossamer drapes, the gown became Marilyn's very own Shroud of Turin. Her appearance was her first step on her Via Dolorosa and her cross was her beauty and her naivety.

At the birthday bash, noticeably shunned by America's First Lady, Jackie Kennedy who was only too embarrassingly privy to husband Jack's string of showbiz lays, Marilyn met Bobby Kennedy once again. The Kennedy brothers not only shared power, it seems they shared pussy. Marilyn could face being dumped on by the Prez as long as she still commanded a hot line to Bobby Kennedy's back office in the Justice Department. When the operators were told not to accept her frantic calls any more, it was Marilyn's cue to get seriously loopy. Fired by Fox, used, abused and forgotten by the two, arguably, most powerful men in the western world, her calls for help to former lover Spyros Skouras pathetically side-stepped, Marilyn was in a bad way. Her drug dependence, aided and abetted by her own and the Fox Corporation's doctors, deepened although she still managed outwardly to maintain a fighting fitness.

Her reluctant psychiatrist Ralph Greenson maintained long and expensive daily sessions with her. He fed Marilyn to herself. It was he who had arranged for the engagement of Eunice Murray, Marilyn's housekeeper and both of whom it is now thought were more in the thrall of Fox than ever they were on Marilyn's side.

But other men were giving orders. Darryl Zanuck himself, recognising the ludicrous rationale of closing down a prospective box office bonanza, engineered a Fox re-think and a new contract was negotiated, giving Marilyn more money, more control, more guarantees, more vetoes ... She'd won. She'd actually beaten the dragon. Yippee!

Which just leaves the little mess with the Kennedy boys. Perhaps buoyed up by the euphoria of having taken on Fox and winning, Marilyn was high on tilting at the windmill of state. She was becoming indiscreet. The word blabbermouth trips off the tongue. People were talking about Marilyn talking. The West Coast movie colony was on a fast-track to every Washington agency via British actor Peter Lawford whose marriage to Patricia Kennedy endowed this clean-cut star of the June Allyson college kid movies with the title Pimp for the Prez. Though it had cost him dear with several super-star friends, Lawford had perhaps reluctantly been Kennedy Klan co-respondent in Hollywood. He had pimped many an 'A' picture lay for the boys from Boston and he was up-to-his-neck, like it or not, in the demise of Marilyn's relations with the men of America's first family. Though this time Bobby wanted her to for good, Marilyn just wouldn't lie down quietly.

He came to persuade her. She was pissed. And got steadily more pissed as she drowned her sorrows in her usual Dom Perignon champagne tipple. Cars came and went from the St. Helena Drive Mexican style house in Brentwood that fourth of September. People saw this, they saw that ... They said it was all too much for her ... That the balance of her mind was disturbed ... That she swallowed over seventy sleeping pills in the course of ten minutes ...

You try it sometime. Take the innards out of seventy standard issue drug capsules and swallow them in ten minutes. Just try it.

Brentwood's now a quiet district, suburban, respectable where nothing more sensational happens between its leafy tree-lined borders and the rest of the world than the frenzied murder of the wife of a black baseball and movie star and her companion by a person or persons as yet unknown.

All very interesting. But Marilyn Monroe, whoever she was, was entirely innocent.

CHAPTER 14

Peggy Lee

Peggy Lee

There was once a tailor in Los Angeles who had a studio on Hollywood and Vine. His name was Sy Devore and he was famous as a gentleman's outfitter in his day. Stars and studio executives alike would wear his clothes to attend important parties or to collect their Oscars as they would today plump for Versace or Cerruti or Armani. Over Sy's premises men like Johnny Mercer and other music business pioneers met and shot the breeze. I'm sure there aren't a lot of people left who'd recognise a photo of Sy Devore but just about everyone who knows anything about records and music will recognise the fabled circular shape of the Capitol Records building, designed by Frank Lloyd Wright, which was erected on the site of Sy Devore's studio. It's as distinctive as the Leaning Tower of Pisa and as symbolic as the Black Tower on the Universal lot in Burbank.

Its building had everything to do with the shift of emphasis in the entertainment industry away from movies and into teevee and finally, what it was built for ... Music.

Its building also had a lot to do with the life and career of Miss Peggy Lee. There were, of course, many other artists male and female both on and off the Capitol label who could with justification call themselves the grandparents of what we know today as The Music Business. Some of these artists were, at least for a time, as blonde as Peggy Lee - Frances Langford, Betty Hutton, Rosemary Clooney, Doris Day, Dinah Shore - and probably as glamorous. But, purely personally, I have elected Peggy Lee as the sublime example of the singer/actress/

performer whose talent, creativity and sensitivity paved the way for later of her ilk in the sixties, and seventies - Carole King, Joni Mitchell, Carly Simon - to be quite properly referred to as artists.

Artists come from life. Artists interpret their own lives' experience so that we who aren't artists can make sense of our own experiences. Peggy Lee sure has had a life and when she sings she reminds us all that we've had one too. And if there ever was a blonde who showed the world that a person *can* make something different *and* better out of life, it's Miss Peggy Lee.

She was born blonde in Jamestown, North Dakota, natural blonde because her parents were both from ice-blue nordic stock, one Norwegian, the other Swedish. She was also born Norma Deloris Egstrom and, like so many of our blondes, she was destined to do her growing up missing one significant parent from a very young age, her mother.

I suppose I identify so much with Norma Egstrom because she grew up entirely rurally. It was not a halcyon childhood but the little girl who became Miss Peggy Lee is thoroughly imbued with the stuff of the earth and the harvest and the make-do-and-mend and the stoic, determined attitude to hardship which country people have all over the world.

Norma was four when her mother died. How can death ever be explained to a four year old? 'Up there' is how heaven, the beyond, call it what you will, is portrayed to most children. It is a totally unsatisfactory explanation. But that was then ... Now is ... Probably just as difficult.

The family almost immediately fell apart. Her mother's father, Grandpa Anderson was unceremoniously packed off to an old people's home and the children, of whom there were seven live-born of a large age range, were soon to be step-mothered as Mr. Egstrom remarried only a few months after his wife Selma's death.

Enter Min. The Hun. Like a witch, like the Wicked Queen, like evil cloaked in clouds of long raven hair. No. I'm not over-dramatising.

Reading Miss Lee's autobiography, MISS PEGGY LEE, I am reminded of the forbearance and quite incredible lack of bitterness displayed by the majority of the human race against people - individuals, not necessarily nationalities - who have done, personally, grave and to my mind unforgivable wrongs. Nelson Mandela and pretty much the whole of non-white South Africa is a case in point, not to mention The Jews both in and outside the state of Israel.

Min was cruel, vindictive and quite inexplicably full of hate. I cannot understand how Mr. Egstrom, an employee of the railroad, came to marry her or remain with her but truth is stranger than fiction and never looks like the movie set these stories usually end up on. A great deal of Min Egstrom's vengeful wrath was vented on Norma. The incidences are many and all recounted by Miss Lee in her own words. Beatings with switches, kicks and punches after an appendectomy with peritonitis complications, burning all photographs of Norma's mother ...

Children when faced with appalling realities are often saved by their imaginations and Norma's was certainly exercised from an early age. It had to be for her to survive sane. There was little or no help from 'Daddy'. Daddy, sadly, was an alcoholic. Not incapacitated, you understand, just alcoholic enough to be oblivious to the suffering of his children.

The railroads which bisected the huge prairie expanses of middle America, many of them private, tiny branch lines only riding for some few tens of miles, were part of this imaginative process. Imagining where the tracks went, what the further-away towns were like, watching passing locomotives and wondering to just where and how the conductor and the engineer went when the locomotive's smoke disappeared on the horizon. And in the Great Depression, just where all the hobos and travelling people came from and went to and how they survived after little Norma'd fed them what little she could.

All this very practical dreaming enabled the growing Norma

to cope with her life of endless chores which called by another name would have conjured up a perfect image of slavery. I get the feeling that her privations somehow empowered her. Death dogged her days. One day, her favourite dog, Rex dies ... Her best friend Ebbie Jordan's crushed by his horse; on another Norma is made by Min to kill the very chickens the children had nurtured from chicks ... Death is ever-present in rural communities.

Of course there were other days, playing with friends and siblings, watermelon time, swimming in water-holes and creeks and waiting for the travelling movie show to visit the Town Hall. Norma remembers seeing in 1927 THE JAZZ SINGER and, later, one of Ginger Rogers's first Paramount New York movies THE THIRTEENTH CHAIR. Ginger Rogers ... Norma loved Ginger Rogers. There were glamorous images. Sure, Norma wanted to be ... Hey, the world was waking up to the fact that there was nothing wrong in dreaming. Little Norma was actually known by her towns fellows in Jamestown as '... our little Hollywood girl'.

And Norma always remembers singing. Remembers that at eight years old, she somehow knew she was going somewhere and that somewhere was to be in show-business. Reminds me of Dusty Springfield's deep-seated certainty that she would somehow be 'all right'.

The Depression forced the Egstroms into vacating their house and into rooms above the railroad depot before goading them to neighbouring Wimbledon, a slightly bigger town but equally overlooked. Her school super Ivar Knapp arranged her first gig with the young Doc Haines and his orchestra. Norma was fourteen when she hitch-hiked to neighbouring Valley City, sang with the band and then on a sponsored radio show for Radio Station Sun Valley. Don't forget that there were almost six hundred radio stations in the states in the mid-thirties and the advertisers were lining up with sponsorship. One nighters with Doc Haines when megaphones not micro-phones were used ... Norma Egstrom was *only* fourteen.

But singing was still only the cream. Norma's bread and butter was still choring and charing in domestic placements and restaurants. She was beginning to date boys in a joshy kinda way. But always singing. Radio gigs here and there, a singing contest or two.

She was fifteen when she left school and returned to Jamestown, her own woman for the first time. By then Jamestown too had a radio station, housed in the Gladstone Hotel and Peggy worked in the hotel's coffee shop. She met Bill Sawyer who took her under his wing but not under his duvet and so much was he gunning for her that he arranged for her to sing in the neighbouring city of Fargo on Ken Kennedy's WDAY Station. It was Kennedy who disabused Norma Egstrom of both the Egstrom and the Norma and re-christened her Peggy Lee. Kennedy died in 1976 and she acknowledged him as the greatest influence on her life.

WDAY paid piece rate. Basic, which was what Peggy got, was dollar fifty a show and fifty cents a line reading commercials. So you didn't like it? There was a line round the block of people who would. It was an apprenticeship of sorts in a very specific economic depression.

Her father blessed her decision to try California and supplied Peggy with a railroad pass to get there. Peggy stayed with her childhood friend Gladys Rasmussen and they got jobs where they could and where they couldn't they starved. Peggy worked in a restaurant in Balboa and then as a barker in a fairground. Roll up! Roll up! For a long time, no one did.

Then, two guitarists, young nephews of one of the fairground's concessionaires, persuaded her to sing with them on the pier at Balboa and on the strength of what they recognised as superb musicianship encouraged her to audition at a club they knew in Hollywood called The Jade. Chuck Barclay hired her. Little money, two bucks a night but it was regular work in the university of life ... Yeah, yeah, yeah. Why is the sweetness of hindsight never a substitute for swallowing the bitter pill in the first place?

Often a godsend for performers who were having lean times in the casting offices at the studios, The Jade was also a haunt of lowlifes of all kinds. The stress of life with little money in a rooming house on Hollywood and Gower and the strain of singing into the late hours in smoky atmospheres brought Peggy low. She needed throat surgery and her family was contacted, sending Sweeney, her first Jamestown boyfriend, to bring her back east.

After surgery, she returned to Fargo where Ken Kennedy gave her work on WDAY and introduced her to the Powers family who ran the hotel and coffee shop where Lloyd Collins played organ and where soon, live entertainment was permanently featured. She was earning $15 a week - sounds a little but it was ten dollars a week more than a secretary was making - and she was able to live with her siblings who shared a house together for the first time in a long time although feeding them all in the midst of the depression was a weekly cliffhanger.

Ken Kennedy then arranged for her to sing for Sev Olsen and his college student band in Minneapolis where she was reunited with Jane Larrabee, another singer with whom she had become best friends whilst Janie was singing at the rival Le Château in Fargo. After further throat surgery during which she suffered a potentially disfiguring accident by falling off an operating theatre gurney, Peggy returned to California with two members of her band and, this time, positively sought out The Jade. She was not there long. She began singing at The Doll House in Palm Springs and it was there that Peggy was able to encash the bond her apprenticeship had invested for her.

It was time for Miss Peggy Lee.

The Mandels, owners of the Detroit Tigers Football team and Mandel's department store in Chicago were staying in Palm Springs and brought along Frank Bering, who with Ernie Byfield owned the Ambassador West and Ambassador East hotels in Chicago. Peggy played for them and she was hired to sing in The Buttery of the Ambassador West.

It must have been a fairy tale come true. $75 a week to sing for an appreciative public and be heard by some of the finest jazz musicians in the world. Jane Larabee had joined her and together they must have dished nightly after the celebrated had been into the Buttery. Claude Thornhill, Glenn Miller and Charlie Barnett. Bands, big bands, were the thing just like four piece electric outfits shaped after the Beatles were the thing in the sixties, like techno computerised keyboard geniuses are the thing as I write. Record company executives like Morty Palitz made for great word of mouth too. Peggy was laying the best foundations.

Ultimately it was Mel Powell, a long time associate of Peggy's, who brought Benny Goodman and his wife to hear Peggy sing. Powell thinks Goodman, faced with the departure of his singer Helen Forrest, made up his mind to hire Peggy on the spot. Band singers moved around in those days from band to band, building their careers unlike today when singers leaving a band will only perform on their own, they won't go join other bands. The money at stake is way too great. 'Oh, QUEEN are minus a singer ... I think I'll go and sing with them!' These days you get just the one swipe at the apple ...

Peggy's first gig with Goodman and his band was totally without rehearsal. Band-leaders in the main regarded their singer as just another musician. Individual instrumentalists weren't granted the dispensation of special rehearsals and Goodman was no different to other band-leaders. It was the band-leaders who were the stars and it was they who were signed to record companies. The Bandleader was in fact a production company who bought out or paid for musicians' services - usually on session rates for negotiated periods of studio time - and it was the bandleader who received the royalties from the sales of a record. Benny Goodman paid Peggy Lee a quaint $10 for recording WHY DON'T YOU DO IT RIGHT? It was a huge, huge hit and Goodman gave her a huge, huge nada.

In 1941, the Goodman band, who incidentally did their fair share of alcohol and marijuana unlike the clean-living bands of the Doris Day days, arrived in New York. They were booked to play the then-fashionable New Yorker Hotel.

Peggy's reputation for 'cool', 'elegant' vocal work quickly spread through the muzocrats who came nightly to see Goodman and her. Count Basie, Louis Armstrong and his wife were all contacts Peggy made at this time and who were to remain lifelong friends. And all the time, the once-faraway war grew closer and closer and started to claim the lives of friends and made ghosts out of flesh-and-blood lovers. At the Paramount Theatre in Times Square in 1941, the Goodman Band were fronted by the current teen-idol heart throb Frank Sinatra whose screaming fans lined the streets for a glimpse of him. Peggy and Frank have been friends for over fifty years. Can it be that neither sought anything from the other except respect? He was one of the first of the pop stars. And where was *his* band?

And in 1941 Peggy met and fell madly in love with guitarist David Barbour. War Bond sales work and hospital visiting and romance ... It was a hectic time, topped by the offer of a movie role in the Charles Rogers production of THE POWERS GIRL for United Artists, released in 1942 in which she co-starred with George Murphy. Going to Hollywood prompted the marriage proposal Peggy had been waiting for and she quit Goodman's band. As man and wife, the Barbours set up house in LA and awaited the birth of their first child. They didn't have any money but Miss Lee writes as if everything was perfect ... Everything except ...

Except that she discovered that her husband was an alcoholic, not the vicious or violent sort, just the plain old self-(and anyone else) destruct sort. Their daughter Nicki was born, healthy and happy ... Except ...

Except that Peggy was told that she would not have any more children. It was at about this time that Peggy's instincts about the spirituality of the universal condition took shape and form when she read the Science and Mind work of Ernest Holmes who became a guru, a friend and the person who enabled her to know that she had resources and reserves of mental strength upon which she could draw to tackle and cope with physical stress and distress. Edna Ferber notes wryly that most adults in worship tend to find the children in them again. To me, Peggy Lee sounds as though she found herself. It does happen. It sounds as though Science and Mind for Peggy Lee equated to a quality of faith which remains untrammelled by the odious judgemental overtones of organised religion. 'You want it? You go get it because no one else will ... But there *is* help *if* you have faith.'

Peggy may not have been earning royalties from her Goodman hits but the success of DO RIGHT got her a top-flight manager and agent, Carlos Gastel and Tom Rockwell respectively. Her self-written songs she had conceived and developed with David whilst she was pregnant, starting with IT'S A GOOD DAY, were snapped up on an independent contract by Capitol records. They were followed by WHAT MORE CAN A WOMAN DO? and I DON'T KNOW ENOUGH ABOUT YOU. The Barbours bought a lovely house for their little nuclear family and all their many musician friends with all their many little habits ... Peggy's kitchens sound like concert hall and theatre Green Rooms the world over.

The work came flooding in during those later nineteen forties. Sponsorship by industrial giants Rexall and Oldsmobile on radio and on television validated Peggy's star status as a broadcaster and the war-enriched American record buyers couldn't get enough of her songs for record hits were now not automatically the songs that were heard in the movies.

MAÑANA, as an example, was a huge millions-selling hit for Peggy and David and also the subject of a long-drawn out court case in which banjo player Hats McKay sued them for three million dollars for plagiarism. This is huge money, the equivalent of $10,000,000 today. They won the case with able backup from many of music's finest exponents and court room performances from the likes of Jimmy Durante.

Although her career and her associations with the créme de la créme of American musicians like George Shearing and artists like Bing Crosby continued apace, Peggy's marriage was melting like the ice-water which David Barbour wasn't adding to his drink.

By 1951, the tide of his boozing hit an all time high. Peggy'd just made the movie PETE KELLY'S BLUES and her father was dying in North Dakota but to save themselves and with no lasting rancour or acrimony whatsoever, the Barbours sacrificed their marriage and divorced. Apart from making the movie MR. MUSIC with Bing Crosby and Gower Champion, their lives as man and wife were over. Peggy bore the sadness of the parting always for memories of love hurt so, so bad. So much worse than the memories of pain and as I said earlier, this is not a vengeful or bitter woman I'm getting here.

The fifties saw her touring. Everywhere. Miss Peggy Lee was never one to shirk the circuit's rougher joints and she was also not one to deny the comforts and benefits of playing plush rooms like those of the early Las Vegas hotels. She brought the best of each world to the other.

The fifties saw her master-works of movie composition and voice-overage. TOM THUMB, JOHNNY GUITAR. You would have thought she could have done anything she wanted but record company executives, like politicians, have to stick their oars in, throw in their tuppence worth, show they're earning their hideously fat salaries ... Peggy wanted to record Richard Rogers' LOVER. Capitol said 'No'. She and her producer Dave Cavanaugh walked and for five years recorded for Decca. She wrote lyrics for Victor Young, performed a poem he had set to music to a huge eighteen thousand audience at the Hollywood Bowl and in 1952 she was asked by Sonny Burke to start work with him for Walt Disney to co-operate on a project that would commute her fame into immortality. LADY AND THE TRAMP is an immortal story. She did immortal work on it and LADY was finished in 1955. However, she was working mortal day rate ... Apart from her royalties which one hopes she received for composition, her Disney pay check for three years work was

$3,500. Oh, Walt ... Did no one tell you that you don't get to take it with you?

Anyway, Peggy sued and won.

I *knew* I oughta been a lawyer.

Although a single gal once again, Peggy wasn't playing hermit. Lana Turner's friend, the ubiquitous and patently oversexed Greg Bautzer squired Miss Lee for a while and ... Hey! Right on time, flaps down and brace yourselves ... Howard! You made it!

Actually Mr. Hughes didn't make it, not with Miss Peggy Lee at any rate. I wonder if Howard Hughes had blondes tatooed on the side of his pork wrench like a fighter pilot had his strike total painted on his aeroplane's fuselage? If he did, it didn't help him any.

Peggy, sans tattoos, made Michael Curtiz's version of THE JAZZ SINGER at Warner Brothers with Danny Thomas who refers to her quite rightly as 'an American treasure'.

She met and married the actor Brad Dexter but knew when she heard him being referred to at the premiere of THE JAZZ SINGER as 'Mister Lee', their marriage wasn't long for the neighbourhood.

Also for Warners, Peggy played Rose in PETE KELLY'S BLUES, directed by Jack Webb, a film which featured a not-yet-blonde Jayne Mansfield. Peggy's image as a singing star had always been on the 'elegant' side of glamorous although I believe she suffered from that fear of 'cross-over' artists that the entertainment industries have. Was she a singer? Was she an actress? Was she a song writer? I think it was her independence in the end which made the movers and shakers in Hollywood movieland hold back. Though nominated for an Academy Award for playing Rose in PETE KELLY'S BLUES, she didn't get it because, as it is rumoured, she was not signed to any studio. Not even a little one. Those men in suits again. They have to have their rules and regs.

And Peggy Lee wasn't your average blonde. She was a highly intelligent woman; she mixed with writers and scientists, appreciated matters intellectual and yet could wear a mink with a diamond or two and look as sexy as she sounded. Miss Peggy Lee was a w-o-m-a-n very much able to say 'no' as 'yes' and ... Well, there were others. Easier.

In Los Angeles, she sang at Ciro's where every movie star on the planet at some time heard her. Peggy was a great admirer of an aforementioned blonde, Marlene Dietrich who heard Peggy sing many times. I can see Marlene, ever appreciative of style and perfection, giving some of her own soon-to-be-staged performances the 'Peggy Lee' treatment on the way home in the limousine after a Ciro's show. That smooth, effortless, almost throwaway delivery which conjures up an eternity in a mere breath.

FEVER and THE FOLKS WHO LIVE ON THE HILL were yet to come although lyric royalties from FEVER were *not* forthcoming. There's no fool like an older fool, I suppose and there are always people to rip a girl off.

It is hard to believe that in 1959 when Peggy played to a packed-out Basin Street East club and had New York and Cary Grant at her feet, that in the audience were people like Quincy Jones and Ray Charles who hadn't even made it then whom she helped to teach by having faith in their talents and, in the case of Jones, employing him for arrangements.

In 1961, she left the USA for the first time on the SS United States and after a fabulously fun-filled yet stormy Atlantic crossing she arrived in England for a long engagement at The Pigalle and a television series. She went to France and had a wonderful time but she returned home to yet another bout of crippling illness, this time double pneumonia with pleurisy complications. She was in bed for seven months.

In 1963, it was Peggy singing I BELIEVE IN YOU not Marilyn Monroe who had top billing at John F Kennedy's birthday bash at Madison Square Garden but it was Marilyn, as we all know, who stole that show. I can tell that Miss Peggy Lee didn't mind a bit. Poor Marilyn ... she was on her way to nothing more pressing than immortality. Peggy had sensibly put hers on a back burner and instead flew back to New York for another sell-out show at Basin Street East.

Her daughter Nicki married David Foster and Peggy became a grandmother. She also became, in the Catholic sense, a widow for David Barbour died just as they were discussing remarriage and four days after the birth of their grandchild. The mid-sixties must have been the start of a part of Peggy's life where death suddenly not only raises its head but roars, like a dark king in an impenetrable jungle of night. You feel it's so useless to even try and run that you find yourself wondering when it will be your turn to be found.

Her stage musical PEG, a dramatised autobiographical affair, was devastatingly received and decimated by the critics on Broadway in 1983 but, though disheartened, Peggy picked up the pieces and put a quintet together and began touring once more. The world. Japan and all over America including New Orleans.

Fate was less than kind and whilst waiting to go on-stage, she suffered heart fibrillation. The irregularity must have been brewing for years. Immediate surgery was scheduled and she was once again an invalid for several months. The double bypass operation was immediately complicated by a serious staphilococci infection.

But she recovered. She still toured. Even after fracturing her pelvis, she still toured. It has to be in her blood. She must love it like she loves life.

Capitol Records didn't want to put out her version of Lieber and Stoller's IS THAT ALL THERE IS? I can't think why. It was a huge hit. People need to be given the perspective. They need to know about sadness and dying as much as they need to know about joy and living. Perhaps the record bosses thought the song was just *too* sad, *too* depressing. *too* much of a downer.

It's my favourite Peggy Lee rendition of all time. When you think you're losing the plot, listen to that song. Like Peggy Lee, it'll enable you to keep on dancing, for as long as it takes.

CHAPTER 15

Grace Kelly

Grace Kelly

Other than the quintessential Marilyn Monroe, Grace Kelly alone deserves to be called a legend in this pantheon of blondes. Not only was she a natural blonde, hindsight condemns her to be a natural legend. Other than magic of course, one of the prerequisite qualifications for the appellation 'legendary' is to be tragic. Grace's progress through life may have been thought magical but there is no doubting the manner of her death was utterly tragic.

The traditional luck of the Irish is patently not inexhaustible.

She was born on the twelfth of November 1929 into a German-Irish family in Philadelphia, the third of four children; Grace had an older sister, Peggy, and brother, John B. Kelly Jr. (Kell) and a younger sister Lizanne. Her mother was Margaret Majer Kelly and her father John B. Kelly.

So much of what has been written in biographical form about Grace Kelly has taken account of her serenely royal apotheosis to an extent that objective assessment of her origins and upbringing has been pale. My reactions to the material I have read is instinctive and might, when compared to the gospel on Grace, be therefore thought barbarian.

I am no hagiographer and Grace Kelly was not a divine being. To begin to understand who she was and, more importantly, what she achieved, I cannot understate how significantly looms the power of her family and her middle-class upbringing. That she ever became a successful actress, let alone a successful Princess is extraordinary.

For any child to have to be a Junior is quite beyond me but that's how it was then and, I believe, still is in much of America. Why, after thousands of generations, men still want and expect their children to be like them is something I can't fathom. To me it displays both ignorance and arrogance, ignorance of the myriad examples of the way such wish-fulfilment has gone drastically wrong in the past and arrogance that anyone could think themselves so perfect that their children should copy them. American fathers, I understand, often employ 'Princess' as an affectionate term of address to their daughters. If there ever was a princess in her father's eyes, it was never Grace but her elder sister Peggy. Poor Jack. He risked disaffecting the wrong daughter.

John B. Kelly, Grace's more than wealthy father would have been my candidate for 'father from hell'. Although I'm sure that, being a good Catholic, Jack Kelly's motivation was god-given, his behaviour and utterances often were hurtful and divisive in the many relationships a husband and father has to maintain in the family context. His children appear to have been no more than personal adornments, left mainly in the care of a 'friend', the family's black gardener Fordie. Jack Kelly had favourites, he was a bully, he was inconsiderate and selfish and rarely at home. As a man he was not above knowing that political muscle didn't always mean democratic majorities; he was autocratic, prejudiced, bore his double standards with a hypocrite's smile and was a spluttering control freak when his authoritarian code was challenged. Not unlike another Irish American patriarch, Joseph Kennedy of Boston, Jack Kelly was a snob and at the same time an inverted snob. He bore grudges and perpetuated lies to give him advantage. He wasn't the gentleman he would have had the world take him for and was a fish out of water when not thrashing in the shallows of his own pond. Grace called him a leader of men. All very well, but it depends where you're leading them. She is supposed to have held him in high ideal and I can only acknowledge her filial dedication but point out how others might have seen him.

Margaret, Grace's mother, was frugal, a disciplinarian and little given to overt emotion. Her displays of affection were as mean as her pocket in regard to both to her husband and to her children. Both Margaret and Jack were, however, very beautiful. Jack knew he was very good-looking and was sensitised to his athlete's body. He was obviously highly sexual and self-aware and not above using his charms wherever they were appreciated. Margaret's looks were merely passed on to her children. She was a social woman, prominent in the charities and fund-raising work whose membership accepted her. Grace and the children must have heard countless times about how beautiful her parents were. But beauty is a cold thing without the warmth of love and it appears that the quality was singularly absent in the house on Henry Avenue. I don't believe any of the Kellys really liked each other that much when they were young.

Extended and close though it might have been, neither Jack's nor Margaret's was the patrician, old-world Philadelphia family that the eager world was later to read about. Jack's roots were securely in the working class and both were Catholic. Though Jack had graduated from laying bricks to making them, his considerable new wealth may have allowed him a brand new posh house but he built it in Germantown, not *the* smartest of suburbs and of course there was his family ... And hers ... And Jack wanted to be assimilated so badly into proper Philly society and he never really was. The old money, the established Protestant families of Philadelphia resisted attempts to be infiltrated and Jack Kelly fumed for years.

His success as an oarsman in international athletic competition to Olympic standards may have failed to help the storming of the social walls but, on the other hand, must have enhanced his mass appeal during his ten year career in local Republican politics. But he didn't last any longer than ten years. Perhaps he backed the wrong horse?

However, where it could be obtained, social and political advantage was always sought by the Kellys who seemed to need as much outward show as possible. Their family became a shibboleth, ultra-sacrosanct to the extent that when suitors were knocking on the girls' doors, they were invariably never good enough. I'm amazed that Rainier of Monaco ever got over Jack Kelly's threshold.

In this very boisterous and extended family - surely the zenith of the ascendant American dream - Grace sought her sanity and equilibrium in a fantasy world, one which couldn't be invaded by the competitive oaring of the men and the grumbling of the love-rationed women, a world where 'could' and 'one day' took the place of 'mustn't' and 'never'.

There were many chances for public performance. Family parties, school plays, the local Old Academy Players am-dram group... The Irish with their love of 'the crack' are never short on available turns and the Kelly family boasted more than its fair share of turns. How much this part of the family was acknowledged must be wondered at although their achievements, I'm sure, were much vaunted. In a way, they were owed more than I'm sure they were ever repaid either in kind or in kindness. Big, butch strong Jack Kelly had two brothers who had gone into the theatre and it was from them he borrowed to establish his brick making and supply business, $5000 from Walter and $2000 from George, very substantial sums in those days. Walter Kelly was huge in vaudeville with several comic routines but it was George, the actor who was to turn Pulitzer prize-winning playwright in 1925 for CRAIG'S WIFE, who was specifically to add his stamp to Grace's passport. I've read nothing about Walter's bachelor proclivities but George is known to have been gay, to the point where his longtime lover - who acted out the charade of being valet-servant - was ignored by the Kelly family at George's funeral. Hey ho! George had taste and money but more than anything he had contacts. And he loved Grace and supported Grace and went out of his way to help Grace where Jack Kelly, even when she won the Oscar admitted that he'd never 'seen' Grace's talent. I think 'the father from hell' is really too kind. Other useful social connections which cannot have disadvantaged the little girl who announced at twelve that she was going to be an actress were the Isaac Levys and the Leon Levys, Philadelphia Jews who were connected by marriage and in business to the Paley family and CBS. Showbiz agents and record business executives like Manie Sachs of Columbia Records and later RCA were Kelly family friends. When Grace made it in the movie business, no 'six month option girl' was she. She was welcomed into powerful inner circles not as a parvenue or an arriviste but as the daughter of old friends.

Grace attended Ravenhill, a Montessori-oriented convent school and then the Stevens School in Germantown in 1943 from which she graduated at eighteen in 1947. She was popular but bouncy, exuberant, sporting Peggy was the dominant sister. The more emotionally substantial Grace knew well when to keep her own counsel.

She had many girlfriends growing up in the War Years which years themselves presumably did not abuse Jack Kelly's business interests. Presumably war-mongering factories were sometimes built of brick? Grace also always had a healthy interest in boys and socialised a great deal around the nucleus of Penn Charter School attended by her bouncy, exuberant, sporting elder brother Kell. (I'm exhausted already.) Socialising included going to the wartime, patriot-packed movies like MRS. MINIVER at which Grace was apparently a great weeper and summer holidays in Ocean City on the Atlantic which she must've enjoyed as she later brought her own Monegasque children on annual beach holidays.

In 1947, Jack Kelly's wish fulfilment obsession was gratified when his son Kell won the Diamond Sculls at the Henley Regatta in England. It was the only competition cup which did not bear the Kelly name. Kelly Senior maintained, as sadly, did Grace, that his exclusion from the competition was because he worked with his hands and wasn't therefore a gentleman. Anyone who cared to acknowledge the reality of English sportsmanship would have known that to be a palpable lie.

Village cricket would never exist if those who worked with their hands were excluded.

In fact Kelly's exclusion was due to a rigmarole dispute between his rowing club Vesper and the Henley authorities although for Irish Jack Kelly, who detested the English anyway, greater capital was obtainable by feeding the fire of the lie. With all the hoo-ha surrounding her elder brother, I shouldn't think anyone took any notice of Grace's announcement that with the help and encouragement of her 'Aunt' Marie Magee and the personal intercession of Uncle George with Emil Diestel, the head of the school, she had secured a place in the fall at the American Academy of Dramatic Art in New York. With the Kelly name finally on the bloody skulls cup, the house on Henry Avenue probably pretended to ignore Grace's departure for Gotham City as her father announced in no uncertain terms that she'd be back home in a week. Such faith! I wonder if the Kellys would have proved as supportive in the face of Grace's defeat as they became in victory. True, at five hundred bucks a semester, Jack provided his daughter with the means to succeed but that magnanimous gesture never implied the right to fail. That namby-pamby philosophy was blasphemy in the American Way and it was left to the likes of the British, namely George Devene at the Royal Court Theatre to give those who grasped it the chance to fail with honour. Honour, to a Kelly, only came with success.

Had Grace fallen into the hands of white slavers or stooped to heroin addiction and prostitution, I doubt that when she left Philadelphia that year that Grace Kelly would have even *wanted* to go back. At any rate, she never did.

The Academy was housed in the Carnegie Hall building on 57th Street and 7th Avenue and Grace lodged at the Barbizon Hotel at 140 East 63rd Street. New York is a walking city and six blocks is no distance. The Barbizon was a women's place, far from luxurious and much, I presume, like the hotel described by Dodie Smith in THE TOWN IN BLOOM. Men weren't allowed in the rooms after ten at night and Grace made some good friends there. She lasted the course and didn't fulfil Jack's gloomy prophesy. She was far too eager to become herself, to establish a persona that wasn't ruled and regulated from Philadelphia. She was popular at the academy although not an outstanding actress by any manner of means. She worked hard and learned deeply, paying most attention to the ironing out of the Philadelphia nasality in her voice and giving it what international Hollywood casting director Rose Tobias Shaw called, 'the cream of tomato soup' quality of its ultimate transatlantic smoothness.

Grace studied costume, dress and make-up as much as the thespian art and augmented the meagre allowance Jack granted with modelling work. She was five seven and one hundred fifteen pounds and worked at that too for she was fond of her food, was Grace. Photographic and fashion modelling as well as television commercials paid between $7.50 and $25 an hour and she wasn't short of work. The rates of pay were more than decent and Grace obviously became used at a relatively early age to having her own disposable income. She became her own woman and loved being in New York. She actively cultivated friendships with sensitive and aesthetic souls almost as an antidote to the boisterous warrior family she'd left behind. Well, not quite left behind for she had to return to pay court. Her family were particularly insensitive, nay boorish on more than one occasion. Bringing home her current boyfriend the gentle and artistic Peter Richardson of whom Margaret and Jack heartily disapproved, Kell was instructed by Margaret to bring home two of the roughest and jockish 'men' and physically abuse the poor Richardson. Not only was Grace humiliated but the Kellys shamed themselves and displayed yet again that they indeed shouldn't be part of polite society. It makes one wonder what they *really* thought of Uncle George.

But life in New York drew her further away from that suffocating family. She once accompanied the Shah of Iran as escort on a week's visit the ruler made to new York. She was not reluctant in announcing that she loved the attention, the secret service bodyguard and being feted by a powerful man. His gift of jewellery to her was reported in the press but despite Margaret and Jack's apoplectic command for her to return it, she didn't. Grace was acquiring muscle as well as an exit visa from the middle class.

She moved from the Barbizon to her own apartment on East 66th and Third avenue and shared with Sally Parrish. She graduated from the American Academy in 1949 and went straight to the Bucks County Playhouse in New Hope Pennsylvania for a repertory season of summer stock.

In her first bill she appeared in her Uncle George's previous Broadway smash THE TORCHBEARERS and also in THE HEIRESS and later in the year had her first crack at Broadway in THE FATHER directed by Raymond Massey. It opened at the Cort Theatre but only lasted a couple of months. Grace's inexperience didn't show and she received a couple of favourable reviews and in 1950 appeared in the first of the eleven movies she was to make, FOURTEEN HOURS directed by Henry Hathaway for Twentieth Century Fox and starring Gary Cooper. This was no starlet arriving on the west coast green and wet behind the ears. She was offered an MGM stock contract but turned it down. Despite her much vaunted confidence to William Allyn that she was going to be '... the greatest film star Hollywood has ever seen', she was obviously in no hurry to fulfil this destiny.

Back in New York, Grace went through two very lean years as far as her professional aim of becoming a considered theatre actress was concerned. She was seen but never cast, often being given the excuse that she was inexperienced. It's a debilitating position, the chicken and egg. No work, no experience. No experience, no work ...

She was cast in ALEXANDER which opened out-of-town in Albany, New York but she had been replaced by the time the play arrived on Broadway. In television, however, she worked. Illustrious names, nay legends, of the future were emerging via television. That superb actress Lee Remick, another cool patrician blonde in Grace's mould, James Dean and Anthony Perkins all worked, as did Grace, for the main sponsored television theatre shows, Philco Playhouse and Kraft television theatre, although of the four, only Grace made it to princess. Premature death was, however, to be the fate of all four and one was to join Grace as a legend.

Grace appeared in over a hundred television plays in the early fifties years and impressed all of those who cast her as not only a beauty but as a nice, sweet girl. She had that ineffable quality which Americans revere most, class. When Americans see real class, they don't envy it, nor mock it, nor seek to rob it. They merely admire it for it makes them feel good. It soothes them. Whether she knew it, God only knows but Grace Kelly was beginning to develop a regality. Always one step removed, somewhat apart, she was nonetheless warm and interested. A fierce guardian of her privacy, she was publicly outgoing and charming. She studied and read widely and deeply but unobtrusively and she was dedicated and committed to doing her job the best she could possibly do it. She tempered duty with obligation, beauty with humility and privilege with work. As a professional, she behaved entirely as would have befitted any British Royal of the time, Queen Elizabeth The Queen Mother is reputed to have said: *"Your work is the rent you pay for the time you spend on earth."*

She landed the part of Isabelle in RING ROUND THE MOON at the Ann Arbor Festival outside Chicago in 1951 and then moved on to Denver where she played in repertory at the Elitch Gardens Summer Stock Theatre. Edith van Cleve her agent had already turned down two film offers for Grace to continue stage work but by the end of the summer in Denver, even Edith conceded that the telegram to Grace telling her to report for work in Hollywood on August 28th to play opposite Gary Cooper in HIGH NOON was not one to ignore.

Produced by Stanley Kramer and directed by Fred Zinneman, HIGH NOON was destined to become a classic western. Grace was chaperoned by her younger sister Lizanne and whilst all acknowledged her inexperience, all acknowledged that she was a refreshingly genuine personality. She disliked her performance which was totally eclipsed both by Coop's and Katy Jurado playing the gunman's mistress. Grace fairly fled back to New York and enrolled in classes with Sandy Meisner to attempt to make her screen acting expressive and comprehensible. The interior stuff of acting is useless for the screen unless it shows on your face and Grace remained stubbornly impassive.

She continued a very passionate love affair with Gene Lyons, an actor whom she had met in Denver and with whom she worked in television back in New York. Once again the family in Philly strove to quash the liaison which ended anyway. Grace was cast in TO BE CONTINUED, a Guthrie McClintic production at the Booth Theatre but that flopped.

HIGH NOON, however, succeeded in achieving four Oscars at the Academy Awards that year, platform enough for Greg Ratoff to want Grace to shoot a screen-test for his movie TAXI for Twentieth Century Fox although the role ultimately went to Constance Smith.

But, hey ... The Greg Ratoff non-event was actually Grace's biggest break. The test she made for Ratoff was seen both by John Ford and Alfred Hitchcock. Grace was to become a star after working with Ford and a princess through working for Hitch.

And so she went to work for MGM at $850 a week although the remaining terms were for an engagement which was entirely dictated by Grace. MOGAMBO's main location was to be in Africa and the movie was a remake of an original Jean Harlow picture of 1932 with Ava Gardner, and Clark Gable in his same role twenty years later. Movies had begun to be shot away from Hollywood on location, a brave and very expensive studio departure. MOGAMBO was not to be movie-make-believe and it was to be shot where it was set, in Africa. Miss Kelly, having mugged up on Swahili before she left for the dark continent, got close to the jungle and, waiting in it, she found Mr. Gable. Yum, yum.

She also got close to Ava and Frank Sinatra. Frank wasn't in the picture and wasn't doing much of anything else at the time but because he was married to Ava, he was in the next tent. Despite other people divorcing, Grace's affections were never to polarise. Ava and Frank would both remain her friends throughout her life.

The studio sequences were shot in London at Borehamwood and Grace, who was beginning to be treated very much like a big star, lived at the Savoy. Perhaps Clark Gable would have gotten an invite for the weekend to Henry Avenue, Philadelphia. For Jack and Margaret Kelly to have disapproved of Clark Gable would have been the same as the Kennedys forbidding the screen actor Peter Lawford into their clan and later the superstar Arnold Schwarzenegger. However, such a dilemma was not to arise for Clark sheathed the pork sword for good (or at least for a while) and Grace returned to New York not to continue her liaison with Gene Lyons but to meet and become friendly with the French actor Jean Pierre Aumont, ten years older than her and a widower.

MOGAMBO opened in October 1953 and Grace's patrician qualities were noted in polite reviews. Grace's film career was usually always criticised for what she was rather than what she might have been for there were many who believed she could never have been otherwise.

Between 1953 and 1954, Grace made six movies, three for Alfred Hitchcock. None of them, however, were for her home studio, MGM who loaned her out on each successive occasion. For a long time, the studio which was in artistic and directional crisis obviously had no idea what to do with their new hot property. The powers that be neither understood her nor had they any vehicles in which to place her. Having some of the same qualities as Greer Garson, Miss Garson was dropped by MGM along with Mr. Gable quite unceremoniously in 1954.

Grace made DIAL M FOR MURDER for Warner Brothers, lived in a suite with her youngest sister Lizanne at the Chateau Marmont and was wooed by Ray Milland, her DIAL M co-star.

Her DIAL M film performance was again seen as patrician by the loftier press but those organs nearer the gutter welcomed the 'blonde, sexy newcomer' who they opined had an earthy appeal which gave boys something to think about ... whilst doing what, may I ask?

In REAR WINDOW, her next with Hitchcock, Grace was cast to type as a society-girl magazine editor although Hitchcock ensured that her performance was underpinned with the quality he had seen in the TAXI screen-test which coupled both the loftier approach to Grace Kelly with the venal. Out of Grace, Hitch was after, and got, sexual elegance. It set the tone for many a star - Candice Bergen, Lee Remick - and entirely complemented fashion's 'New Look'. Grace also managed to shuck the family chaperones for a while. Not much of a life for either Peggy or Lizanne in fact. Get a life girls! During REAR WINDOW Grace shared an apartment with actress Rita Gam who would also never leave Grace's life.

MGM loaned her out again, this time to Paramount, for THE BRIDGES AT TOKO-RI. She was paid the tiny salary of $10,000 whilst MGM cleared $15,000 on the loan-out deal. This girl was not being overpaid! The director/producer was George Seaton who, with his associate William Perlberg was impressed by Grace's dedication to acting as opposed to the machinery of becoming a movie star. They wanted her for their next Paramount production, Clifford Odets' Broadway success THE COUNTRY GIRL.

MGM only agreed to her doing so after she had committed herself to one of their productions called GREEN FIRE and a major renegotiation of her contract. Grace became committed to an extra contractual picture for MGM plus an option for them to make three others with her. Her money went up too, at last, and for THE COUNTRY GIRL, Dore Schary at MGM charged Perlberg and Seaton $50,000, twice the fee she warranted for BRIDGES OF TOKO-RI. But it was worth it. Grace knew that THE COUNTRY GIRL was her picture. And, for a while anyway, her co-star William

Holden was her man. After Bing, that is. And, before Oleg. That's Mister Cassini to you and I.

COUNTRY GIRL wrapped and Grace went straight into making GREEN FIRE, an in-house MGM potboiler co-starring Englishman Stewart Granger all about emeralds and Columbia and an uncomfortable location probably better used by our Kirk's little boy Mikey Douglas and Kathleen Turner many years later.

There was no let-up in the work department in 1955, for no sooner had Grace finished with sweaty Colombian emeralds than began the promised loan out once again to Paramount for her last movie with Hitchcock, and probably her most sublime, TO CATCH A THIEF in which she was to co-star with Cary Grant. Yet another location picture, this time on the Cote d' Azur of southern France. The sexual elegance was now extended into John Michael Hayes' wonderful dialogue which oozed with lascivious doubles entendres.

And Oleg Cassini was to come too. Probably quite often. Suave and dark and international and sophisticated and a bit of playboy, he suited Grace down to her branded white gloves, the old ravisher! As could have been expected, the son of Russian parents who'd had a flighty upbringing in decadent Europe of all places was entirely un-American and therefore loathed by the flag-waving family back home in fer ... fer ... Philly.

The movie finished and Oleg Cassini's chances too bit the dust. Whether it was his twice-divorced track record, I don't know. Faced ultimately with the marriage question, it must be borne in mind that Grace was in that respect deeply religious and the prospect of being unable to marry without the blessing of the church would I hazard have made any thought of a domestic future with Cassini a non-starter.

Also a non-starter was the prospect of doing QUENTIN DURWARD for MGM. The studio's previous suggestions had all been similarly stereotyped - pretty period dresses, gung-ho chaps and demure, ravishable virgins - and Grace refused. The studio therefore put her on suspension - a standard step in front office dealings with recalcitrant stars - on seventh March 1955.

The suspension was to last all of two weeks because Grace's performance in THE COUNTRY GIRL was nominated for an Oscar by The Academy and she duly took possession of her gold-plated, long-stated ambition on March thirtieth 1955. John B. Kelly was still publicly announcing his bewilderment at his second daughter's success over Peggy's.

John B. Kelly who?

In May, to promote TO CATCH A THIEF, Grace flew to France to appear at the Cannes Film Festival. She did so with no little reluctance, overcome by much encouragement from her friend and future press aide Rupert Allan and that ghastly family again telling her she was Irish American and that she owed it to her country. I suppose they couldn't stress the *German*-Irish-American because of the two world wars. Hey ho.

Whilst in Cannes, Grace was bamboozled by *Paris Match*, then the *Hello! Magazine* of its day, into being driven with no proper frock and in a great hurry and dash an hour's drive to Monte Carlo where the somewhat Ruritanian personage of Rainier the Third, ruler of Monaco, one of Europe's jokier independent princedoms had graciously agreed to have his picture taken with the world's most popular movie star. Gee, thanks, Rainier.

But of course, there were wheels within and behind wheels ... There always are and there always will be.

Grace had her picture taken in a frock she didn't particularly like and seemed to have a nice afternoon with Rainier who, unlike his realm, let's face it, was no picture postcard. But Grace never came close to saying she'd fallen in love ... Even when it would have been alright to have said so.

Jean Pierre Aumont had again surfaced in Grace's periphery and it seemed she could have had her pick of the bunch. But available royals ... There's a teaser. They were few on the ground then. Never abundant after the unification of Germany and democracy and nationalisation in Italy, they were in the post second world war boom a very threatened species. I think

Rainier's bachelorhood was before the Belgian marriage, certainly before the Spanish and a whiffle too early even in the life of our own dear Prince of Wales. And despite what everyone may have thought, American patrician-*looking* actresses weren't exactly what even the most desperate of royal houses were looking out for.

But it was what Aristotle Onassis was looking out for vis a vis the ruler of the little country which housed one of the most famous gambling casinos and tax-break facilities in the world. Onassis had invested heavily in the Société des Bains de Mer, the company which ran the casino and, ergo, Monaco for there was little else in this four hundred acre enclave. Monaco and the Monegasques needed to come into the twentieth century and be made profitable. The casino, the opera house, the royal palace and the fading stucco villas were dilapidated and falling apart. The country had to be saved and so lacking a Marshall Plan ...

Grace returned to America and agreed to do THE SWAN opposite Alec Guiness for and at MGM. It was a picture-postcard film in which Grace had to be .. well, Grace, of course. She was to play a princess who is to save her country by marrying the rich Prince Albert and who instead falls for the tutor. Who wrote this stuff? MGM of course but at least they were getting the message about Grace. A little late, if I may say, as things were to soon turn out.

Those wheels were sure a-turnin'. Rainier and Grace had gotten along, absolutely as only absolute princes' wheels turn. But there must have been other candidates for the, aheem, position. One hears that even Marilyn Monroe's name was once mentioned in a giddy moment. Rainier might have even listened for he was certainly no blushing flower. He too had had experience of *life* (nudge wink), specifically a long-established affair which had been politically terminated. Now inward investment was being sought by the board of the S.B.M and heirs to the house of Grimaldi were being looked for and Grace's were the best qualifications.

Catholic, single, pure (but don't quote me) and not averse to relocation. Background not a problem and with a little re-writing by the publicity department, quite a plus. Have I said Catholic? Oh, yes. I have because one of those turbulent priests who have popped up throughout history like Thomas a Becket and Thomas More duly pops up here in the story except this one's *really* on the side of the king. Fate let it fall to Father Francis Tucker to play Dolly Levi and bore Rainier's Onassis-validated suit to Pa Kelly in America before Rainier came to call in person at Henry Avenue.

It was Christmas, Grace had just finished shooting THE SWAN and Bing Crosby could have been singing in the most perfect Christmas setting ever when ...

It seems that Pa Kelly was convinced Rainier had enough money despite being European and not a democrat even of the Republican variety; it seems Ma Kelly's social face would not have to be lifted as long as Grace behaved herself; it seems MGM were pretty pleased because they immediately put THE SWAN on ice to be thawed at the time of the time of the wedding; it seems that The Société de Bains de Mer were in agreement although it equally seems that the several tens of thousands of Monegasque residents were overlooked in the love story that was set up to blossom between Rainier and Grace with the blessing of the catholic cupid Father with the fairy wand.

The day after Rainier arrived in Philadelphia, only the second time they'd ever met, the couple went for a drive around Pennsylvania and her Prince gave our Grace a ring. January first 1956, they were engaged and they told the world four days later.

She'd become the movie star she said she'd become and now she was to be a princess. It was an apotheosis, although of the lay variety. She is supposed to have said, merely, *"I have made my destiny."*

I should say.

America, nay the world, went crazy. Grace's after all was the ultimate fairytale love story and it really seemed that the pair were in love. Arranged? Of course! It beat the hell out of arranged, but then so did TRUE LOVE, the song Grace sang with Bing Crosby in HIGH SOCIETY, the last film she would ever make. She got a gold disc for it too, this girl whose very life seemed touched by Midas.

In fact she owed another movie to MGM but Dore Schary proved himself totally graceless when he uttered his famous retort to being told by Rainier that Monaco was only some five square miles big ... *"That's no bigger than our backlot!"* Ouch. Not clever, Dory. For Grace to have made another movie would have been impossible. The world's press would have seen to that.

In any event, W. R. Hearst's yellow-fanged rags gave her life a thorough dissection with the inadvertent help of the rather silly Ma Kelly. Grace didn't deserve that sort of treatment. It wasn't the limelight. Grace knew all about that. It was the foretaste of the operating theatre light under which her every future move would be scrutinised, the arc lights at the disaster scene when future family ructions occurred, the flash lights of the paparazzi cameras wherever she was to appear ... No wonder for the first year of her marriage, she remained virtually a recluse behind those pink palace walls.

On March 12th Grace arrived by ship in Monaco for her two weddings, the civil marriage on the eighteenth April and the cathedral ceremony on the nineteenth. The beau monde and quite a lot of cafe society turned out to join movie land and the braver royals in the Grimaldi-Kelly nuptials. As Grace herself later admitted, had she not been an actress, she wondered how she would have coped with both the event and the life it presaged.

As Her Serene Highness, Princess Grace of Monaco, Grace Kelly rather transcends being a glamour blonde at this stage. She did her job as princess superbly. In her early fifties, she had rejoined the film industry not as an actress but as the only female board member of Twentieth Century Fox and she had rejoined the thespians she loved touring the world reading her poetry to great acclaim. Whether she was really happy or not, we will never know. For us, it shouldn't matter for she fulfilled all our fantasies and made us happy. Characteristically, she never went over the top about her own happiness.

What, sadly, our Serene Highness did go over the top of was a French mountain road's crash barrier on the thirteenth of September 1982, having borne Rainier his three living heirs and suffered the loss of several unborn ones. Like in the movies, like in THE SWAN, she had saved her country and she had only ever had eyes for the prince.

The car - a British Rover wouldn't you know, Jack Kelly - which she was supposed to have been driving on the day of her death, accompanied by her youngest child Princess Stephanie, crashed down the mountain-side. Stephanie survived. Grace didn't. She sustained many injuries, sank deeper into a mortal coma and her grief-shattered family gave permission for her life support system to be switched off when doctors pronounced her brain dead on September fourteenth 1982 at ten thirty at night.

Utterly, senselessly, repugnantly tragic.

But, as my friend Freddie Mercury used to say, there you have it, dears. Another one of human life's irrefutable equations: $M + T = L$. Magic plus tragedy equals the stuff of legends.

The wonderful thing about fantasy is that you can always change it. It's not like a vow or a promise or a faith. It's our internal gyroscope, keeping us going and keeping us upright. Always a creature of fantasy, it has been made known by friends that Grace Kelly Grimaldi's current one when she died was of being able to be normal again.

CHAPTER 16

Dusty Springfield

Dusty Springfield

Dusty Springfield has enjoyed the fruits of a thirty five year career. Such a long lease on success is only remarkable if the career still has meaning. I think it does and I hope that Dusty Springfield, whoever she is now, does too.

I have included Dusty in this book because according to the original and inherent meaning of glamour, I believe she was both bewitched by blonde and, having created the image which we know as Dusty Springfield, bewitched *AS* a blonde. Her audience was certainly bewitched and still is. Trouble is, as trouble was, it was an image that was shown, in the context of the times, to be seriously flawed.

The structure of the frail hull supporting the blonde superstructure sprang some serious leaks. Whoever is or was the person who lies behind the facade of Dusty Springfield, is and was seriously compromised by a sexuality which, in the way-back-when nineteen sixties, was considered incompatible with a career. Probably right thinking but ... times changed. However, the career that sprang from Dusty's enormous initial talent is and was proportionately compromised.

It's an interesting situation. What would *you* have done, dear reader? What did so *many* other stars do?

The problems for Dusty set in when the corrosion started to eat away at the human being behind the image for in Dusty's case, that human being was and is a sensitised and sensitive artist, confused and vulnerable as well as highly motivated, singularly focused and very much in charge.

I have also included Dusty Springfield in this book because when she started singing it was in the very early years of the new music business. She had to forge her way without a map. She was a pioneer. Her mistakes became the rules which others learned by, her career became the map that others followed through the minefield. She sacrificed her career to some vague notion of her 'private' self, terrified that she should be revealed as lesbian. It was a career that couldn't have happened in pictures. The ladies of rock who came after her, have also learned from Dusty's public pain. They should thank her.

Dusty has often said she is lazy. So? Anyone who has ever felt the need to communicate anything - painter, novelist, composer, songwriter, actor, singer - feels that emotion which, because of trepidation or guilt that you're not doing a 'proper job', you brand laziness. To an artist, their work can be almost alien, something that exists above and outside themselves but which only has form via them. Often afraid, sometimes scared to death, revealing the finished work is like walking naked down a street for the artist is asking to be judged, to be shot down. And the judges are the fans, the people who, although professing their love, expect never to be disappointed, year after year, album after album, film after film.

And all this has to be done in public. There is no private in show-business as all our glamour blondes have discovered to their cost.

However, when Dusty started out, she was called an artiste with an 'e'. There was no music industry as we know it today. There was variety and there were acts and it was England. Dusty Springfield took shape and form as an act, first with her brother, Tom Springfield, then as part of a bigger act, the fabulous *Lana Sisters*, then, with Tom and Tim Feild she graduated into yet another act, *The springfields.*

By the time she went solo in 1963, we had only just witnessed the arrival of *The Beatles.* Singers and bands went out on tour around Britain and even into Europe in tinny, rattly coaches, seven or ten 'acts' on a bill, gear and cozzies crammed on board too. The tours played mainly in cinemas, the Odeon as opposed to the Orpheum circuit in America, usually using the cinemas' ropey speaker systems to try and get across a sound which approximated to the yardstick of the original record. PA's? Computerised on-stage monitors? Multi-track mixing desks? Forget it. The technology wasn't even available to achieve the sound Dusty knew she needed to hear.

Luckier than most who start on the same road, Dusty started out with a lot. Whether it was enough, I'm sure both we and she would debate. Dusty must have often wished for a different set of luggage. But, you get what you get in life.

On April 16th 1939 as the civilised world again teetered on the brink of auto-destruction, Dusty got dealt her basic hand; she got her mother and father, Kay and Gerard (OB) O'Brien and she got an elder brother, Tom, christened Dion. Dieu-Donne - given by God. Dusty also got dealt London and, her only real bonus, a wild card. Turning it over later in teenage, the card read VOX, just when she needed it most.

Kay was in her mid-thirties when she had her children. She came from an Irish Catholic background and she was outgoing and loved 'the crack'. She dreamed strong dreams, especially for her daughter Mary Catherine Isobel Bernadette, as Dusty was baptised. OB was a steadier personality but was nonetheless as musical and as supportive an influence as Kay on his children's choice of future. The parents loved music of all sorts, jazz, classical and ethnic but, formatively, American music. The children listened, read and were influenced. Things American became an integral part of Dusty's soul. Images blonde and beautiful also instilled themselves into her psyche. Real escape for mother and daughter was found in the diet of Hollywood movies they consumed at their weekly picture palace. The creators of Dusty Springfield borrowed from only one source - The Hollywood Blonde. American movies and popular culture saved Britain from going crazy after the war.

Singing at home, en famille, and in choir and class in school is one thing. To be taken seriously as a singer in the real world is a quantum leap. By fourteen and, so it seems, by chance, Kay read Dusty's wild card. VOX. Kay realised Dusty could sing, differently, quirkily. 'The voice' became noticed. The dreams and ambitions that had been Kay's became Dusty's. Dusty could be a singer. Vital parental encouragement was lavished on her and living in the suburb of Ealing, on London's doorstep, Dusty only had to take the subway to sing for her one guinea nightly fee at the clubs, bars and private parties in the West End and Belgravia where she started off. OB even came and collected her.

And she had Tom. The two grew up at home beating out rhythms and singing and they later went out performing together on their degree courses at the university of life. Useless to pretend that their parents' marriage was idyllic. It wasn't. Kay and OB argued, often, it would seem, mightily. Certainly it was enough for Dusty to remember significantly. As the younger sibling, she has also maintained that a lot of her natural assertion and independence was compromised. Tom was the older and, so she says, the cleverer. He certainly did very well at school, was a natural linguist to the extent of speaking and reading Russian fluently in those cold war days. Dusty, little sister, has forever since compared herself. Was it out of defiance that she never properly learned a musical instrument and never learned to read music?

Being the youngest was to have as important an effect on her character as her having been continuously educated in Catholic schools - motto *Goodness Is Excellence*. Thinking yourself inadequate and not as good as your nearest and dearest, coupled with fierce pangs of guilt borne through religious adherence to seemingly unattainable goals of goodness, rightness and don't-argue-girl makes for a deep need to succeed, to please and to be loved. The dread possibility of failure engenders insecurity which breeds concern. Anticipation of being lost, of being wrong, of being seen in a bad light breeds worry. Dusty came through adolescence a worrier. She also came through with an acute awareness of loving, and, most poignantly, of being unloved.

What better way for an un-confident yet defiant teenager to be loved by as many people as possible as well as to be as different as she could than to sing and to be applauded and to be paid for the pleasure?

I find it fascinating that Dusty has said recently that she was always brought up to be a part of singing, one of a number, half a duo, a third a trio, a part of the band. She maintains she was never brought up to sing lead. But sing lead she did, in the *Springfields* and, when that award-winning, pioneering trio determined its existence, Dusty found herself suddenly alone in the spotlight. By that time, the young Mary O'Brien had constructed what she must have felt was a fairly sturdy doppelganger to take the strain.

Mary O'Brien's was a psychological virgin birth, her off-spring being Dusty Springfield, her of the, finally, big blonde Hollywood hair, her born from Twentieth Century Fox and MGM musicals and American dreams, her of the sparkly and expensive frocks, the sports car and dark glasses; Dusty Springfield, as the gossamer dried on her wings, was assumed to have been constructed with a pretty broad back and skin like a rhino's. Way to go! Dusty Springfield soared and left myopic red-headed Mary O'Brien standing blinking at the gate.

Dusty has confirmed that from her Springfield base, she took the step into the solo unknown knowing she was going 'to be alright'; she knew from her advisers and confidantes, Ivor Raymonde who worked as the *Springfields'* musical arranger and wrote her first hits, from Emlyn Griffiths the *Springfields'* manager, from her mother, her father and from Tom. But most of all she knew it herself when she felt 'the buzz' as she has described it. When Dusty Springfield sang I ONLY WANT TO BE WITH YOU, she instantly established a lasting audience.

The voice became synonymous with a generation. It has never been equalled or bettered in British pop music for individuality, expression, timbre, pitch or colour. The voice is indefinable except in terms of what it does. It puts whoever listens to it in touch with their feelings. It is an instant conduit to joy, to pain, to laughter or to tears. It grabs you and forces you to listen to the words. That aching vibrato, the vocal quiver that sends shivers through the waiting lyrics ... Dusty's vocal performances sear, they soar, sometimes triumphant, sometimes infinitely reflective. She sings and the sound becomes a mirror in which we see all the times we've felt just like her ...

I can't have been the only lonely teenager shut up in a boarding school who can still, thirty years later, weep on cue when I hear the intro to I JUST DON'T KNOW WHAT TO DO WITH MYSELF. I still remember that aching pit of loneliness I scrabbled in and the desperation to have anyone just to hug me. Dusty's songs made all that painful growing up seem bearable, 'cos there was someone else who knew what I was going through. She became my friend. I danced with her to LA BAMBA, drunk on illicit cider in the cricket pavilion and sang along with MOCKINGBIRD at many a teenage party. The sound of the voice makes me know I'm alive.

Multiply me by several hundred thousand and no wonder she sensed 'the buzz'. No wonder she sensed she would be 'all right'. But did she know she was going to have to be 'all right' for so long? There were no boyfriends, no husbands, no level emotional playing field to support help her. As she revealed at the end of those magical sixties, she, Dusty, the flesh-and-blood person behind Dusty Springfield would have been just as likely to have walked from the spotlight into the supportive, loving arms of a woman as into a man's. Then, her situation must have caused confusion and pain. The burden she carried of being Dusty Springfield was made immeasurably more intolerable by the pressure of keeping secrets, of living a lie, of endless double-speak and truth-avoidance measures. Oh that she could have been Dusty Springfield *now* and learned from k.d. Laing, from Madonna. But, like I said, they instead learned from her.

Gay girls aren't like gay boys. Gay girls, in my humble

assessment, are *much, much* more to do with the heart. Much more to do with grand passions, huge crushes and obsessive, often violent, relationships, gay girls are, in the majority, much less visible than gay boys. At least, they were in the nineteen sixties. Released from being pinned between two men in a trio, no wonder those arms and hands flailed like combine harvesters as Dusty milled every ounce of meaning and significance from her songs. Dusty sang a love song like no white British woman has sung it before or since.

Dusty had been developing her art and craft for five years by the time she went solo. Watching and listening to Johnny Franz her recording manager in the studio, learning from arrangers like Ivor Raymonde, noting and filing away the properties and potential of different musical instruments and the primitive, mainly four track recording techniques available at the time, Dusty embarked on the role she has always fulfilled but seldom been fully accredited, that of being ultimately her own producer.

She had recorded in Nashville, visited New York, was expertly acquainted with American pop music in a way that most tired session players in England found encyclopaedic and threatening. Walking past a New York record store in the early sixties, she heard the sound of The Exciters blasting out onto the side-walk. Dusty had heard the future of pop music and she knew it worked.

Fundamentally, Dusty sees her voice as an instrument, as a part of a band. She knows its limitations and now knows she has to take care of it when stray infections and overuse threaten. She sees herself not as the music she makes but as a part of the music with which she is associated. The voice rises up, sometimes like a trumpet over-riding the guitars of a mariachi backing, sometimes like a flute or clarinet in a wildly swinging jazz band, sometimes sounding like a silk stocking being dragged over barbed wire, sometimes like the same silk stocking floating hidden in viscose tears. Instruments make sound and sound communicates mood and feeling.

She speaks now almost enviously of the expertise and technology available today compared to the sixties. Certainly, the means by which her recordings have been made over the years may have changed enormously but the way she makes them is the same. As with all artists, yesterday's ends become tomorrow's means.

She has a keen sense of what is right for her voice and she has said, though I choose not to believe her completely, that a song's lyrics are far less important to her than the music, than where the notes are, how the song sounds. And she will do a song over and over and over again until either exhaustion or the sheer impossibility of improvement forces her to quit. Fabled stories of yelling at truculent musicians abound. *She* knew the sound a Fender bass could produce. *She* had heard that sound. The bass player hadn't. He didn't believe her. Result? She's been branded difficult. Worse. She's a difficult woman.

Then, the music business was a man's world. Now, I think it is still. Then most of Britain's singers, men or women, went into the studio, sang and went away. If a man wanted another take, okay. If a woman wanted another take when a man had said he didn't, she became, at the angry snap of a fader, 'difficult'. Difficult usually heralds perfectionism. Controlled perfectionism often makes for efficient hit production. Way back then, Dusty was rarely treated with the commensurate seriousness she sought, perhaps contributing, along with an her mother's bequeathed propensity for 'the crack', to her fabled exhibitions of over-the-top fun. Cream pie throwing, plate-chucking. What larks! But was it ever realised that only an inch beneath the bravado, was a very committed young woman?

Most of Dusty's early songs were written by men for women to sing. Songs by women about how women feel about men for women to sing came later, almost too late for a woman like Dusty to have properly profited from. The way men love is different to the way women love. The way men love women and the way they express that love is entirely different from the way a woman loves a woman. Dusty has always battled in a man's world. I think she will still be battling now despite Joni, Carole and Carly, Tammy and even Dolly and Madonna. Work and business are as much about power as is love ... And gender, sadly, is so much about power. Dusty has had little confidence in either gender or proclivity and her power has been concomitantly curbed. This was no Marlene Dietrich who, by allowing herself to be courted by men and women equally, merely fanned the flames of her 'fatale' image even further and was forgiven indiscretion forever. Dusty Springfield protested too loudly and too much and suffered accordingly. Like all our blondes, she has been sustained by a huge gay following which, like Mae West, she has been reluctant to acknowledge except when forced. I am writing during years in which her gay audience could have benefited enormously from her public espousal of their current problems. Privately, I'm sure she is more than generous.

Her initial hits gave Dusty at least a little power and by avoiding being hoist by her own petard she was allowed to go on being successful in the days when the song, the single 45 rpm. rather than the artist, was paramount. In the days when a single sold in predictable hundreds of thousands, the album, the expression of the artist's core of self-expression, were almost secondary and certainly not conceptual.

Dusty was one of the first to brook this tradition and in 1964 came out with her album A GIRL CALLED DUSTY. She paved the way for the women who were to follow although she remained reliant on other people to write the material which mirrored her soul.

If she'd only written her own, although the 'if' game can make for lonely graves. Tom Springfield had amply realised the financial significance of writing as well as performing, so pioneering with *The Springfields* the path for later groups who wrote for themselves. I believe Dusty realised the importance of the singer songwriter too as the sixties progressed although she wasn't doing or didn't do anything about it, preferring perhaps, if indeed she chose at all, the road of least criticism, of least confrontation. Songwriters naturally confront themselves and Dusty was only in the business of being honest in private.

She admits that her early method of selection was 'swiping' material which she either had heard others singing or which she knew was earmarked elsewhere. On the way, there were some that got away. AIN'T NO MOUNTAIN HIGH ENOUGH was one. She confesses that she would have 'killed for that song'. But, as my granny said about love and missed buses, 'another'll be along in a minute' although Dusty's buses, like American Greyhounds, made too many stops.

She promoted her British singles in America where she had great success, meeting many of both her musical influences and crushes alike along the way. She still quotes her experiences at The Fox Theatre, Brooklyn on the Murray the K shows in the mid-sixties where the bill, played some six times daily along with the movie, included *The Supremes* and *Martha And The Vandellas*. Being an off-stage honorary Vandella when one or the other of the real ones was playing hookey obviously fitted snugly into Dusty's predilection for being 'just part of a group' as they sang 'Hitchhike, hitchhike, baby' accompanying Marvin Gaye. She has fond memories of three black beehives and a blonde beehive crammed quite convivially into a tiny dressing room.

In Britain, some had already dubbed her with black epithets and she herself was quite content to bask in the 'brown-ness' of her voice. Her undeniable love of black American music, notably the Motown material, led her to crusade selflessly for that label to be heard and its artists to be recognised worldwide. That Tamla-Motown, however, never asked her to join was, as Dusty has confirmed, 'probably not a bad thing'. Though the label might have triumphed, not all Motown artists had good experiences.

Dusty has always, utterly unselfishly, praised others where credit has been due, acknowledging many times that 'no one sings Bacharach like she does', referring to Dionne Warwick, one of her earliest influences. Burt Bacharach, then writing with Hal David, she credits with changing the course of pop music more than *The Beatles*. Carole King, creator of GOIN' BACK and other Dusty favourites with Gerry Goffin, was another writer Dusty obviously admired, coming from a Californian corner that was later to bring Carole Bayer Sager and Lesley Gore songs into her repertoire.

Dusty's solo debut had been into a world where management was not the industry byword it had become by the early seventies. The business face of Dusty Springfield belonged to Vic Billings, now sadly dead. Vic understood Dusty well although their relationship seemed to allow more for Dusty's capricious over-view of her career than it did for the pursuit of common policy.

The albums WHERE AM I GOING? and DUSTY DEFINITELY added to Dusty's covering of the sixties ground. She had from the outset always worked live, incessantly, tirelessly touring and playing the many British club and cabaret venues. Starting with *The Echoes*, an independent unit who always supported her, her show was always augmented, often by a sixteen piece band, musicians whom she worked relentlessly but paid highly on session rather than contract rates. Sound checks and rehearsals went on for hours. Again and again she would check for the 'dead' areas of a room, miking yet further sections of the band should she discern even one voice of criticism of the sound after an otherwise sell-out show.

Television appearances, recording sessions singing French, Italian and German translations of her hits, subsequent European tours to promote the translations, brushes and scrapes with the press and the establishment, once for refusing to appear before segregated audiences in South Africa ... The halcyon sixties highs as well as the down-and-dusty days lasted over six years. Not much time away from giddy Dusty Springfield and there was stolid old Mary O'Brien still waiting at the gate for it to be her turn.

226

DUSTY IN MEMPHIS, her fifth album was the validation from the American record industry that she was world-rated, that she had finally arrived. 'Them up there', the latter-day studio moguls, deemed it essential she should stay ... Jerry Wexler, Tom Dowd and Arif Mardin and Atlantic Records. 'Long distance information give me Memphis, Tennessee ...' It was a time when Dusty sensed the call of her own wild frontier. Thirty *is* a dangerous age.

In the making of MEMPHIS, there were certainly, as the bumpy road sign says, 'Men at Work'. Dusty must have found it not only hard to be true to herself and to stick to her guns in the face of so many assumptions having been made about her but also intimidating to stand and sing and lay down work on the spot where so many of her heroes and heroines had worked before.

The painful feeling of comparing herself to incomparables she wrought within herself exquisitely. With each track, with each album it seemed Dusty had more and more to lose. It seems as though Marilyn Monroe really had died in vain.

Actors and performers who change their names and who think they've created a convenient alter ego to inhabit usually find that instead of being able to come and go at will in and out of these 'other selves' that they are inevitably trapped by them and that the demands made on and by their real selves are insupportable. Most hack their way through with or without their mothers or any little helpers; some go under completely and only a very few get out un-scarred. But Dusty, like all the others, seemed blinded by the brightness of her chosen yellow brick road which led her west, to Los Angeles. I wonder if she wanted Mary O'Brien to come too?

She made three albums after she'd dipped her finger into the lotus licence of LaLa land. FROM DUSTY ... WITH LOVE, SEE ALL HER FACES and CAMEO. None continued or were part of an artistic and career development and although there were some gems, Dusty didn't do much for Thrillsville, middle America. Dusty was understood in Britain and Europe. She wasn't even mildly comprehensible in most of the U. S. of A.

Did she feel that Britain knew too much about her and was turning fickle prior to 'the rot' as she called it setting in? Did she think that America would finally validate her in a way that it hadn't done to any other women artists since Peggy Lee, Dusty's much vaunted icon?

Dusty didn't want to play clubs and cabaret. Peggy did. Dusty wanted to play theatres. But she had no band. Peggy had her pick and from her own cultural back-yard of supreme musicians. Even in contemporary terms, Dusty wasn't a rock act in the seventies idiom like Elton was, like Cat Stevens, Rod Stewart and the other British writer/performers. Peggy of course wrote songs. Dusty didn't. Dusty was still working away in the only way she knew how. Selecting the songs, putting down the tracks, laying on the voice and then ... she refused what was on offer. No substitutes were forthcoming. Dusty kind of de-mobilised herself.

That she was living and having fun on her own terms for the first time in a long time in a location she had always dreamed of, driving the freeways in a pink Jensen was undeniable. That she was loving real loving and dreaming big dreams was obvious. That her vocal interpretations were in many ways benefiting from this ex-patriot life are for me to assert and others to argue. Our Dorothy had indeed settled in the Emerald City but, despite the tin gods, the straw polls and the neutered MGM lion, she found that the grass wasn't as bright green as the yellow bricks reflected. And, what's more, her Wiz turned out to be a new management she couldn't even get on the 'phone, let alone meet to dish over lunch. We all thought our Dust'd mis-read the road signs; her yellow brick road seemed to have turned into a cul-de-sac.

The first of two big holes appeared in her career from 1973, after CAMEO. Dusty seemed to stop fighting, she quit battling and dropped out, waiting, biding her time. The enforced inactivity drove her, as she has explained, crazy with frustration and sedentary sloth and thence into the clutches of some pretty heavy chemical substances, not to mention some confusing personal situations and personality warps. Ouch!

With Dusty not around so much, Mary O'Brien started demanding attention. Great, except that Mary was still a schoolgirl. Dusty had been too busy being Dusty for years to pay sufficient attention to Mary. Mary O'Brien began to appreciate just how much Dusty Springfield was not a thing of the broad back and thick skin but a thing of sound and fury and not a lot else. Dusty Springfield was, after all and as you will recall, Mary's invention. Mary ... Dusty ... Who the hell? As she has admitted since, 'Mother' found them both in deep trouble and in great need of help. Sadly, Mother's little helpers gave Mary and Dusty a rotten bashing.

Eventually, the determination of contractual difficulties allowed Dusty to re-materialise, re-establishing her working base in 1978 with a new manager in the person of Barry Krost ... But Barry's had never been a one horse stable.

And so it began again. All over again.

IT BEGINS AGAIN and LIVING WITHOUT YOUR LOVE were produced in Los Angeles by Roy Thomas Baker, (lately producer of QUEEN) and David Wolfert respectively and for once Dusty was credited as Production Associate. She'd cleaned herself up and she looked great, she sounded great. Hollywood had again worked its magic influence but this time directly, not via the anonymous, faraway silver screen. She sang songs which were part of contemporary West Coast experience. Many of them were written or co-written by women, at the forefront of a women's vanguard in music. Dusty had lived this life and had experienced the casualty rate at first hand.

Dusty showed that she was beginning to consummate her own artistic relationships, especially between herself and her art and craft. The three were visible in tandem. Her work appeared heartfelt, from *her* heart not from the pen of a writer her audience couldn't see or hear. This was *real* .

But the reality buckled under its own weight. Dusty's management relationships fell apart as did her relationships with her recording company and once again, the well dried up. She recorded WHITE HEAT for Casablanca Records in 1983, unreleased except in America.

After that, the politics ensured that the eighties, like Quentin Crisp's apartments, got dustier and dustier. To pile irony onto injury, Casablanca had been ultimately bought up only to rewrite history and place Dusty once again in the hands of Phonogram. Too much musical chairs, too much politics and far too much for a white girl. Dusty must have been bone-weary.

But unbeknownst to her, her reputation was growing in younger, curious and appreciative minds. It was alive and well. To her obvious delight, she had become a cult as she found herself metamorphosed yet again from pop singer passée to prototype pop diva.

A fabulous foray into club-land hype in 1985 led to an association with club owner Peter Stringfellow. Dusty however, was a record maker. Nightclubs *play* records, they don't make them but the venture restored Dusty to the public eye and, particularly, to the field of vision of Neil Tennant and Chris Lowe, collectively known as *Pet Shop Boys*.

Dring-dring. Dring-dring. Twenty four hours later, Dusty was back in London. She was being very cautious. She didn't come to stay, only to see.

The resulting duet with Chris and Neil, WHAT HAVE I DONE TO DESERVE THIS? gave Dusty yet another extension to her ladder. In 1989, a solo single, NOTHING HAS BEEN PROVED recorded for the film SCANDAL heralded an album co-operation which produced REPUTATION, only half of which was produced by the *Pet Shop Boys*. Dusty had her way with the other half in co-operation with Brian Spence, Dan Hartman and Rupert Hine with Andy Richards credited for REPUTATION. That's a real little pie for so many fingers. Hadn't she always wanted to do so much production herself? Or had she battled so hard for so long that she now longed that the onus for perfection be taken out of her hands? Was she willing to allow someone else to tell her how good she was and believe them? 'We just want you to sing,' she was told when she finally asked what she was supposed to do. Sing? Just sing? It was something she wasn't used to.

She is still blonde, still glamorous and is currently signed to SONY records. 1995 sees the release of an album she recorded in Nashville, country-flavoured and co-inciding with the happy announcement that she appears to have rebuffed the onslaught of breast cancer. She truly is a glamour blonde of worthy longevity.

Viva Dusty. Arriva! Arriva!

CHAPTER 17

Dolly Parton

Dolly Parton

My friend Colin Higgins who wrote and directed NINE TO
FIVE and BEST LITTLE WHOREHOUSE IN TEXAS told me that in all
the weeks of pre-production and shooting of both movies, he
never once saw Dolly Parton without *full* make-up and *full*
coiffure. Not once. Not even a glimpse. Not at five in the
morning nor at mid-night. Never.

The reality of Dolly Parton is as distant as our perception of
her is intimate. Our's is the wedding of the painted doll to the
little girls and boys who've loved her.

To be so public, yet so private takes some doing. It's something definitive that stars do. Joan Crawford did it. Her fans
waiting at the studio gate never saw what lay beneath the
Crawford maquillage. What they did see was absolutely real
but void of any reality. It was the truth, yet a lie. It's one of the
basic tenets of all relationships between stars and fans, deities
and believers. It can appear a massive contradiction.

In the same way that country life and country living engen-
der personalities equipped with gritty survivalist philoso-
phies, country music has, generically, spawned stars to match.
The glitter and rhinestones and sequins which are applied to
the basic homespun are just that ... mere decoration, for all to
see and for all to know. Dolly Parton is like the inside of a
tinker's van, the cornucopia of a rural travelling shop, a mag-
pie's hoard, a drag artist's wardrobe. She's geegaws and
playpretties and sugar and spice.

And Dolly Parton only works because although it's easy to

pick holes, to ask awkward questions, to point and giggle and titter and know that no one really believes for a moment, when looked at un-dissected, like the walk-down at the end of an otherwise tacky out-of-town pantomime, we find the Dolly Parton we behold perfectly credible and heartwarmingly affirmative. Dolly Parton, her records, her movies, her Dollywood theme park, her whole life and being is the most wonderful souvenir for the most hardened amongst us to take back to our particular reality and display, like a gaudy fairing, in pride of place on our mantels.

This, of course, is the middle-class view. The view across the bridge. But Dolly does not merely cross cultural boundaries, she straddles class ones too. Dolly has none of the urban trim which makes for the urbane. She has none of the city slick which makes for pose, vogue and attitude. Whether she is what she has made Dolly Parton appear is almost a matter of no concern. What matters is that we continue to buy what it is she's selling. We've been doing it for years.

I confess unashamedly an inordinate preference for country music and wish I knew more about it. I know I know nothing about opera and I don't care. I do care that I don't know more about country songs and singers. I know what I like and I like Dolly Parton.

She has just published an autobiography. It must have been reviewed a thousand times all over the world by those who have an opinion about Dolly and her work. Most of the critique I read was patronising and schoolboyish and missed the point entirely. Dolly's most thrustingly obvious prime pieces of property are her tits. She says so, don' care who knows so and, way to go, rightly so. So men like 'em, may even drool a little over 'em but most men have to answer to most women and most women wouldn't let their men drool over Dolly Parton's titties if'n they didn't let 'em.

Maybe that paragraph is a little on the country side but it hits my spot and it reminds me that Dolly, like all our blondes, is a star because women made her one and then allowed their men to like her too. It's like the difference between prostitutes and mistresses. The former are forgivable, 'cos Lord knows, there but for fortune ... The latter, however, are dangerous. To any woman, home wrecking's unforgivable in every walk of life.

Dolly's Nell Gwynn, roll-up, roll-up, heckle-me-if'n'y'dare vulgarity is seen as nothing more dangerous than plain speaking. To women it is never threatening but chummily reassuring. Dolly tells it like it is and says a lot of things that most folks think but usually never say. And what she says is couched in terms that ordinary folks have no problem with. It's the glory of country performance.

Dolly Parton is one long hen night. And she's loved all the more because the following day she'll give the same sassy, come-on cheek 'n' thigh to those same women's husbands and boyfriends, maybe a battalion of America's finest waiting, perhaps, to go off to war. Or a factory full of assembly workers. Or a construction site brimming with hard hats.

Though treason it might be to say both to Mr., Mrs. and Ms. American who might likely believe that no class system operates in the land of the free, Dolly Parton is all about class and yet has absolutely none. She doesn't seek the upper crust, has no need for it, wouldn't know what to do with it if she was covered in it because she is very, very rich and she is a big, big star. It's supposed to be what the *whole* of the American dream is about, not just what *some* Americans dream of.

But although Dolly's winning combination buys a lot of life-miles, it buys only so many. Take away the stardom and I fancy Miss Dolly would be in a bit of a pickle. Take away the money and she'd just spend the rest of her life earning it back for Dolly Parton is a business woman as much as she is an artist.

She was born on January 19th 1946 in a primitive cabin in the Smoky Mountains of Tennessee, the fourth child of Avie Lee and Robert Lee Parton. Avie Lee and Robert were married when they were fifteen and seventeen respectively. Avie Lee had had twelve children by the time she was thirty five. Dolly and her sisters once found her mother's diaphragm beneath her parents' bed. Sure must've bin dusty.

These Parton people were poor. Not food-stamps poor, not welfare poor. These people lived in unsupported poverty and not a little ignorance. They did, however, it seems, live in an awful lotta love 'though to Dolly's annoyance, they found it difficult to say so. She has, may it be so recorded, changed a lot of all that now.

It was a time way before political correctness, way before Doctor Spock filtered down through its middle-class apprenticeship. Robert Parton - we shall call him Daddy - was a sharecropper, farming a parcel of land, the produce of which he shared by paying part in kind to the landowner, Martha Williams. It is a land and a time so far away and yet I can reach out and touch it in my mind for I am the same age as Dolly Rebecca Parton. The comparison over time is as third world to our first.

Had Dolly been born fifteen years sooner and had she arrived, like Doris Day via the boondocks bandstands onto the Burbank back lot in the early fifties, the front office would have told the back office to invent another pedigree for our hillbilly mountain gal. A sanitised lie would have been put about and Dolly would have lived up to it. But when Dolly arrived in Hollywood, like Mae West, she was already a star.

When Dolly was gettin' started, however, the climate was so much more lenient than in Mae's day. It wasn't a sin to be or to have been poor. Admission was deemed good for the country's soul and 'sharing' was the stuff of the new rock 'n' roll America and its renewed egalitarianism. Elites were being breached like sandbags in a gathering flood. Without this trend for revelation, we would never have had Joan Rivers and Oprah and Doctor Ruth and teevee evangelism.

The Partons' lives hardly improved when Daddy paid $5000 for a farm of their own. Newspapers pasted to the wooden walls kept out the draughts. Breakfasts were biscuits (scone bread) and gravy. Discipline was rough and readily administered. Life was hand-me-down and make-and-mend. Store-bought was a luxury and there was nothing cute or admirable about home-made. You looked death in the face as it lay at wakes in rustic plank coffins and you were introduced to sex as animals rutted in front of your very eyes in the farmyard. Home-made? Might as well hang out a sign - *"Poor white trash"*.

Dolly claims such privation fostered creativity. Mebbe for *her* family but what about the other ten million children from the likes of all the other East Tennessees in the Union? Never saw no ten million other kids writing songs about patch-work coats that earned no million dollars!

But what the heck ... Whatever some Parton did, they did it right because Dolly grew up with an imagination brighter than a thousand palettes and an ear for sound and cadence that would rival any impressionist's eye for colour and light so maybe hunger does sharpen some senses? I think the Parton in question was Uncle Billy Owens but that'll all come later in the story.

The growing up was accomplished in a close gaggle of girlfriends, Dolly's closest being Judy Ogle. They met when they were seven and they are still friends forty years later. The prurient and the pusillanimous are desperate for these two women to be lesbian lovers. I don't think they are and if they are who's to give a heck? Any loving friendship, whether sexually based or not, that survives forty years is an institution to be celebrated and praised not a social mugging to be censured and derided. People who make mucky observations, much like the petardiers, usually find themselves well and truly hoist for they display their ignorance about non-middle class female relationships.

Most working class women are closer to their women folk than ever they are to a man. Other than fathers or brothers, husbands or sons most working class women are unused to the friendship of men and to have such a relationship would be virtually taboo. The sexes everywhere invariably know little about each other but working women, whether urban or country ones, only ever really know a man in terms of his family role. Tammy Wynette, after all, refers to the male in her famous song as *"... just a man."*

Dolly and Judy call each other Sis or Sissy, exploding another sentimental myth about brothers and sisters being naturally close because of blood ties. Though it occasionally changes in later life, I've found that the only blood that kicks in during childhood and adolescence between most siblings is that drawn and shed in anger and deadly rivalry for space and attention. The girlfriends and boyfriends with whom I explored the really important things of life like sex and truancy and stealing apples and chocolate bars were never my family. So, I'm toasting Jude 'n' Dolly. You're more than lucky, ladies. You're blessed.

But the ceremonies of childhood soon commute into the deadly serious rites of passage involved in becoming either a man or a woman. In a house jam-full of people, privacy is an unheard of luxury. Spits and spats tone up the tongues of adolescents seeking identity when confronted in a small house with twelve others vying for the space to be themselves. Dolly and her sisters obviously gave as good as they got from the boys and by the time she was a precocious twelve, I have this picture that Dolly was already imbued with the spirit of Mae West in a Jane Doe body.

And however well-intentioned, Robert Lee's and Avie's discipline took its tumble. Forbidden cosmetics, Dolly was drawn like a magnet to this unobtainable commodity, made instantly more desirable. Plant juices were smeared over lips and eyes, burnt matches and corks supplied eyeliner and a little added spit furnished mascara. However dangerous, peroxide was employed from an early age to heighten, in this case, what nature had intended but hadn't entirely pulled off. Flour went for face powder and in the absence of reddener, Dolly employed what she calls in her autobiography, 'the rouge of pain'. She pinched her cheeks like a flagellant before the altar of pulchritude. Even her expressions sound like song titles or punch lines in a middle eight hook.

She admits to always having an ear for music. Certainly singing was endemic both in her own home and in church where she and her sisters were always giving voice. Tin cans, pots and pans, old mandolins and guitars were all recruited into the ensemble. And all around them, other people were singing and playing too, not for gain but as an antidote to the pain of living outside the pale of civilised America. Sawdust, a dirty, ill-clad old man who lived in a chippings-strewn shack in abject poverty and yet who played the banjo like an angel on a cloud sang with Dolly each day she passed by to school. That Sawdust had travelled, had been out of Tennessee and across oceans to fight, to possibly be killed ... Who knows the sights he had seen, the death, carnage and destruction he had witnessed to have caused him to abandon all the niceties of life except the joy of making music.

Dolly says that Sawdust taught her that it was okay to be different. That it was alright to be able to proudly advertise your priorities. And Dolly does. She's a veritable neon marquee. Her priorities are God, Love and Sex and not, she tells us, necessarily in that order.

Her hormones are so healthy she should bottle them. Perhaps she will. Her avowed atavistic affinity between her sexuality and the countryside, the elements and the primal open air will I fear be lost on many city folk who have either never experienced or never indulged in those wonderfully liberating and ultimately erotic acts of rolling naked in new grass, or lying naked between the curling roots in the hollow from where an uprooted birch or beech has been wrenched by a gale force storm. Set against the rages and the calm of Mother Nature, Dolly observed the equal extremes of the behaviour of men and women. Country music has as much black hate and pure white love as Mother Nature has ever engendered crackling storm clouds and soft, refreshing rain.

She was effectively taught guitar by both her Uncle Louis

and Uncle Bill Owens although it was the said Uncle Billy, a songwriter and performer on his own account, who must have noticed a quality in Dolly's singing and the admitted way in which she pushed herself to the fore of her sisters' singing groups.

Uncle Billy Owens single-handedly fostered and nurtured Dolly's career. It was he who introduced her to Tennessee sponsor Cas Walker, a multi-millionaire grocer who took spots on radio and TV stations to advertise and promote his grocery chain. Dolly was eleven when she started singing on those shows which were broadcast out of close-by Knoxville where Uncle Bill would faithfully drive his protegee whatever the weather. Radio, in this case WIVK, was a firmly established medium, rather more than television and in 1956 was ready and waiting to play its part in the fanning of the flames of the new music. The local teevee station in Sevierville, Sevier County only had eight hours of daily programming. Remember. It was only 1956, now. The year Elvis first made it big.

It was Uncle Billy who also, with her Uncle John Henry, arranged for the twelve year old Dolly, chaperoned by her grandmother, to take the bus from Sevierville the hundreds of miles to Lake Charles, Louisiana where Henry had fixed up for Dolly to record for Ed Schuler's GoldBand records. The 'A' side they cut was PUPPY LOVE, co-written by Bill and Dolly. It got a lot of air play but very little real pay. But it was the first step, as was Johnny Schuler, son of the GoldBand owner, who kissed her a lot as they lay studying biology beneath the tall oaks, hidden by veils of festooned Spanish Moss.

For the next months, until she was thirteen Dolly continued with her radio and teevee work in Knoxville, earning something like $20 a week. Uncle Bill continued his managerial efforts on her behalf and they carried on writing together.

Bill Owens knew that it was the walls of Nashville's citadel which had to be breached one day if he and Dolly were ever to make headway and so off they went, taking trumpets to Jericho, when Dolly was thirteen.

Here, a word about Nashville. It now, of course, potentially rivals Los Angeles and New York in significance as a seat of power and as a town has changed a great deal in thirty years. But it's still a town where God is the staple industry. It is the centre of religious publishing in America and there's a great deal of money in religion. In Nashville's banks and savings-and-loans and social centres, God is spoken of in very personal terms. God is like the invisible friends many of us had as children. He's (for God is certainly not a she or, forbid, sexless) talkable to and is asked more things than there are ever answers. He usually says no but is still asked in case, like the lottery, a prayer is granted. I am being neither glib not flip, not even middle-class. God is a fact in Nashville. The fact that AIDS is currently a fact in Nashville puts some of the followers of God on the spot for love is something that only ever applies to the righteous and is something only god-fearin' folks can properly do ... Previous generations of country music stars have been a little short on the tolerant and more catholic Christian values but if they hadn't been, they wouldn't have had an audience. Today's artists are widening Nashville's horizons. God works not only mysteriously, but often very very slowly.

For Dolly in 1964, caught in Nashville's jungle landscape of artistic selection, although help was available in the shape of Carl and Pearl Butler who had befriended Dolly in Knoxville, it wasn't until Jimmy Newman offered Dolly his spot on The Grand Ole Opry that she took any positive steps.

Her appearance on the famed WSM-networked Opry show sure set Dolly ablaze but any expectations she and Billy may have had about the spread of the conflagration were decidedly contained. The next year saw the pair travelling the road-houses and country auditoria of the southern states in Billy's old brown Ford, sleeping in the car and generally paying dues. It's an essential exercise to make a lasting bed. Basically, the philosophy works like this: Too little paid in, not enough to take out. Like a pension scheme, really.

The career saw yet another false start with Buddy Killen and Tree Publishing whom Dolly and Billy browbeat into granting an audition by refusing to budge from his office. The result was a short-lived arrangement with Mercury for whom she recorded several tracks produced by Jerry Crutchfield. IT MAY NOT KILL ME (But it's sure gonna hurt) was the 'A' side and I WASTED MY TEARS, the 'B'. Though played to death by WIVK and on the Sevierville station, IT MAY NOT KILL ME didn't kill, it died, instead, a death un-sustained by airplay any place else.

And of course, there were four more years of school to get through. Dolly and Billy had to play troubadour to fit in to an extent with Dolly's schooling and these last years until graduation must have passed very slowly for Dolly who blazed her light of ambition like a beacon. She was certainly growing up differently. Her approach to dress and appearance was already coming definitely from the trash corner of the fashion ring and it had its repercussions in that many of her peers and their relatives regarded her as a whore. A story about her being gang-raped did the rounds and her facing up squarely to the untruth and challenging those who thought it true ensured her graduation early from that academy where thick skins are acquired.

She graduated from high school the year after Kennedy was shot. Each event affected her deeply but she declared her ambition to be stage-struck and with her newly applied 'big hair' she set off once again on the bus for Nashville.

She met Carl Dean, the man she was to marry, almost as soon as she arrived. He picked her up off the street but was a perfect gentleman for an awful lot longer than she obviously thought necessary. Handsome, tall, undeniably attractive, Carl Dean was and is a man of few words and none of those in public. He was generally undemonstrative - "... 'cept in those special ways when he'll pick me a bunch of wild-flowers" - but solid and dependable; they had a good long courtship before they married. Shit, seems she might as well have married his horse. But in a country where a woman's a woman and a man's a man ...

If'n I was being honest, here ... Well, hell ... I am. Dolly's marriage is one which I feel millions would like. Most of the time, Carl does his thing and Dolly does hers often quite intimately, with other people, but not for long and never forever and I'm sure if a white lie here and a white lie there has been told or a little economy with the truth indulged in, so much the better. The twentieth century has, at its end, irrevocably acknowledged that monogamous marriage is not for human beings as a species. It's only for certain others in the animal kingdom. That marriage in general is for humans is for sure but not marriage immutable, not in terms of his and hers but theirs. Men and women are not gods and neither are they God. What Dolly and Carl do is no one else's business but their own and that goes double for the rest of us. But until there are more Carl Deans in the world, new men but their own men, all my ranting'll come to nothing.

Their marriage must have been special because it was solemnised in Ringgold on the thirtieth of May 1966 and flew in the face of Fred Foster who finally signed Dolly and Uncle Bill to a deal with his Combine Publishing and Monument records and who had forbidden Dolly to make such a dumb career move.

Fred Foster took over from Uncle Billy booking Dolly on American Bandstand and booking her into a juke box convention in Chicago. Foster was ignorant of Dolly's marriage for twelve months. The stable and long-lived foundation of her marriage to Carl has proved the most solid platform on which Dolly could have ever sung. Theirs was the monument, not Fred Foster's.

But she sang PUT IT OFF UNTIL TOMORROW with Bill Phillips for Monument and it was a hit on the country charts as well as the follow-up DUMB BLONDE. PUT IT OFF became the BMI song of the year in 1966. From this point, Dolly's career took off. For better or worse, she worked for seven years with Porter Wagoner on his syndicated television show after his original girl singer Norma Jean Beasler moved on. Dolly was twenty years old and she was being paid $60,000 a year. It was a huge amount of money for which she had to eat a lot of humble pie but the diet can't have been that unpalatable because she stayed two years longer than her original five year contract stipulated. Dolly acknowledges that although she already knew how to sing, Wagoner taught her how to perform. Working on the commercials that accompanied the show also must have taught her about timing, spontaneity and the huge business network which underpins the whole creeping institution of American television and radio. Dolly wanted her own show and she wanted what Mae, Marlene and Madonna all enjoyed ... control. A lot of men, including Wagoner, would have preferred her to remain in her second string position as a woman ...

Dolly inevitably moved from Monument to RCA and the seventies saw her life's fund of living being inexhaustibly but sensitively exploited to furnish songs like JOSHUA and OLD TIME PREACHER MAN. Moving on always implies someone else standing still. Being left behind, maybe. Fred Foster and Uncle Bill in their turn were supplanted by the influence of Porter Wagoner and then RCA made Wagoner step aside. RCA New York weren't just signing a country artist. They were signing someone they knew they were going to make money on. Dolly knew that too and was prepared to go full along with their intention. To do that, she knew had to make 'the crossover'.

Not another godly allusion to the River Jordan, 'cross over' needs a word.

As much as the stand-off between the respective fans of the opera and the theatre musical, there was a traditional rift - in the purely topographical sense, of course - between country and mainstream pop. There are always divides and human divides usually occur because of sex or money. Power. In the sixties, the musical divide was money based. Dolly's hit song JOLENE, number one on the country charts, sold in the region of sixty thousand copies. A number one or even a number twenty in the pop charts sold millions. Country sold less because country's appeal had been traditionally patronised as redneck, unsophisticated and 'poor'. But America was once again in the melting pot. It was re-inventing itself out of dire necessity. Old industries (including agriculture) and traditional demarcations were being toppled everywhere in the mid-sixties. Racial prejudice was being fought, gay and female liberation were buzz causes. Anyone could be unemployed, not just poor people. Teevee was supplanting communal activities like going to the movies.

The time was ripe for a musical crossover as well, for country to become cosmopolitan despite those who fought bitterly and trenchantly against it in Nashville.

But this crossover at the many bridging points still had to be managed. In the music business, management by the early seventies had also become a buzz word and Dolly duly arrived at Sandy Gallin's door. Sandy Gallin's world was coming out of the closet as fast as country music. Whilst so many celebrated manager/client relationships have floundered or fallen by the wayside through lack of trust or loss of love, the empathy between Dolly and Sandy has stood the test of time. Sandy Gallin persuaded her much against her inclination to accept the Weill/Mann composition HERE YOU COME AGAIN instead of one of her own.

It happened for her. HERE YOU COME AGAIN was a hit in the national pop charts. Dolly had made it. She finally had something to be in control of. The circumstances also go a long way to prove that, unlike the customer, the artist is not always right.

Dolly was one of the first of a new generation of country music realists who, whilst sticking to the principle of being artists of the people, no longer depended on playing at state and county fairs or hillbillying at hoedowns to sell records. She helped pave the way for the current generation of women in Country music such as Kathy Mettea, Suzy Boguss, Pam Tillis, Mary Chapin Carpenter and Martina MacBride. These and many other woman have had a huge influence on country music, making it the biggest grossing section of the US recording industry today. Though I feel a new divide has been created, this time based on sex, I do believe and shoot me down y'all, that women have adopted country and have shooed their men to metal. We shall see.

Dolly's 'crossover' was cemented by her finally having her own teevee show, networked out of Nashville and called, unsurprisingly, DOLLY! She has always done well on television, especially chat shows such as Johnny Carson's TONIGHT show, David Letterman's programme and even, famously, once winning over the gritty Barbara Walters.

Helped by Gregg Perry, Mike Post and other producer/ arrangers, Dolly swept through the remaining years of the 1970's before she arrived in Hollywood in 1981 for the movie NINE TO FIVE. The film was not only good for Dolly's career but also for her sister Rachel's who played the character Dolly created in the subsequent television series. It was good for a lot of other people too. It helped soften Jane Fonda's image and reconfirmed Lily Tomlin's mass appeal. My friend Colin Higgins also told me that he believed he was the first director to benefit from the music copyrights spawned by his film. Dolly's composition NINE TO FIVE was most likely a bigger hit than the film with the Mike Post produced accompanying album.

Dolly's subsequent work on BEST LITTLE WHOREHOUSE IN TEXAS was not happy for her and in her autobiography she apologises for what she sees as the hurt she caused some people. My belief is that a lot of hurt was caused by a lot of people on that movie. Illness and exhaustion played havoc with her own health and she once again had recourse to a god-based self-renewal programme. Unlike the work produced by an individual writer/recording artist/performer, movies are art made by committee. The process can be frustrating and confrontational and Dolly also had to cope with not being an actress. If she was to be cast, it would only ever be to type, 'cos wherever she went that wig, all that slap and both those damn tits were contracted to come too. Like it or not, the image of

Dolly Parton is already frozen in time. She's gonna be Dolly Parton 'til she dies.

But although Dolly learned stuff, she must, like Bette Midler have sussed that singers making movies were finding it tougher than Doris Day ever did.

But then Doris usually did what she was supposed to. What she was told.

Dolly's co-operation with Sylvester Stallone on RHINESTONE didn't produce a hit. Her screen career sagged until STEEL MAGNOLIAS quite sometime later and another teevee show didn't serve her as well as she would have liked.

Her music making, however, has continued unabated. Wonderful co-operations with Tammy Wynette and Loretta Lynn and then with Emmy Lou Harris and Linda Ronstadt, HONKY TONK ANGELS and TRIO respectively confirm her position in the pantheon of country music. Her entrepreneurial spirit has been confirmed both by the creation of her theme park DOLLYWOOD which celebrates the 'country' life and her recent founding of Blue Eye Records whose first release was an acoustic set of Old Country and Smoky Country tracks produced by Steve Buckingham.

Whether, like Cat Stevens, she will prove to be another music star running up to an apotheosis is to be seen. If she does, it will be when she too is 'written out', fresh out of new songs and feeling unable to compete with or contribute to the current entertainment scene she helped to create. I can only conclude that from what she proclaims now she will never become judgemental as a prospective religieuse. From what she writes and from what I sense, I don't think Dolly Parton would ever risk alienating the love of anyone.

CHAPTER 18

Madonna

Madonna

Madonna is as famous for her utterances as Mae West and so here's a conceit for you, prompted by my reading the following words that the lady herself *m'a donné.*

"Power is a great aphrodisiac and I'm a very powerful person."

Mention of aphrodisiacs conjures up Aphrodite, the great goddess whom the Ancient Greeks saw as the Goddess of Life. She had many names - Athene, Artemis amongst them and being the mistress of life could never be conceived of in too powerful terms. Aphrodite, because she governed life was also the goddess of death and the Ancient Greeks imagined her retinue to embrace an army of women. Despite other peoples seeing the demons of death in female form, the Greeks saw in women only the human being, not the gender. When their bards and poets wrote therefore about the battles of life, the myth-makers dared the impossible and united masculine strength with feminine charm and improved on nature itself. The Amazons, that celebrated race of warrior women, were therefore eulogised by the Greeks who saw these women as sharing equally with men in the heroic tragedies of life in the full face of the limits set by the gods themselves.

"It's a great feeling to be powerful. I've been striving for it all my life. I think that's just the quest of every human being: power."

Phew! Heavy.

But then she is. However much I admire Madonna, I really would get scared knowing that I had to *know* her. Her friendship would be a fizzing, fused bomb which I feel I would be tempted to throw, cartoon-style, to anyone else whom I thought could catch it. Madonna Ciccone was, is and always will be a heavy trip.

"I am ambitious but if I weren't as talented as I am ambitious, I would be a gross monstrosity."

These lines ... They really could have been said by Mae West.

Madonna's father, Silvio, known as Tony, was the youngest of the six children of an immigrant Italian peasant couple hailing from Pacentro in Abruzzi, southern Italy. They settled near Pittsburgh and never really learned English. Tony worked his way through college and after serving in the Air Force in Alaska, settled in Detroit where, in 1955, after a whirlwind courtship in which he eschewed his engagement to another, the zealously Catholic Tony married Madonna Louise Fortin who was of French Canadian stock.

They had two sons, Anthony and Martin, before the birth of their first daughter. Yes, *her* . Sixteenth of August, 1958. The little girl was named for her mother, Madonna and known as little Nonni. 1959, 1960 and 1962 saw the arrival of Paula, Christopher and finally Melanie.

Momma Madonna worked as hard as Poppa Tony, in her case as an X-Ray technician which may or may not have contributed to her developing breast cancer whilst she was pregnant with her youngest child Melanie. The family lived in Pontiac, some twenty five miles north west of Detroit. Poppa Tony, perhaps somewhat over-zealously, had his children reveille at six in the morning to do an hour on their knees in church before going on to school.

The neighbourhood was nice, it was good and god-fearin' and the bossy demanding little girl named for her momma who shared a room with her two sisters, was totally unprepared for the tragedy that was to befall them.

I'd like to bet matchsticks that the children were never told what was wrong with momma. It's usually the way and such a wrong and cruel way but in the early nineteen sixties that was the perceived wisdom. That momma Madonna was ill was obvious to anyone but a child. She grew weak, exhausted and when urged to play and couldn't, would often cry. Madonna is said to have remembered comforting her mother who was simply unable to join in the children's games. At the tender age of four, Madonna avers that whilst holding her mother she remembers feeling very, very strong whilst knowing her mother was very, very weak.

Momma Madonna spent almost the last year of her life in hospital and died in December 1963. Had she lived, I probably wouldn't have been writing this but then the dance of death frequently creates unholy partners.

And who wouldn't have become obsessed by death, by dying and all the wild scenarios that a child's boundlessly fertile imagination creates to terrify them at bedtime? Who wouldn't at four or five years of age have become obsessively involved with keeping hold of the love of the only parent you had left, a man, your father? Who wouldn't have gotten a little confused as the priests wittered on about God the Father? Who wouldn't have flirted and shimmied and squirmed all over anyone, especially your very own daddy, to get and keep the attention which only your mother had previously bestowed?

But then ... There's always another hand. On this other hand, Tony Ciccone had to work; he had *six* children to deal with in the emotional fair-shares stakes. In most situations of temporary caring, the carer won't be able to last more than a couple of months. Any longer and the tension and stress caused by dealing with emotional and physical needs of people who have nothing to do with you in blood or in love can cause some pretty ugly scenes. Thus the series of temporary housekeepers whom Tony engaged was finally terminated when he married the latest of them, blonde, fit Joan Gustafson.

The reaction from the children was predicatable, especially from a little girl who desperately sought her mother. 'Dead' and 'heaven' are highly sophisticated concepts to a four year old child. The family moved to Rochester, Michigan to an open, friendly, middle class neighbourhood where two other Ciccones arrived, Madonna's half-sister Jennifer and her half-brother Mario. There were now *eight* kids. Perhaps if they had been a little less antagonistic to their step-mother, Tony would have been less of a disciplinarian but they weren't and he wasn't. They were not allowed teevee nor was idle time condoned.

Madonna's was a childhood of 'got to', 'should' and 'must'. Domestic discipline was bolstered by the nuns at St. Andrews where the Ciccones were educated. It seems to have been standard Catholic fare. Little mouths were washed out with soap for foulness - all that kinda stuff. And yet, Madonna at age nine and ten, still desperately seeking love, became obsessed with becoming a nun. She idolised the very women who often inflicted punishments on her and her classmates. God oversaw her every waking childhood moment both at home and at school and to a ten year old, God must have seemed a very unforgiving, stern and unrelenting shadow, a long way from the God of Love. Loving God was fearing God and the young Madonna had a lot of fear to cope with. She had a 140+ IQ and an imagination to match. She was still haunted by fears of cancer - again a very sophisticated concept for a little girl to deal with - and of dreams in which she was murdered by a brutal and faceless man.

Her waking hours were surely full. Initial piano lessons had given way to childhood dance lessons. At West Junior High and later at the well-to-do, lushly appointed Rochester Adams High School, she was actively participant in school sporting and drama activities.

She admits her teenage years were real angry. Her mother's family, the Fortins, where she spent a summer, were free and easy and loose. Her uncles had a rock band and she was able to practise being a teenager without the constant censure of home and school. Coming back to Rochester must have been a bummer.

At fourteen, something happened which would change her life. We probably all need only *one* thing back to which we can trace our lives other than our parents and family. It's usually a person. Madonna's was Christopher Flynn in whose dancing school she enrolled. He saw potential in her. He lit a fire under her and Madonna started cooking. He saw curiosity, he saw daring, he saw rebellion, he saw sex and he saw enormous talent. And he was the first man to tell her she was beautiful.

Thank God he was gay. They might have married and been *really* unhappy although at least Flynn might still have been alive. As well as introducing her to the plastic arts, museums and galleries, Madonna experienced with Flynn the gay discos he frequented. Madonna took to that just post-gay liberation dance-and-trance culture more often drug-enhanced although she herself never was - like the ugly duckling took to becoming a swan.

Madonna was into that gay scene, not like, but with Flynn. To begin to understand the effect that this social life had on her is to begin to understand the whys and wherefores of Madonna vis a vis other women. In her little pond, she became a big fish. People looked at her. She was a happening, volcanically ener-gised dancer. She danced with guys whose friends and lovers got jealous and argued over her, she danced with guys who treated her as just matter-of-fact, she danced with really at-tractive, raunchy guys who'd pick each other up, go out back and have sex and be back on the dance floor whilst buttoning the flies of their 501's.

Madonna learned that sex wasn't *that* special not in *that* way. It didn't have to be courted like virgins would. She learned it could be enjoyed and had fun with rather than worried about and then endured. She learned the freedom that gay men seem to have had which their straight counterparts don't have - gay boys get to check out what they're being offered and have a chance to say 'no' without wasting time. She learned that passive doesn't mean punchbag.

Most of all she learned that sex was the kick start which fired the human race and she realised that sex was a passport ... She was kinda one of the boys.

Straight 'A' graduate, she enrolled in the University of

Michigan's School of Music at Ann Arbor, Iggy Pop's old stomping ground. She beatnikked-out on the poetry of Sylvia Plath and Ann Sexton and punked-out in her clothes and got close for a moment to drummer Steve Bray. Christopher Flynn had moved to Ann Arbor with her but Flynn realised the town wasn't big enough for Madonna and encouraged her to move to New York. She didn't graduate and although her father objected strongly to her dropping out, I have a feeling that they didn't exactly hang out a sign, 'Madonna - Phone home'.

Her one way ticket dated July 1978 flew her to New York's La Guardia airport and she arrived in Times Square with less than twenty dollars in her pocket. Her part time jobs took second place to the dance classes she took with members of the Alvin Ailey company before she joined the Pearl Lang Dance Company in November.

She danced but it was pure dancing ... Madonna needed more. It was as though she was acknowledging the call of the very origins of modern ballet which had been developed in Europe as the light relief, an audience eye-pleaser in the middle of an opera performance. Dance to Madonna was *part* of something else. Madonna wanted to *be* that something else. She wanted not only to dance, but to sing and to act ...

She now realised that she needed to *be* the whole creation.

To keep the wolves from the doors of the various unwholesome squats and less than salubrious tempaccoms she inhabited and which so upset her father when he came to visit, Madonna got into nude modelling. $100 a day for that was better than $50 for eight hours waiting tables. She posed for painters and also for photographers such as Bill Stone and Martin Schrieber and she posed as Madonna. Solo. Somewhere, she'd dropped the Ciccone. The photographs would later both haunt and enhance her reputation and her career.

She was lonely too even though she was all-but a resident at the many Manhattan discos which thudded and strobed their way from late 'til dawn. Such a transient night life makes for many a passing ship. You meet, you greet, maybe you eat and then usually, that's eet! Madonna was luckier than most although her now immutable growing-up had left her way outside the pale.

Whilst literally scavenging for food, Madonna also scavenged for people and whilst doing that, she attracted some really interesting ones. Musicians, actors, deejays and dancers, street and spray-can artists like Futura 2000, Keith Haring and the young Jean Michel Basquiat BW. Before Warhol. These her ship passed in the night as it passed all the denizens of midnight Manhattan.

Through T-Shirt artist Norris Burroughs she is supposed to have met Dan Gilroy, a musician with whom she took up and who she just as quickly dropped when she got the break that *most* material girls would have only dreamed of.

Madonna arrived for backing singer/dancer auditions being held by Jean van Lieu and Jean Claude Pellerin, the French producers of Patrick Hernandez' worldwide hit BORN TO BE ALIVE. She impressed them and they offered her fame, fortune and France. She arrived in Paris in May 1979, took everything that was afforded her - clothes, limousines and a fairly crazed night life - and by August was nowhere near being a star. She had the trappings but no substance. She didn't much like France or, it seems, the French and when pneumonia curtailed her clubbing and her libido, she found it easy to turn her back on the Eurotrash she had met and limped home to Dan Gilroy and his brother in Queens.

She appeared in A CERTAIN SACRIFICE for director/writer Stephen Jan Lewicki for a fee of $100 - the entire budget he had for actors. It was another piece of work which would return to haunt her although its implications were un-apparent as she and the Gilroy brothers formed their first band, THE BREAKFAST CLUB. Madonna drummed and Angie Smit sang. Out front. Drummers have to get used to looking folks in the ass. It wasn't Madonna's style and engineering the removal of Ms. Smit from the band and assuming her stance at the mike was, six years on from the last big moment, Madonna's *really* big moment.

The Gilroys saw her singing as well as moving and they also saw her flexing her acumen. The acumen is the muscle most people don't have. Madonna, they say, has one of the biggest around. Way bigger than Schwarzenegger's or Sly's. Madonna, aged twenty and on her own, displayed an acumen that only one showbiz woman had hitherto rivalled. Mae West. Madonna gave great 'phone and she hustled clubowners and bookers like the whole of the William Morris.

Her ability to move quickly and alone, like a cat, enabled her to leave the Gilroys and their band and she moved from Queens into Manhattan. She started a new band The Millionaires, commuted to Modern Dance and later changed to EMANON, the reverse spelling of NONAME. As Emmy, one of many nicknames by which she was successively known, Madonna fronted a $25 a night act and was miles from nowhere unlike the women she admired, Chrissie Hynde and Pat Benatar and Deborah Harry. She desperately wanted to call her band MADONNA.

A blast from the past in the form of Steve Bray from her Ann Arbor days arrived and, with nowhere else to live, they managed to squat for months in The Music Building on 8th Avenue in mid-town Manhattan. A sort of latterday Brill building where Carole King, Neil Sedaka and the other major writers from the thirties to the sixties had written the songs that changed the face of pop music, the Music Building's floors housed production, publishing and management companies one of which was Adam Alter's and Camille Barbone's Gotham Productions.

Madonna hustled, first Adam and then Camille who saw EMANON at the venue called Kansas City. It should have been another turning point as the women were much attracted to each other, physically and emotionally. They shared a birthdate, the sixteenth of August, the day in 1977 when Elvis died, a moment which Madonna later claimed (seriously?) to have been when his soul passed into her body. Being seven years older, Camille Barbone displayed the sort of indulgent, mother-figure characteristics Madonna has often sought in female friends. The wilful, wily Madonna has always loved to be babied.

In return for fifteen percent of zilch, Camille offered to manage Madonna, put her on salary, found her a place to live and introduced her to a new band. Madonna's foot-stamping, gimme-gimme tactics were swiftly in evidence. She insisted Camille sack Bob Riley, the band's drummer and substitute Steve Bray. Though Madonna was never greedy, never extravagant, never took drugs, Camille was nevertheless embroiled in a spiral of excess fuelled by Madonna's ceaseless, exhausting, restless outrageousness. No sooner had Barbone entrusted the feeding and walking of her two poodles to Madonna than Madonna spray-painted the dogs SEX and FUCK. Mindless it might appear but think of seeing them on Fifth Avenue! Entirely newsworthy. You wouldn't forget it, would you?

The spiral of excess turned into a vortex of waste. Barbone and Alter's Gotham Productions were financially wiped out and after the band had finally recorded four tracks at Media Sound Studios, the unpaid band split up. The tape was Madonna's stepping stone and Barbone's millstone. Its triple ownership has never been sorted out to anyone's financial advantage. It has remained un-released and Barbone's investment has therefore remained, even recently, un-recouped.

At one point, nine record companies were interested in signing Madonna having been played the tape. Barbone and Alter succeeded in signing *no* contracts. There must lie a tale. A cat with nine lives? It takes real talent or sublime ill-luck or a major implosion of trust to bypass a break like that. Twice Madonna seemed to have avoided joining the music biz proper.

She continued to dance her way through New York nights in Danceteria, Paradise Garage, The Continental and The Pyramid. Her new best friend who saved her from her garbage can existence was Erica 'Rica' Bell, a graduate, moneyed girl who owned The Lucky Strike Club. Where Madonna danced, people congregated and they looked. She admitted to Rica and her other new best friend Martin Burgoyne, Rica's barman who was to outlast all other friends until his sorry death from AIDS, that she, Madonna was desperately seeking fame.

People looked but when in 1982 the brunette Madonna bleached her hair blonde one wild weekend with her current lover Joe Jones, the world sat up and took notice.

One of those who noticed was Mark Kamins, the deejay at Danceteria. They met, they bonked and the rest is really history. He played her tape at the club and the crowd loved it especially when *"Who's that girl?"* turned out to be *that* girl, that *fabulous* dancer! Bleached blondes sure did seem to have more fun, didn't they Debbie?

Or did they? Debbie Harry must have been Madonna's major inspiration and was yet another career - writer/performer/solo-artist-to-be - kissed kindly by peroxide. A career perhaps overcome by peroxide? Five or six years earlier, Debbie Harry had ploughed (professionally of course) the same furrow as Madonna. She was, I contend, more beautiful, more shocking because of her cool elegance and, therefore, entirely more glamorous. She too launched herself and her band Blondie on the New York dance scene, at the club CBGB's. Debbie Harry took full advantage of the cheap trashy image which so many identified with her blonde up-front persona and which fitted so excellently into the punk image which she purveyed. DEF, DUMB AND BLONDE and ONCE MORE INTO THE BLEACH have never really rebuilt her Punk Blondeness as a solo artist back to the heights she quit when Blondie's career self-determined.

When it came to the crunch, there was no doubting where the beef was ... Madonna quite simply lacked Debbie's delicacy. And her true devotion to friends.

But Debbie Harry was certainly up front. Madonna, of course, went one step further. Madonna was in your face and if necessary I'm sure she'd have sat on Mark Kamins' who, experiencing the Madonna charm blitzkrieg, of course wanted to produce her. He took her tape first to Chris Blackwell at Island Records. He turned it down but Chris is as famous for his no as he is for his yes. He also turned down Boy George but found Cat Stevens and Bob Marley. Hey nonny, no!.

Then Kamins went to the Warners office where he saw Michael Rosenblatt, the A and R man at Seymour Stein's Sire records. Sire weren't afraid of pre- or post-punk, having successfully marketed the Ramones amongst others. Rosenblatt flipped, Stein agreed and, third time lucky, Madonna done deals were at last successfully brokered.

She'd made it. Now she had to make it.

That she was standing on a hill of broken hearts and promises seemed un-troublesome. It might just as well have been a hill of beans. Other people may have made Madonna but once made, she also made sure she threw away the mould.

Steve Bray, natch, was elbowed in favour of Kamins and two tracks, AIN'T NO BIG DEAL and EVERYBODY were given a big, *big* promotion budget based on photo-images of the blonde Madonna who crafted a high energy dance show involving her best friend Martin Burgoyne and two other dancers which galvanised the ravers on the club circuit in early 1985.

When Madonna returned to Manhattan for the video shoot for EVERYBODY she did so as a brunette. Rosenblatt and Sire freaked and Madonna went back to blonde. It really was a *BIG* promotion budget. Ed Steinberg produced the $1500 promo video which topped the dance charts and crossed over.

Seymour Stein ordered a twelve-inch mini-Album to be made to further test the waters and ensure EVERYBODY hadn't been a fluke. It was Kamins' turn to fall (or was he pushed?) by the wayside and it was Reggie Lucas who produced PHYSICAL ATTRACTION, a track he wrote in direct response to seeing Madonna move which she did in her mysterious way her wonders to perform. PHYSICAL ATTRACTION too topped the dance charts.

Madonna's night-living continued, unabated. Her boredom quotient was on maximum. Like the gay boys were all doing then before they knew what the strange new 'gay cancer' was all about, no sooner had Madonna had someone than she tired of them. There were lots more where the last one had come from. Her fantasies were made words and the words she made flesh. Her celebrity allowed her to 'score' lovers even more easily and people seemed to want not only to be seen with her but to allow themselves to become her scalps.

Like Mae, Madonna knew the value of shock.

She met and engaged Maripol, a publicist who not only ensured that Madonna was *only* seen with the *right* people but fulfilled the role left vacant by Camille Barbone as surrogate parent. Madonna didn't need encouragement in the desperate search for publicity. She was a great manipulator and the press duly fell prey. She would lie, make things up, invent stuff and merely shrug or laugh if ever challenged or found out. She made herself famous. She worked hard at it and she deserved what she got and for a change, what she got was what she wanted. Exactly. She became the symbol of everyone's dreams of a good time.

Madonna *was* the club scene of New York in 1983. It was how her career had been borne, branded and brokered and now video validated her permit to perform.

Madonna's new longer-lived love affair with John 'Jellybean' Benitez, also produced his song HOLIDAY which replaced the iffy AIN'T BO BIG DEAL as the putative hit single from her first album MADONNA. Benitez, apart from being her sexual type - light-skinned Latino who muscled on the edge of dangerous - also understood the club, street and music scenes from the inside out being, amongst other things, the mix-master at Danceteria's big rival club, The Fun House.

No fewer than three singles from MADONNA had gone top ten by 1984. She publicity-toured a little in Europe to promote herself but returned no fonder of France to consolidate what was a coming position in the music industry. Her clothes, her Boy Toy logo, her street cred was making her an institution and she realised that although she needed control, she also needed help.

She took on Freddy de Mann, Michael Jackson's manager, as her own. Must've been one of de Mann's better days. And to think that when he first met her he couldn't see it, couldn't understand what all the fuss was about! Perhaps the fifteen percent thing was why she treated him like an employee. Perhaps the fifteen percent thing was why he let her. Fifteen percent of Madonna? Work it out.

Loving liaisons were gettin' dangerous. Madonna went through at least one abortion whilst supposedly with Benitez. Though she became officially engaged to him, she was certainly seeing others all the time. Benitez, surprise surprise, found himself passed over in pleasure for journalist Steve Newman whilst Reggie Lucas was passed over as producer on Madonna's second album LIKE A VIRGIN for Nile Rogers who had worked with Diana Ross and, quintessentially, with David Bowie.

LIKE A VIRGIN had been written as a ballad some years before but Rogers re-jigged it onto a dance format. Mary Lambert filmed the video in Venice. Hey presto. Madonna magic.

MATERIAL GIRL followed and meantime, DESPERATELY SEEKING SUSAN director Susan Seidelman, a neighbour of Madonna's in New York, cast her in the movie that Madonna came to steal. When *Rolling Stone* featured Madonna on its November 1984 cover, the other stars of SUSAN knew they had been permanently eclipsed. Madonna's ambition to conquer the silver screen as well as the small is evinced in her citing Carole Lombard and Judy Holliday as her idols. These gals made some combination to live up to and, in the living up to, some target to be shot down.

Like Mae West's DIAMOND LIL, Madonna was becoming more famous than any other woman alive and in a press which was not naturally on her side. It was her peer, Cyndi Lauper who was more favoured. Cyndi was more, sorta, female, cuter ... Like Margaret Thatcher, the other material girl of the front page, Madonna was thought too strident, especially by the womens' movement against whose politically correct standards, Madonna fell far short.

With LIKE A VIRGIN album having sold three and a half million albums in twelve weeks and whilst Warners executives saw Madonna material selling eighty thousand units a day, the video of MATERIAL GIRL showed Madonna as Monroe, blonde on blonde, in a gown designed by Travilla, out-legending a legend. Travilla was said to be miffed because he didn't get a credit. In fact, a lotta other people were beginning to be miffed. Even her own staff, the staff at management and record companies were uneasily observing the contagion of her confrontational style. Madonna was aggressive both in offence and defence, in love and in lust, in tryst and trust. Cruising the East side in her limousine and picking up Rican boys whilst kissing her girlfriends is pretty confrontational stuff. Violence also proved to be a part of the cocktail which Madonna loved to swallow.

Mary Lambert, her video director, first introduced Madonna to Sean Penn although at the time Madonna was more interested in the mutual advantage she perceived in gettin' acquainted with Prince. Prince kinda saw it the same way. What an ego rub that date would have been. Do you think they spent time comparing sizes? I bet Madonna's was biggest.

The business of creating mutual advantage Madonna orchestrated like the front office would run a blonde career in the Hollywood 'thirties because, in mutual advantage, love doesn't need have a lot to do with it. So when love did get to have a lot to do with it, Madonna was somewhat at a loss in the final instance 'cos love does have a habit of getting in the way. Having sex is so much easier.

The simmeringly violent, gun-toting, fag-hating shortish Sean Penn was not the ideal Front Office candidate to marry Madonna. In the *his* and *hers* stakes, any advantage would have seemed to have been his.

The wedding guests were orchestrated and so was the

wedding. Sean lost his temper, Madonna didn't seem to mind and they went off to honeymoon in Carmel. She said then and she kept saying that she loved him. I believe her. With Sean she broke out of her racially fenced compound where her sexuality only seemed to function when stimulated by a stereotype. Sean was totally different.

He was an actor and he was a white American; thanks to his parents and his own not inconsiderable efforts, he was Hollywood establishment. He was also dangerous. He liked guns. He showed he could and would fight for her by fighting over her. He threatened her ex-lovers with death and mutilation and was known to have stalked one Bobby Martinez whilst packing a handgun. What did Madonna think? She thought he was the coolest guy in the universe.

But did Sean beat up on her? Did he get a little beyond the Hanky Spanky which had always excited her? Were their bonds those abused words like 'Sorry' and 'I didn't mean it' and 'I'll never do it again'? Goddam it, it's all love, you know. The power of love. S and M is all about control but it's also about the willingness to be controlled. I don't think Sean perhaps quite understood it like Madonna.

When they got back off honeymoon, their togetherness spawned a Malibu estate and a joint venture in SHANGAI SURPRISE, a movie for ex-Beatle George Harrison. Madonna was also due to start her third album, TRUE BLUE. Their relationship went up and down like a seesaw in their playground around whose perimeter, Sean was parading his violence like a rottweiler. After several skirmishes with photographers, Penn gave his ultimate exhibition when he hit on old friend of Madonna's and threatened to further beat the guy over the head with a chair. David Wolinski had merely kissed Madonna hello.

Penn's violence thereafter became the biggest issue in the gradual breakdown of their marriage. He had been her inspiration. TRUE BLUE had been *his* title. Controlled, his violence excited her. She didn't know how to handle this careering situation. She released PAPA DON'T PREACH. The single and its video provoked new heights of controversy and also proved that in a strange way, Madonna didn't need Hollywood. Her work was creating new areas where both the old and the new Hollywood came to her. TRUE BLUE sold seventeen million copies by 1986.

But it was another bummer of a year.

She was working for Jamie Foley, her oft-times video director, on his movie originally entitled SLAMMER but now called WHO'S THAT GIRL? She was also taking a deep interest in the career of Nick Kamen, a young, British model-singer-musician. He was another wedge. Penn loathed her involvement with the pretty young protegé. What was Madonna doing? Goading Penn? Could she not leave him? Did she want to make *him* leave *her*?

After a long struggle, AIDS finally caught up to Madonna's front door. Martin Burgoyne, her old friend died in New York. She was at his bedside and had paid for over $100,000 of his medical expenses. Sean had been sympathetic but he really *didn't* like gays. It would seem that Burgoyne's dying was hardly an issue which cemented their relationship. It was rather yet another wedge for Madonna refused her husband's insistent demands that she be tested for HIV. She also was not keen to have his child. HIV and babies for a young couple like the Penns, went hand in hand.

Testing is a contentious issue even with gay couples. Knowing she hadn't practised what had become known as 'safer sex' whilst AIDS had been taking hold in her social arena, Madonna was not quick to have her fate determined. Martin's death sobered her up. I think she must have grown up a lot that year and it was only just the beginning. Her image certainly changed. She began to get glamorous and she attended to her health and her diet by exercising and eating with rigorous discipline. But then she had always been a self-disciplinarian. She had also been a perfectionist.

She covered the world with the WHO'S THAT GIRL? tour. Sean

meanwhile was seething and slip-sliding away back home and on the day Madonna was flying back from Japan at the end of the first leg of the tour, Penn was sentenced in Miami to sixty days for another infringement of the law, this time for driving whilst under the influence.

There was time before Penn was due to go to jail and they had a passionate making-up. They tried so many times. No one can say that the poisonous Penns didn't eschew rancour on many occasions to attempt reunions and reconciliations. But none of them worked. The WHO'S THAT GIRL? tour trundled almost endlessly on whilst the world's press wondered endlessly whether the marriage was still on.

Madonna started to date other men. She had a fabled liaison with John F Kennedy Junior of which his mother, the redoubtable Jackie O was said to have disapproved heartily. Madonna also started to date another woman. Her probing friendship with the actress/singer/performance-artist Sandra Bernhardt was conducted openly by both of them in the face not only of the American public on the David Letterman Show one night but also in the face of Madonna's infuriated homophobic husband.

Her continued acting roles including the television adaptation of Damon Runyon's BLOODHOUNDS OF BROADWAY she made for the dying director Howard Brookner gained her bad reviews. No one however reviewed her loyalty. In the Broadway production of David Mamet's SPEED THE PLOW, she was equally badly reviewed but because of her the play was big box office.

Although they celebrated her thirtieth birthday together, the Penns' marriage was measurable in days. There was no baby and Sean must have realised that there would never be one. Madonna came out of SPEED THE PLOW as Sean went into a Los Angeles theatre production of HURLY BURLY. Madonna, for reasons best known to herself, showed up to the first night with Sandra Bernhardt and Sean, understandably, went crazy. First nights are for first night audiences to come and bolster up the good opinions of the press for the good of the play. Madonna's actions showed bleak regard for the company integrity of HURLY BURLY and publicly humiliated her husband.

More violence marked the weeks running up to New Years 1990. After a physically violent contretemps, Madonna fled their home and took refuge at Freddy de Mann's. She finally filed for divorce.

Because of their pre-nuptial agreement, the parting of the Penns was quickly settled. Madonna, worth by current estimates over $70,000,000 went out and bought a new home in the Hollywood Hills which her younger brother Christopher decorated. She bought paintings and artefacts both past and present extravagantly and expansively,

The LIKE A PRAYER album release schedule also brought her into contact with Pepsi Cola who paid her $5,000,000 to endorse their product. She went brunette for the video and the Pepsi commercial. Madonna wanted to use the old Mae West line: *"Is that a (Pepsi) in your pocket or are you just happy to see me?"* The agency had other ideas but the one thing they couldn't control was the LIKE A PRAYER video. The record itself when released caused such accusations of blasphemy and outrage from catholic and church leaders, that Pepsi pulled the plug on their association. Madonna knew she would sell many more records as a result and got to keep Pepsi's $5,000,000.

"... Madonna? Oh yeah! Seen her, shagged her, sussed her ... Oh yeah?" Was that dumb of Pepsi or what?

She went back to blonde immediately for EXPRESS YOURSELF and stayed blonde for Warren Beatty and Breathless Mahoney. I know of only one woman who ever turned down Warren Beatty. We all know it wasn't Madonna. Mr. Beatty was no spring chicken. Their age difference of course was nothing Freudian. Nor their personalities. Warren seemed almost avuncular, almost charmed by the outrageous antics of his paramour. Far from being disturbed by Madonna's continuing friendship with Sandra Bernhardt, Mr. Beatty seems to have gotten hard over it. Madonna invoiced the movie magnate a mere $27,360 for her nineteen weeks work on DICK TRACY. Her rewards would be more and would come later when the I'M BREATHLESS album was released.

Whilst Warren was busy cutting DICK, Madonna eschewed her vow never to tour again and began producing her BLONDE AMBITION extravaganza. Huge, imperial, obsessed ... The arrangements would take months and would see Madonna at the height of her hire 'em, fire 'em, fuck 'em and forget 'em megalomaniac behaviour and also at the height of a fevered creativity. She told the director Vince Paterson that she was going to fulfil the world's perceptions of her. She got gay French fashion designer Jean Paul Gaultier to help her give her Blonde Ambition a form. He did. In a pointed conical bustier.

The show was liberally structured around themes of sex and religion and both seemed to take on a new and greater importance for her. She was developing an almost messianic self-importance and yet still knew she couldn't do it all on her own. Once again she turned to inspiration from the streets.

Seeing dancers Jose Guitierez and Luis Camucho dancing 'en vogue' at The Sound Factory in New York, Madonna once again sucked in a little something from the streets and made it her own. She annexed the style and employed the dancers. Auditions for the remaining male dancers were underpinned with a qualification only understood by the Empress Catherine of Russia and several wayward Roman Caesars. But I still bet Madonna has a bigger one than anyone of those boys!

Whilst rehearsing, the second of Madonna's very close friends to die from AIDS succumbed. Keith Haring, the artist, whose paintings now sold for millions, died. Later that year, Madonna was voted America's smartest businesswoman by *Forbes* Magazine. The epithet and her reputation for having a big acumen infuriated her. Madonna was said to be worth over $150,000,000 and was America's highest earning woman at $40,000,000 a year. When, finally, Christopher Flynn too was to die, she must have really wondered what all that money was for.

BLONDE AMBITION started in Japan in April 1990. The fans were treated to one hundred and five minutes worth of androgyny, homosexuality, sado-masochism with a just a passing reference to the straight erotic here and there all hung on the eighteen songs of the set. Crosses of electric lights were blazed, incense burners smashed and a crucifix was thrown to the ground. They sure got their money's worth those fans! All four and a half million dollars of it!

She financed the making of Alek Keshishnian's documentary IN BED WITH MADONNA herself. It was a coup de theatre and turned out to be a coup de cinema. It covered the exhausting BLONDE AMBITION TOUR and all its outrageousness which, incidentally, she toned down when the juggernaut rolled into Detroit and her father and family were in the audience. The Italian Italians had not been spared however much the Vatican castigated their errant daughter. I wonder if they ever seriously thought of excommunicating her? Probably not. They'd probably learned. They were the Pepsi generation after all.

The woman who was said to have had a *"brain for sin and a body for business"* was now in her mid-thirties. The woman who was hailed by Vogue's Leon Talley as being a 'Goddess of Fashion' still looked good and shaped up at 32:23:33.

Though Miss Madonna sure wasn't cryin' into her C-cups, despite the continuing moan of romance, the lady was still alone. She must have started to feel acutely alone as she watched Sean, the love of her life, marry actress Robin Wright and have a baby and the libidinous Mr. Beatty finally succumb to Annette Bening with whom he too started a family. Even Tony Ward, who had come nearest, lately, to being a permanent fixture, didn't wait to be ditched but went off and married Amalia Papadimos.

Maybe the problem about Madonna marrying was that she would have to be a wife? I think she wanted to be the husband. She wanted to be in charge. Marriage is mutual charge. I don't think she knew that. By blurring the edges of everything - sex, role, gender - I think that in the end she could recognise nothing. Not even friendship.

But she still had her career of which she *WAS* indubitably in charge. JUSTIFY MY LOVE video 'surprised' her by being banned by MTV. Did she care? Like all the way to the bank. She was seen around with Michael Jackson when it was cool to be seen with Michael Jackson and Alek Keshishnian's IN BED WITH MADONNA opened to wild acclaim in May 1991 at the Cannes Film Festival attended by the Goddess herself.

She has continued to be alone. She has continued to produce wonderful work. Her albums and videos are inspirations and every one a gem. She is currently in the world charts with TAKE A BOW, her homage to Valentino and BLOOD AND SAND, a worthy successor to the traditions of that ancient black and white paradise known as Hollywood, the original Dream Factory. In TAKE A BOW she appears as the matador's lover, closely photographed in a veil and looking like Mae West, her severe coiffure and exquisite mouth promising only that which a blonde can fulfil.

Like Mae, like Harlow, Marlene, Ginger, Lana and Marilyn ... True to their memory and a proud tradition, Madonna has never yet failed to give us new ways to dream.

Outroduction

I feel passionately about artistry, about actors, about performers, about creativity and writing and audio-visual skills, about the administration and acumen and technology that is poured into lives to turn them into careers. I am personally deeply grateful to those careers for having enriched our own lives with magi and dreams and laughter and tears.

Other than deep religious faith, for those of us who can't quite manage that particular quantum leap, the power of words and music and flickering images to re-inforce our belief in life and love and ourselves is just as endowed and, presumably, equally blessed.

Now, the twelve women included in this book are my personal choice. I realise only too well that having so chosen, I stand with my head above the parapet waiting to be shot down with criticism about those blondes that I have omitted.

To those who will call for my head for excluding Betty Grable, Alice Faye, Kim Novak, Brigitte Bardot or Diana Dors and all the dozens of others from these pages, I can only apologise and promise that if this book goes anywhere to kindling renewed interest in the lives and times of those women whose talents and tears have lent extra dimensions to our own lives, Glamour Blondes II is already on the stocks.

But first, we should give the Brunettes a chance...

Acknowledgements

I would like to thank Gillian Firman at Bryan Forbes Ltd., Jacki Wadeson whose articles on hair and beauty I read with great interest, John V Simmons whose book on Cosmetics is full and fascinating, Patricia Spencer whose book *HAIR COLOURING* was most informative, Georgine de Courtais and her book *WOMEN'S HEADDRESS AND HAIRSTYLES,* James Stevens Cox and his volume *A DICTIONARY OF HAIRDRESSING AND WIGMAKING,* Nadia Vella at Jo Hansford in Mount Street, Ann Ortman for her introduction to Nadia, my mother, Mary, for her observations on hairdressing in provincial England in the 1930's, Mae West for her autobiography *GOODNESS HAD NOTHING TO DO WITH IT,* Neal Gabler for his book *AN EMPIRE OF THEIR OWN,* John Coblenz at Crusaid, Gibson Grenfell, Cheryl, Darren and Monica Towrie at the Kobal Collection, Christopher Anderson for his book *MADONNA, UNAUTHORISED,* the late Edna Ferber for her not only insightful but compassionate and compelling autobiography *A PECULIAR TREASURE, HARLOW AN INTIMATE BIOGRAPHY* by Irving Shulman, *DORIS DAY HER OWN STORY* by A. E. Hotchner, Matilda Quiney for her proof-reading and superb comments, *MARLENE* by Maria Riva, John and Jackie Jesse, The Sunday Times Magazine, Lana Turner for her autobiography *THE LADY, THE LEGEND, THE TRUTH* and Joe Morella and Edward Z. Epstein for their biography *LANA,* Peggy Lee for her autobiography *MISS PEGGY LEE,* Dolly Parton for her own book *DOLLY, MY LIFE AND OTHER UNFINISHED BUSINESS,* Ret Turner, Arlen Stewart, Sarah Bradford and Gwen Robyns for their biographies entitled *PRINCESS GRACE*, Bernard Taylor for his comments on Dinah Shore, Kris Ellam, Denise Ellam-Bell, Gloria Steinhem for her book *MARILYN/NORMA JEANE*, Peter Harry Brown and Patte B. Barham for their book *MARILYN THE LAST TAKE*, Anthony Summers for his book *GODDESS*, Mike Ashwell for his perspicacity and proof-reading, Edward and Gillian Thorpe for their observations, Sarah Standing, Peter Straker for reminding me about Montgomery Clift, Suzanne Parks at Chrysalis for information on Deborah Harry, Fiona Jackman.

And for his library, his collection of lobby cards, his wisdom, his love, his support and his obsession with the subject in general and in particular, my Ni.